Methods of Critical Discourse Analysis

INTRODUCING QUALITATIVE METHODS provides a series of volumes which introduce qualitative research to the student and beginning researcher. The approach is interdisciplinary and international. A distinctive feature of these volumes is the helpful student exercises.

One stream of the series provides texts on the key methodologies used in qualitative research. The other stream contains books on qualitative research for different disciplines or occupations. Both streams cover the basic literature in a clear and accessible style, but also cover the 'cutting edge' issues in the area.

SERIES EDITOR
David Silverman (Goldsmiths College)

EDITORIAL BOARD
Michael Bloor (Cardiff University and University of Glasgow)
Barbara Czarniawska (Göteburg University)
Norman Denzin (University of Illinois, Urbana-Champaign)
Uwe Flick (Alice Salomon University of Applied Sciences, Berlin)
Barry Glassner (University of Southern California)
Jaber Gubrium (University of Missouri)
Anne Murcott (University of Nottingham)
Jonathan Potter (Loughborough University)

For a list of all titles in the series, visit www.sagepub.co.uk/iqm

Methods of Critical Discourse Analysis

Second Edition

Edited by
Ruth Wodak and Michael Meyer

Los Angeles | London | New Delhi
Singapore | Washington DC

This second edition first published 2009
First edition published 2001

SAGE Publications Ltd
1 Oliver's Yard
55 City Road
London EC1Y 1SP

SAGE Publications Inc.
2455 Teller Road
Thousand Oaks, California 91320

SAGE Publications India Pvt Ltd
B 1/I 1 Mohan Cooperative Industrial Area
Mathura Road
New Delhi 110 044

SAGE Publications Asia-Pacific Pte Ltd
33 Pekin Street #02-01
Far East Square
Singapore 048763

Library of Congress Control Number: 2008932562

British Library Cataloguing in Publication data

A catalogue record for this book is available from the British Library

ISBN 978-1-84787-454-2
ISBN 978-1-84787-455-9 (pbk)

Typeset by C&M Digitals (P) Ltd, Chennai, India
Printed in Great Britain by TJ International Ltd, Padstow, Cornwall
Printed on paper from sustainable resources

Mixed Sources
Product group from well-managed
forests and other controlled sources
www.fsc.org Cert no. SGS-COC-2482
© 1996 Forest Stewardship Council
FSC

Contents

Acknowledgements

This book could not have been written without the help of many people. We wish to express our gratitude to them all.

Our endeavour to provide readers with a comprehensive book introducing the different approaches to Critical Discourse Analysis started in the form of a seminar on CDA at the Department of Linguistics (University of Vienna) in 1999. We appreciate the discussion and work with the student participants which provided an important stimulus for our plan to publish the first edition.

We appreciate the collaboration with the authors of the contributions to this book: Norman Fairclough, Siegfried Jäger, Florentine Maier, Gerlinde Mautner, Martin Reisigl, Teun van Dijk and Theo van Leeuwen. Not only did they write instructive and interesting chapters, they submitted them on schedule, and were very open to our criticism, comments and suggestions.

Bryan Jenner has been indispensable in helping to recast some of our more idiosyncratic pieces of non-native English into an acceptable form. Anahid Aghamanoukjan, Ulla Ernst and Edith Fazekas contributed to fine-tuning the manuscript in an essential way. Claire Lipscomb at Sage has been an extremely supportive editor who has made a very positive contribution to the final results. Last but not least we thank the six anonymous reviewers who helped us to avoid a number of shortcomings in the first edition but who are not responsible for those in the second.

Notes on contributors

Norman Fairclough is Professor Emeritus of Language in social Life at Lancaster University in the UK. He has written extensively in the field of Critical Discourse Analysis. His main publications include: *Language and Power* (1989), *Discourse and Social Change* (1992), *Media Discourse* (1995), *Critical Discourse Analysis* (1995), *Discourse in Late Modernity* (1999) (with Lilie Chaouliaraki) and *New Labour, New Language?* (2000). His main current interest is in language (discourse) as an element in the contemporary social changes that are referred to as 'globalization', 'neo-liberalism', 'new capitalism', the 'knowledge economy' and so forth. Over the past three years he has been working specifically on aspects of 'transition' in Central and Eastern Europe, especially Romania, from a discourse analytical perspective (see www.ling. lancs.ac.uk/profiles/263). Email: n.fairclough@lancaster.ac.uk

Siegfried Jäger has been a Professor for German Language at the University of Duisburg/Essen (Germany) since 1972, and since 1987 he has also been head of the Dusiburg Institute of Linguistic and Social Research. His major research areas are Discourse Theory and Critical Discourse Analysis based on Michel Foucault's theory. He has conducted several projects dealing with a broad range of topics, e.g. language barriers, right-wing extremism, immigration and racism in mass media and everyday talk, media coverage of crime, Jewish publications in the 19th century, Christian fundamentalism and anti-Semitism in the German and Polish mass media. For his publications, see diss-duisburg.de. Email: s.jaeger@diss-duisburg.de

Florentine Maier is a research assistant at the Academic Unit for Nonprofit Management at the Wirtschaftsuniversität Wien (WU, Vienna University of Economics and Business). Her primary fields of research are the spread of managerialism into Non-profit Organizations, and the employment of older workers. Before entering the Academic Unit for Nonprofit Management, she was a Research Assistant at the Institute of Human Resource Management at the WU. She has also worked as a lecturer in Human Resource Management at the University of Applied Science at the Vienna Chambers of Commerce, and as a teacher of Chinese. She gained her doctoral degree in social and economic sciences from the WU in 2008. Email: florentine-maier@wu-wien.ac.at

Gerlinde Mautner is Professor of English Business Communication at the Wirtschaftsuniversität Wien (Vienna University of Economics and Business).

A graduate of the University of Vienna, she has spent a year at each of the linguistics departments of the universities of Birmingham (UK), Lancaster, and, most recently, Cardiff. Combining critical discourse analysis with corpus linguistic methodology, her research focuses on corporate and marketing communications, as well as on the discourse of the public and nonprofit sectors. Email: gerlinde.mautner@wu-wien.ac.at

Michael Meyer is Professor for Business Administration at the Unit for Nonprofit Management at the Wirtschaftsuniversität Wien (WU, Vienna University of Economics and Business). Since 1989, Michael Meyer has held a range of academic positions, such as Assistant Professor for Marketing and Cultural Management, and Social Researcher in various interdisciplinary projects. Currently, he is head of the Research Institute for Nonprofit Organizations at the WU. He is an experienced lecturer and researcher in the field of Organizational Behaviour. His areas of specialization and current research include: Managerialism, Nonprofit Organizations, Civil Society and Civic Participation, Social Systems Theory, Organizational Theory, and Careers (for his publications, see: www.wu-wien.ac.at/npo/english/team/mm). Email: michael.meyer@wu-wien.ac.at

Martin Reisigl has a PhD in Applied Linguistics and currently teaches Applied Linguistics at the University of Vienna. He is also working on his habilitation project supported by research fellowships of the German Alexander von Humboldt Foundation and the Austrian Academy of Sciences (APART). From May 2006 until January 2007, he was a visiting professor at the university La Sapienza in Rome, Italy. From February until June 2007, he was a visiting fellow at the Institute for Human Sciences/Institut für die Wissenschaften von Menschen (IWM) in Vienna. His research interests include (critical) discourse analysis and discourse theory, text linguistics, academic writing, sociolinguistics, (political) rhetoric (language and discrimination, nationalism, racism as well as populism), language and history, linguistics and literature, argumentation analysis and semiotics. Email: martin.reisigl@univie.ac.at

Teun A. van Dijk was Professor of Discourse Studies at the University of Amsterdam until 2004, and is at present Professor at the Universitat Pompeu Fabra, Barcelona. After earlier work on generative poetics, text grammar and the psychology of text processing, his work since 1980 has taken a more critical perspective and has dealt with discursive racism, news in the press, ideology, knowledge and context. He is the author of several books in most of these areas, and he has edited *The Handbook of Discourse Analysis* (4 vols, 1985), the introductory book *Discourse Studies* (2 vols, 1997) as well as the reader *The Study of Discourse* (5 vols, 2007). He has founded six international journals: *Poetics*, *Text* (now *Text and Talk*), *Discourse and Society*, *Discourse Studies*,

Discourse and Communication and the internet journal *Discurso and Sociedad* in Spanish (www.dissoc.org), the last four of which he still edits. His most recent monographs in English are *Ideology* (1998), *Racism and Discourse in Spain and Latin America* (2005), *Discourse and Context* (2008), *Society and Discourse* (2008), and his last edited books (with Ruth Wodak), *Racism at the Top* (2000), and *Discourse and Racism in Latin America* (2008). Teun van Dijk, who holds two honorary doctorates, has lectured widely in many countries, especially also in Latin America. For further information, see his website: www.discourses.org. Email: teun@discourses.org

Theo van Leeuwen is Professor of Media and Communication and Dean of the Faculty of Arts and Social Sciences at the University of Technology, Sydney. He has published widely in the areas of critical discourse analysis, multimodality and visual semiotics. His books include: *Reading Images – The Grammar of Visual Design* (with Gunther Kress); *Speech, Music, Sound: Multimodal Discourse – The Modes and Media of Contemporary Communication* (with Gunther Kress); and *Introducing Social Semiotics and Global Media Discourse* (with David Machin). His latest book *Discourse and Practice* was published in 2008. He is a founding editor of the journal *Visual Communication*. Email: theo.vanleeuwen@uts.edu.au

Ruth Wodak is Distinguished Professor of Discourse Studies at Lancaster University. In addition to various other prizes, she was awarded the Wittgenstein Prize for Elite Researchers in 1996. Her research interests focus on discourse studies, gender studies, language and/in politics, prejudice and discrimination, and on ethnographic methods of linguistic field work. She has held visiting professorships in Uppsala, Stanford University, University of Minnesota, University of East Anglia and Georgetown University. In 2008, she was awarded the Kerstin Hesselgren Chair of the Swedish Parliament (at the University of Örebro). Recent book publications include *Ist Österreich ein 'deutsches' Land?* (with R. de Cillia, 2006); *Qualitative Discourse Analysis in the Social Sciences* (with M. Krzyżanowski, 2008); *Migration, Identity and Belonging* (with G. Delanty and P. Jones, 2008), *The Discursive Construction of History: Remembering the Wehrmacht's War of Annihilation* (with H. Heer, W. Manoschek and A. Pollak, 2008) and *The Construction of Politics in Action: Politics as Usual?* (2009). See www.ling.lancs.ac.uk/profiles/265 for more information on her ongoing research projects and recent publications. Email: r.wodak@lancaster.ac.uk

1

Critical Discourse Analysis: History, Agenda, Theory and Methodology[1]

Ruth Wodak and Michael Meyer

CDA – What is it all about?

In this chapter, we first provide a brief 'story' – how it all began; then we present an overview of some important research agendas in CDA and discuss new challenges for CDA research. Secondly, we discuss the various theoretical and methodological approaches assembled in this volume from a sociological and epistemological perspective.[2] There, we focus mostly on three central and constitutive concepts: power, ideology and critique. We also, of course, summarize some of the salient principles which are constitutive of all approaches in CDA. In addition, we mention some important criticism which CDA has been confronted with in the past years (see Billig, 2003, 2008; Chilton, 2007; Chilton and Wodak, 2007; Wodak and de Cillia, 2006 for an extensive discussion of these issues).

The terms Critical Linguistics (CL) and Critical Discourse Analysis (CDA) are often used interchangeably. In fact, recently, the term CDA seems to have been preferred and is being used to denote the theory formerly identified as CL. Therefore, we will continue to use CDA exclusively here (see Anthonissen, 2001; Chilton and Wodak, 2007 for an extensive discussion of these terms and their history). The manifold roots of CDA lie in Rhetoric, Text linguistics, Anthropology, Philosophy, Socio-Psychology, Cognitive Science, Literary Studies and Sociolinguistics, as well as in Applied Linguistics and Pragmatics.

Nowadays, some scholars prefer the term Critical Discourse Studies (CDS). For example, Teun van Dijk provides us with a broad overview of the field of (C)DS, where one can identify the following developments: between the mid-1960s and the early 1970s, new, closely related disciplines emerged in the humanities and the social sciences. Despite their different disciplinary backgrounds and a great diversity of methods and objects of investigation, some parts of the new fields/paradigms/linguistic sub-disciplines of semiotics, pragmatics, psycho- and sociolinguistics, ethnography of speaking, conversation analysis and discourse studies all deal with discourse and have at least seven dimensions in common (see Van Dijk, 2007a; Wodak, 2008a):

- an interest in the properties of *'naturally occurring' language use* by real language users (instead of a study of abstract language systems and invented examples)
- a focus on *larger units than isolated words and sentences* and, hence, new basic units of analysis: texts, discourses, conversations, speech acts, or communicative events
- the extension of linguistics *beyond sentence grammar* towards a study of action and interaction
- the extension to *non-verbal (semiotic, multimodal, visual) aspects* of interaction and communication: gestures, images, film, the internet, and multimedia
- a focus on dynamic (socio)–cognitive or interactional moves and strategies
- the study of the functions of (social, cultural, situative and cognitive) *contexts of language use*
- an analysis of a vast number of *phenomena of text grammar and language use*: coherence, anaphora, topics, macrostructures, speech acts, interactions, turn-taking, signs, politeness, argumentation, rhetoric, mental models, and many other aspects of text and discourse.

The significant difference between DS and CDS (or CDA) lies in the *constitutive problem-oriented, interdisciplinary approach* of the latter, apart from endorsing all of the above points. *CDA is therefore not interested in investigating a linguistic unit per se but in studying social phenomena which are necessarily complex and thus require a multi-disciplinary and multi-methodical approach.* The objects under investigation do not have to be related to negative or exceptionally 'serious' social or political experiences or events – this is a frequent misunderstanding of the aims and goals of CDA and of the term 'critical' which, of course, does not mean 'negative' as in common-sense usage (see below). Any social phenomenon lends itself to critical investigation, to be challenged and not taken for granted. We will return to this important point and other common misunderstandings of CDA below.

We would also like to emphasize right at the beginning of this volume that it is obvious that the notions of *text* and *discourse* have been subject to a hugely proliferating number of usages in the social sciences. Almost no paper or article is to be found which does not revisit these notions, quoting Michel Foucault, Jürgen Habermas, Chantal Mouffe, Ernesto Laclau, Niklas Luhmann, or many others. Thus, *discourse* means anything from a historical monument, a *lieu de mémoire*, a policy, a political strategy, narratives in a restricted or broad sense of the term, text, talk, a speech, topic-related conversations, to language per se. We find notions such as racist discourse, gendered discourse, discourses on un/employment, media discourse, populist discourse, discourses of the past, and many more – thus stretching the meaning of *discourse* from a genre to a register or style, from a building to a political programme. This causes and must cause confusion – which leads to much criticism and more misunderstandings (Blommaert, 2005; Reisigl, 2007; Wodak, 2008a; Wodak and de Cillia, 2006). This is why each contributor to this volume was asked to define their use of the term integrated in their specific approach.

A brief history of the 'CDA Group'

CDA as a network of scholars emerged in the early 1990s, following a small symposium in Amsterdam, in January 1991. Through the support of the University of Amsterdam, Teun van Dijk, Norman Fairclough, Gunther Kress, Theo van Leeuwen and Ruth Wodak spent two days together, and had the wonderful opportunity to discuss theories and methods of Discourse Analysis, specifically CDA. The meeting made it possible to confront with each other the very distinct and different approaches, which have, of course, changed significantly since 1991 but remain relevant, in many respects. In this process of group formation, differences and sameness were laid out: differences with regard to other theories and methodologies in Discourse Analysis (see Renkema, 2004; Titscher et al., 2000; Wetherell et al., 2001; Wodak, 2008a) and sameness in a programmatic way, both of which frame the range of theoretical approaches. In the meantime, for example, some of the scholars previously aligned with CDA have chosen other theoretical frameworks and have distanced themselves from CDA (such as Gunther Kress and Ron Scollon); on the other hand, new approaches have been created which frequently find innovative ways of integrating the more traditional theories or of elaborating them (see below).

In general, CDA as a school or paradigm is characterized by a number of principles: for example, all approaches are problem-oriented, and thus necessarily interdisciplinary and eclectic (see below). Moreover, CDA is characterized by the common interests in de-mystifying ideologies and power through the systematic and *retroductable* investigation of semiotic data (written, spoken or visual). CDA researchers also attempt to make their own positions and interests explicit while retaining their respective scientific methodologies and while remaining self-reflective of their own research process.

The start of the CDA network was marked by the launch of Van Dijk's journal *Discourse and Society* (1990), as well as by several books which were coincidentally (or because of a *Zeitgeist*) published simultaneously and led by similar research goals.³ The Amsterdam meeting determined an institutional start, an attempt both to constitute an exchange programme (ERASMUS for three years)⁴, as well as joint projects and collaborations between scholars of different countries, and a special issue of *Discourse and Society* (1993), which presented the above-mentioned approaches. Since then, new journals have been created, multiple overviews have been written, and nowadays CDA is an established paradigm in linguistics; currently, we encounter *Critical Discourse Studies, The Journal of Language and Politics, Discourse and Communication* and *Visual Semiotics*, among many other journals; we also find several e-journals which publish critical research, such as *CADAAD*. Book series have been launched (such as *Discourse Approaches to Politics, Culture and Society*), regular CDA meetings and conferences take place, and handbooks are under way. In sum, CDA (CDS) has become an established discipline, institutionalized across the globe in many departments and curricula.

The common ground: discourse, critique, power and ideology

When deconstructing the label of this research programme – we view CDA basically as a research programme, the reasons for which we will explain below – we necessarily have to define what CDA means when it employs the terms 'critical' and 'discourse'. Michael Billig (2003) has clearly pointed to the fact that CDA has become an established academic discipline with the same rituals and institutional practices as all other academic disciplines. Ironically, he asks the question whether this might mean that CDA has become or might become 'uncritical' – or if the use of acronyms such as CDA might serve the same purposes as in other traditional, non-critical disciplines; namely to exclude outsiders and to mystify the functions and intentions of the research. Most recently, Billig has reiterated this question under a new frame: do scholars who employ CDA write in the same way mainly by using nominalizations extensively, like the many texts which they criticize (Billig, 2008)?

> The problem with talking about the unconscious, repression, mental representations, mirror-stages, etc., is that it is easy to assume that we have solved problems by discovering 'things'. And the more we write about these 'things', the more we take their existence for granted. Analysts might have once understood these concepts semi-metaphorically, but soon they write about them literally. In my view, the cognitive psychology of 'mental representations', or the psychoanalysis of 'the unconscious' and 'repression', makes psychology too easy and too non-materialistic – too prone to accept that non-material entities provide the solution to the puzzles that, in effect, analysts are avoiding. And that is why I advocate that we should be examining nominalizing (not nominalization), representing (not representations), repressing (not repression) and so on.

Billig (2008) ends his quite provocative argument by stating:

> [t]here is no reason for supposing that for academics, writing their academic articles, the active forms are psychologically primary. In my article and in this reply, I have struggled to resist the grammatical forms with which my fingers are so familiar. I have redrafted,

often with a struggle, many sentences which spontaneously spilled out in the passive form. I have probably used the first person singular here more times than I have done in all the rest of my publications put together. And so now, I do not want to end by promoting a new label. To adapt a very famous phrase, the point is not to categorize language, but to change it.

We cannot follow Billig's recommendations in detail or answer his questions in this chapter extensively. However, we believe that he points to potentially very fruitful and necessary debates for CDA. More specifically, Billig points to the danger which can befall any discipline (or school or group) when it becomes established and institutionalized after having been marginalized for a long time. Once established, he argues, one might forget the basic desiderata and become corrupted by the system – in our case, the Knowledge-based Economy (KBE) which influences all our lives in so many ways (Billig, 2008).

At this point, it is important to stress that CDA has never been and has never attempted to be or to provide one single or specific theory. Neither is one specific methodology characteristic of research in CDA. Quite the contrary, studies in CDA are multifarious, derived from quite different theoretical backgrounds, oriented towards different data and methodologies. Researchers in CDA also rely on a variety of grammatical approaches. The definitions of the terms 'discourse', 'critical', 'ideology', 'power' and so on are also manifold. Thus, any criticism of CDA should always specify which research or researcher they relate to. Hence, we suggest using the notion of a 'school' for CDA, or of a programme, which many researchers find useful and to which they can relate. This programme or set of principles has, of course, changed over the years (see (Fairclough and Wodak, 1997; Wodak, 1996).

Such a heterogeneous school might be confusing for some; on the other hand, it allows for continuous debates, for changes in the aims and goals, and for innovation. In contrast to 'total and closed' theories, such as Chomsky's Generative Transformational Grammar or Michael Halliday's Systemic Functional Linguistics, CDA has never had the image of a 'sect' and does not want to have such an image. This heterogeneity of methodological and theoretical approaches that can be found in this field would tend to confirm van Dijk's point that CDA and CL 'are at most a shared perspective on doing linguistic, semiotic or discourse analysis' (Van Dijk, 1993a: 131). Below, we summarize some of these principles, which are adhered to by most researchers.

The notion of discourse

CDA sees 'language as social practice' (Fairclough and Wodak, 1997), and considers the 'context of language use' to be crucial. We quote one definition which has become 'very popular' among CDA researchers:

> CDA sees discourse – language use in speech and writing – as a form of 'social practice'. Describing discourse as social practice implies a dialectical relationship between a particular discursive event and the situation(s), institution(s) and social structure(s), which frame it:

> The discursive event is shaped by them, but it also shapes them. That is, discourse is socially constitutive as well as socially conditioned – it constitutes situations, objects of knowledge, and the social identities of and relationships between people and groups of people. It is constitutive both in the sense that it helps to sustain and reproduce the social status quo, and in the sense that it contributes to transforming it. Since discourse is so socially consequential, it gives rise to important issues of power. Discursive practices may have major ideological effects – that is, they can help produce and reproduce unequal power relations between (for instance) social classes, women and men, and ethnic/cultural majorities and minorities through the ways in which they represent things and position people. (Fairclough and Wodak, 1997: 258)

Within this definition, the term 'discourse' is of course used very differently by different researchers and also in different academic cultures (Wodak, 2006a,b). In the German and Central European context, a distinction is made between 'text' and 'discourse', relating to the tradition in text linguistics as well as to rhetoric (see Brünner and Graefen, 1994; Vass, 1992; Wodak and Koller, 2008 for summaries). In the English speaking world, 'discourse' is often used both for written and oral texts (see Gee, 2004; Schiffrin, 1994). Other researchers distinguish between different levels of abstractness: Lemke (1995) defines 'text' as the concrete realization of abstract forms of knowledge ('discourse'), thus adhering to a more Foucauldian approach (see also Jäger and Maier in this volume).

The discourse-historical approach relates to the socio-cognitive theory of Teun van Dijk (1998) and views 'discourse' as structured forms of knowledge, whereas 'text' refers to concrete oral utterances or written documents (see Reisigl and Wodak in this volume).

The critical impetus

The shared perspective and programme of CDA emphasize the term 'critical', which in the work of some 'critical linguists' can be traced to the influence of the Frankfurt School and Jürgen Habermas (Anthonissen, 2001; Fay, 1987: 203; Thompson, 1988: 71ff): 'Critical Theory' in the sense of the Frankfurt School, mainly based on the famous essay of Max Horkheimer in 1937, indicates that social theory should be oriented towards critiquing and changing society, in contrast to traditional theory oriented solely to understanding or explaining it. The core concepts of such an understanding of critical theory are:

- Critical theory should be directed at the totality of society in its historical specificity.
- Critical theory should improve the understanding of society by integrating all the major social sciences, including economics, sociology, history, political science, anthropology and psychology.

What is rarely reflected in this understanding of critique is the analyst's position itself. The social embeddedness of research and science, the fact that the research system itself and thus CDA are also dependent on social structures, and that criticism can by no means draw on an outside position but is itself well integrated within social fields, has been emphasized by Pierre Bourdieu (1984). Researchers, scientists and philosophers are not outside the societal hierarchy of power and status but are subject to this structure. They have also frequently occupied and still occupy rather superior positions in society.

In language studies, the term 'critical' was first used to characterize an approach that was called Critical Linguistics (Fowler et al., 1979; Kress and Hodge, 1979). Among other ideas, those scholars held that the use of language could lead to a mystification of social events which systematic analysis could elucidate. 'For example, a missing by-phrase in English passive constructions might be seen as an ideological means for concealing or "mystifying" reference to an agent' (Chilton, 2008).

Nowadays, this concept of critique is conventionally used in a broader sense, denoting, as Krings argues, the practical linking of 'social and political engagement' with 'a sociologically informed construction of society' (Krings et al., 1973; Titscher et al., 2000: 88). Hence, 'critique' is essentially making visible the interconnectedness of things (Fairclough, 1995a: 747; see also Connerton, 1976: 11–39). The reference to the contribution of critical theory to the understanding of CDA and the notions of 'critical' and 'ideology' are of particular importance (see Anthonissen, 2001, for an extensive discussion of this issue).

Critical theories, thus also CDA, want to produce and convey critical knowledge that enables human beings to emancipate themselves from forms of domination through self-reflection. Thus, they are aimed at producing 'enlightenment and emancipation'. Such theories seek not only to describe and explain, but also to root out a particular kind of delusion. Even with differing concepts of ideology, critical theory seeks to create awareness in agents of their own needs and interests. This was, of course, also taken up by Pierre Bourdieu's concepts of 'violènce symbolique' and 'méconnaissance' (Bourdieu, 1989).

In agreement with its critical theory predecessors, CDA emphasizes the need for interdisciplinary work in order to gain a proper understanding of how language functions in constituting and transmitting knowledge, in organizing social institutions or in exercising power (see Graham, 2002; Lemke, 2002; Martin and Wodak, 2003). In any case, CDA researchers have to be aware that their own work is driven by social, economic and political motives like any other academic work and that they are not in any privileged position. Naming oneself 'critical' only implies specific ethical standards: an intention to make their position, research interests and values explicit and their criteria as transparent as possible, without feeling the need to apologize for the critical stance of their work (Van Leeuwen, 2006: 293).

Ideology and power – a kaleidoscopic view

The critical impetus of CDA and other 'critical' research programmes is certainly the legacy of enlightenment (Horkheimer and Adorno, 1969/1991). Critique regularly aims at revealing structures of power and unmasking ideologies. Ideology is then not understood in a positivistic way, i.e. ideologies cannot be subjected to a process of falsification. Nor is it the Marxian type of ideology according to the economic base/superstructure dichotomy that is of interest for CDA.

Political scientists name four central characteristics of ideologies:

1. Power is more important than cognitions.
2. They are capable of guiding individuals' evaluations.
3. They provide guidance through action.
4. They must be logically coherent. (Mullins, 1972)

Although the core definition of ideology as a *coherent and relatively stable set of beliefs or values* has remained the same in political science over time, the connotations associated with this concept have undergone many transformations. During the era of fascism, communism and the Cold War, totalitarian ideology was confronted with democracy, the evil with the good. If we speak of the 'ideology of the new capitalism' (see Van Dijk and Fairclough in this volume), ideology once again has a 'bad' connotation. Obviously, it is not easy to capture ideology as a belief system and simultaneously to free the concept from negative connotations (Knight, 2006: 625).

It is, however, not that type of ideology on the surface of culture that interests CDA, it is rather the more hidden and latent type of everyday beliefs, which often appear disguised as conceptual metaphors and analogies, thus attracting linguists' attention: 'life is a journey, social organizations are plants, love is war', and so on (Lakoff, 1987; Lakoff and Johnson, 1980, 1999). In daily discussion, certain ideas arise more commonly than others. Frequently, people with diverse backgrounds and interests may find themselves thinking alike in startling ways. Dominant ideologies appear as 'neutral', holding on to assumptions that stay largely unchallenged. Organizations that strive for power will try to influence the ideology of a society to become closer to what they want it to be. When most people in a society think alike about certain matters, or even forget that there are alternatives to the status quo, we arrive at the Gramscian concept of *hegemony*. With regard to this key concept of ideology, Van Dijk (1998) sees ideologies as the 'worldviews' that constitute 'social cognition': 'schematically organized complexes of representations and attitudes with regard to certain aspects of the social world, e.g. the schema [...] whites have about blacks' (Van Dijk, 1993b: 258).

Furthermore, it is the functioning of ideologies in everyday life that intrigues CDA researchers. Fairclough has a more Marxist view of ideologies and conceives them as constructions of practices from particular perspectives:

Ideologies are representations of aspects of the world which contribute to establishing and maintaining relations of power, domination and exploitation. They may be enacted in ways of interaction (and therefore in genres) and inculcated in ways of being identities (and therefore styles). Analysis of texts ... is an important aspect of ideological analysis and critique ... (Fairclough, 2003: 218)

Power is another concept which is central for CDA, as it often analyses the language use of those in power, who are responsible for the existence of inequalities. Typically, CDA researchers are interested in the way discourse (re)produces social domination, that is, the power abuse of one group over others, and how dominated groups may discursively resist such abuse (e.g. Van Dijk in this volume). This raises the question of how CDA researchers understand power and what moral standards allow them to differentiate between power use and abuse – a question which has so far had to remain unanswered (Billig, 2008).

There are as many concepts of power as there are social theories. There is almost no sociological or socio-psychological theory which does not provide a distinctive notion of power, with a Weberian definition as the lowest common denominator: power as the chance that an individual in a social relationship can achieve his or her own will even against the resistance of others (Weber, 1980: 28).

At least three different approaches to power can be distinguished:

- power as a result of specific *resources* of individual actors (e.g. French and Raven, 1959)
- power as a specific attribute of *social exchange* in each interaction (e.g. Blau, 1964; Emerson, 1962, 1975)
- power as a systemic and constitutive element/characteristic of society (e.g. from very different angles, Foucault, 1975 and Giddens, 1984).

Michel Foucault focuses on 'technologies of power': discipline is a complex bundle of power technologies developed during the 18th and 19th centuries. Power is thus exercised with intention – but it is not individual intention. Foucault focuses on what is accepted knowledge about how to exercise power. One way of doing this is by threatening with violence. However, suggesting how 'happy' people will become if they buy specific consumer products is also an exercise of power; marketing provides us with a large body of knowledge of powerful techniques. Though Foucault also combines the notions of power and domination in a Weberian tradition, he focuses primarily on structure. Foucault recommends an analysis of power with a rather functionalist strategy: in his historical analysis in *Surveiller et Punir* (Foucault, 1975), he always asks and answers questions concerning the social functions and effects of different technologies of surveillance and punishment. How do things work at the level of ongoing subjugation, at the level of those continuous and uninterrupted processes which subject our bodies, govern our gestures and dictate our behaviours?

Within CDA, power is mostly perceived in the third way, not only because Foucault is one of the theoretical 'godfathers' of CDA, but also because the text in CDA is often regarded as a manifestation of social action which again is widely determined by social structure. Besides, CDA researchers rarely work with interactional texts such as dialogues (Chilton, 2004; Lalouschek et al., 1990; Wodak, 2009 as exceptions). Consequently, it is not the individual resources and not the specifics of single-exchange situations that are crucial for CDA analyses, but the overall structural features in social fields or in overall society. Power is central for understanding the dynamics and specifics of control (of action) in modern societies, but power remains mostly invisible. Linguistic manifestations are under investigation in CDA. This relation between social power and language is a permanent topic not only in CDA (Fairclough, 1989/1991; Wodak, 1989) but also in sociology (Bourdieu, 1991) and sociolinguistics (e.g. Ng and Bradac, 1993; Talbot, 2003; Young and Fitzgerald, 2006).

An important perspective in CDA related to the notion of 'power' is that it is very rare that a text is the work of only one person. In texts, discursive differences are negotiated; they are governed by differences in power that is in part encoded in and determined by discourse and by genre. Therefore, texts are often sites of struggle in that they show traces of differing discourses and ideologies contending and struggling for dominance.

Thus, the defining features of CDA are its concern with power as a central condition in social life, and its efforts to develop a theory of language that incorporates this as a major premise. Closely attended to are not only the notion of struggles for power and control, but also the intertextuality and recontextualization of competing discourses in various public spaces and genres (Iedema, 1997; Iedema and Wodak, 1999; Muntigl et al., 2000). Power is about relations of difference, and particularly about the effects of differences in social structures. The constant unity of language and other social matters ensures that language is entwined in social power in a number of ways: language indexes and expresses power, and is involved where there is contention over and a challenge to power. Power does not necessarily derive from language, but language can be used to challenge power, to subvert it, to alter distributions of power in the short and the long term. Language provides a finely articulated vehicle for establishing differences in power in hierarchical social structures.

In sum: CDA can be defined as being fundamentally interested in analysing opaque as well as transparent structural relationships of dominance, discrimination, power and control as manifested in language. In other words, CDA aims to investigate critically social inequality as it is expressed, constituted, legitimized, and so on, by language use (or in discourse). Most critical discourse analysts would thus endorse Habermas's claim that 'language is also a medium of domination and social force. It serves to legitimize relations of organized power. Insofar as the legitimizations of power relations ... are not articulated ... language is also ideological' (Habermas, 1967: 259).

Main research agenda and challenges

In this section, we summarize some important research agendas which are currently of interest in CDA. We then also list examples of research linked to these agendas and challenges. Although we, of course, encounter a vast amount of research and also many methodological and theoretical approaches, we have decided to restrict ourselves to six major areas and related challenges:

1. Analysing, understanding and explaining the impact of the Knowledge-based Economy on various domains of our societies; related to this, the recontextualization of KBE into other parts of the world and other societies ('transition').
2. Integrating approaches from cognitive sciences into CDA; this requires complex epistemological considerations and the development of new tools. Moreover, we question in which ways such approaches depend on Western cultural contexts and how, related to these issues, Eurocentric perspectives could be transcended.
3. Analysing, understanding and explaining new phenomena in Western political systems, which are due to the impact of (new) media and to transnational, global and local developments and related institutions. More specifically, phenomena such as 'depoliticization' and 'participation' need to be investigated in detail.
4. Analysing, understanding and explaining the impact of new media and related genres which entails developing new multimodal theoretical and methodological approaches. Our concepts of space and time have changed, and these changes interact in dialectical ways with new modes and genres of communication.
5. Analysing, understanding and explaining the relationship between complex historical processes, hegemonic narratives and CDA approaches. Identity politics on all levels always entails the integration of past experiences, present events and future visions. The concepts of intertextuality and recontextualization are inherently tied to interdisciplinary approaches.
6. Avoiding 'cherry picking' (choosing the examples which best fit the assumptions) by integrating quantitative and qualitative methods and by providing retroductable, self-reflective presentations of past or current research processes.

Of course, the many issues of *Discourse and Society*, *Journal of Language and Politics*, *Visual Semiotics*, and *Critical Discourse Studies*, to name but a few, have published a huge variety of CDA-oriented research over the past decade which we cannot review in detail. We therefore necessarily have to refer readers to the many handbooks and journals in the field.[5]

Language of the New Capitalism and the Knowledge-based Economy (KBE)

In Jessop et al. (2008), many aspects and dimensions of the impact of KBE on higher education are explored from sociological, educational and CDA perspectives. KBE has penetrated most domains of our Western societies and is also colonizing other parts of the world. Indeed, *globalization and competitiveness rhetoric* (Muntigl et al., 2000) seem to be ubiquitous, and the quantification and economization of knowledge serve to rank social institutions and individuals. Through detailed case studies, the recontextualization of more global policy strategies can be illustrated on the micro level (Falkner et al., 2005). This, of course, requires interdisciplinary research as well as new theories on transition and social change (see Krzyżanowski and Wodak, 2008).

Chouliaraki and Fairclough (1999) explain and elaborate how CDA is useful in disclosing the discursive nature of much contemporary social and cultural change. Particularly the language of the mass media is scrutinized as a site of power, of struggle and also as a site where language is often apparently transparent. Media institutions often purport to be neutral, in that they provide space for public discourse, reflect states of affairs disinterestedly, and give the perceptions and arguments of the newsmakers. Fairclough reveals the fallacy of such assumptions, and illustrates the mediating and constructing role of the media with a variety of examples. He has also been concerned with the 'Language of New Labour' (Fairclough, 2000a) which, of course, is part and parcel of KBE ideology.

In this vein, Jane Mulderrig (2006) develops a methodology and interdisciplinary theoretical framework for historically analysing the exercise of governmental power in a specific policy field, thus addressing at least three of the above-mentioned challenges. At the theoretical level, this work employs an interdisciplinary approach to CDA by grounding close textual analysis in both educational sociology and neo-Marxist state theory. It thus contextualizes the linguistic findings in terms of historical developments in the capitalist state over the last four decades. This research also develops novel ways of using corpus tools in CDA, and in particular it demonstrates their heuristic value in directing the analyst's gaze in unexpected and often fruitful directions (see Mautner in this volume; and Baker et al., 2008). More specifically, the themes explored in this research include the rise of a more personalized form of governmental identity, and the prominent role of the pronoun 'we' in legitimizing government action and deflecting its public accountability. A further strand to this research makes a direct link between the verbs used to perform government actions and the increasing social significance of 'governing at a distance' or 'networked governance' as described by, among others, the social theorist Nikolas Rose (1999).

Phil Graham also elaborates the problems of New Capitalism while integrating a strong historical perspective (Graham, 2002). The historical investigation of hortatory genres, for example, compares the emergence of, and struggles between, the Church, 'divine right' royalties and secular forces over legitimate uses of the sermon form in Western Europe between the 10th and 14th centuries, with contemporary struggles over genres that are used to motivate people on a mass scale. The main focus of Graham's research is to explore and explain the relationships between new media, new genres, institutions and social change at a macro level. The perspective is primarily historical, political–economic, relational and dynamic. Genres are produced, textured and transformed within institutional contexts over long periods of time. In turn, institutions invest years – in some cases, millennia – in developing, maintaining and adapting generic forms to changing social conditions in order to maintain or gain power. Graham believes that at certain times in history, certain genres become very effective in motivating or manipulating large sections of society. Because genres are developed within institutions, and thus within the realms of vested interests, they display inherent axiological biases. The nature of knowledge and its status as a commodity form immediately become problematic. In the tradition of dialectical argumentation, Graham accepts the claims that knowledge can become a dominant commodity; that a global economy can be built on such forms; and that our new media must, in some fundamental way, underpin the emergence of this new form of political economy. The research problem is therefore formulated as an historical investigation into the relationship between language, new media and social perceptions of value.

Focusing cognition

The seminal book by Teun van Dijk and Walter Kintsch, *Strategies of Discourse Comprehension* (1983), triggered research in discourse and cognition from interdisciplinary and critical perspectives. In this book, they considered the relevance of discourse to the study of language processing. Currently, interest in cognition has grown, and many scholars attempt a combination of new cognitive theories (on conceptual metaphors, for example) with CDA (Charteris-Black, 2006; Musolff, 2004). Some of this research draws on earlier attempts which integrated cognition, sociolinguistics and discourse analysis (such as Lutz and Wodak, 1987; Wodak, 1986a, 1996; Wodak and Schulz, 1986) by proposing new approaches (see below).

Much of the focus in this area has been placed on researching social inclusion and exclusion. Teun Van Dijk, for example, has recently paid special attention to the discursive reproduction of racism in Spain and Latin America (Van Dijk, 2005). The study by John Richardson on the '(mis)representation of Islam', and research on the representation of migrants, asylum-seekers and refugees in the British Press, have elaborated research on racism, antisemitism and xenophobia in intricate ways, by combining quantitative and qualitative methods, and by focusing on argumentation as well (see Baker et al., 2008; Delanty et al., 2008; Richardson, 2004; Wodak, 2008b, 2008c).

Moreover, the focus on theorizing *context and knowledge* is apparent. Van Dijk argues that whereas (critical and other) discourse studies have paid extensive attention in the last few decades to the structures of text and talk, they only paid lip-service to the necessity of developing the relations between text and context (but see Panagl and Wodak, 2004). Most approaches, also in CDA, define the influence of the social context on language variation and discourse in terms of objective social variables such as gender, class, race, ethnicity or age. Van Dijk argues that no such direct influence exists, because social structures and discourse structures cannot be related directly, and need the mediation of an interface. He shows that this interface must be cognitive, in the sense that it is not 'objective' social situations, but the *subjective definitions of the relevant properties of communicative situations that influence text and talk*. These definitions are then made explicit in terms of a special kind of *mental model* (see Van Dijk, this volume). In sum, Van Dijk emphasizes that CDA should also not limit itself to a study of the relationship between discourse and social structure, such as racism and other forms of power abuse, but that language use always presupposes the intervening mental models, goals and general social representations (knowledge, attitudes, ideologies, norms, values). In other words, the study of discourse triangulates between society/culture/situation, cognition, and discourse/language.

Paul Chilton, who is a cognitive linguist, has never explicitly applied the term CDA to his own work and has always worked within a cognitive framework, principally on the discourse of politics and the international relations framework (cf. Chilton, 1994a, 1994b, 1996a, 1996b, 2004, 2005a, 2005b; Chilton and Lakoff, 1995). His most recent (2004, 2005a) and ongoing work departs from CDA's tendency to allegedly reify social structures and processes and raises major research questions relating to the relationship between language and social cognition in the evolution of the human species. More particularly, he has drawn on cognitive evolutionary psychology to ask whether there might exist an innate 'critical instinct'. If this was the case, he argues, then what is the role of critical discourse analysis? Chilton's argument is that the most fundamental issue is whether societies provide the freedom to enable the 'critical instinct' to operate. This position is, of course, extremely vulnerable and has been challenged by other CDA researchers (Fairclough in this volume; Van Dijk, 2007a; Wodak, 2007). Linked to this approach is a concern with universal aspects of language and the human mind, a concern that is also reflected in his current collaborative work on comparative discourse analysis that crosses linguistic, cultural and political boundaries (Chilton, 2007; Chilton et al., forthcoming). Comparative discourse analysis, he argues, is the most serious challenge facing practitioners of CDA, if CDA is to overcome its Euro-centric drift and respond to a globalized scholarly environment.

The emergent blend of CDA, cognitive linguistics and corpus linguistics has become a huge priority that is also recognized by many other scholars (see, for example, Koller and Davidson, 2008). However, what remains unsolved is the apparent contradiction that CDA starts from a complex social problem or phe-nomenon; cognitive linguistics, however, starts from the individual mind, and corpus linguistics from the largely (but not fully!) decontextualized text. Thus, integration will have to address these epistemological considerations. Both Chilton and Koller (and many other CDA researchers) state that the analysis of powerful, even hegemonic discourse(s) which however do not necessarily dis-criminate against a particular social group has to be enhanced, for example, by aspects of corporate self-presentation, as well as the impact of new genres, and so on (Koller, 2008).

Multimodality and 'new' genres

Recognition of the contribution of all the aspects of the communicative context to text meaning, as well as a growing awareness in media studies in general and in the importance of non-verbal aspects of texts in particular, has turned attention to *semiotic devices in discourse other than the linguistic ones*. In particular, the theory put forward by Kress and van Leeuwen (1996) provides a useful framework for con-sidering the communicative potential of visual devices in the media. Currently, van Leeuwen is focusing on the semiotics of handwriting and typography and the question of colour, as well as on the constraints imposed by certain software, PowerPoint templates, and so on. Thus, it is important for social semiotics to pro-vide models of semiotic practice that are appropriate to the practices they model, and as different semiotic practices are very differently organized, it is not possi-ble to apply a single model to all. Van Leeuwen claims that the role and status of semiotic practices in society are currently undergoing change as a result of the fact that it is increasingly global corporations and semiotic technologies, rather than national institutions, which regulate semiotic production and consumption (see also van Leeuwen, this volume).

Jay Lemke's recent work has emphasized multimedia semiotics, multiple timescales and hypertexts or *traversals*. This work emphasizes the implicit value systems and their connections to institutional and personal identity in new multimodal genres. The work on multiple timescales, for example, is an exten-sion of earlier work on ecological–social systems as complex dynamical systems with semiotic cultures. It is very important in considering all aspects of social dynamics to look across multiple timescales, i.e. how processes and practices which take place at relatively faster rates are organized within the framework of more slowly changing features of social institutions and cultures (see the concept of 'non-simultaneity' or *Ungleichzeitigkeit*) (Lemke, 2001, 2002). Lemke's work has combined both these themes to develop the idea that although we tell our lives as narratives, we experience them as hypertexts. Building on research on the semantic resources of hypertext as a medium, he proposed that postmodern lifestyles are increasingly liberated from particular institutional roles, and that we tend to move, on multiple timescales, from involvement in one institution to another, creating new kinds of meaning, less bound to fixed genres and registers, as we 'surf' across channels, websites and lived experiences. This is seen as a new historical development, not supplanting institutions, but building up new sociocultural possibilities on and over them.

Moreover, Lemke – while building on CDA and extending the tools from systemic linguistics – has increasingly investigated combinations of language, visual media and dynamic–interactive effects. The most advanced part of this work concerns computer games. Here, one has to take into account not only the semiotic and semantic affordances of an interactive environment, but also the phenomenological experience and particularly the feelings and emotions of the user. This requires developing a number of new tools to think about and analyse categories of feelings, and their combination with other sorts of meanings. In this vein, the semantics of evaluations and judgements is a key link, as is re-thinking feelings, at least in part, as social and distributed, rather than as totally individual and internal. Of course, there are also cultural dimensions to feelings; this point addresses similar issues to those mentioned by Chilton (see above), namely that CDA has to move away from a Eurocentric focus.

Another branch of this work is the critical analysis of *transmedia*. This is the term now used for sets of related media (e.g. a book and film, a website and a game, merchandise, stories written by fans of the movie or games, etc.) that either form a commercial franchise (e.g. *Harry Potter, Star Wars*) or some more loosely connected intertextual set (see the remarks on KBE above). In either case, there are economic and material relationships as well as textual and semantic ones (see also the research by Graham above). Thus, these cases are particularly revealing for a study of the *political economy of signs*. Commercial interests and their ideologies interact with consumer interests and consumer beliefs and desires. Of special importance is the appearance of collectives of consumers who also become producers of parallel or counter media: for instance, readers write their own stories changing the values and practices of famous characters from popular movies, fiction, games, and so on, and these are widely read and distributed on the internet, for example in blogs. Something similar is also happening with art, games and music. Fans edit commercial movies, add a musical soundtrack, and create new montage effects with completely different ideological and narrative meanings from the original works, which illustrate creative and subversive processes of the recontextualization of multiple genres and modes in detail.

Therefore, Theo van Leeuwen (2006: 292) argues that:

> [c]ritical discourse analysis has also moved beyond language, taking on board that discourses are often multimodally realized, not only through text and talk, but also through other modes of communication such as images … Overall, then, critical discourse analysis has moved towards more explicit dialogue between social theory and practice, richer contextualization, greater interdisciplinarity and greater attention to the multimodality of discourse.

Political discourse

The study of political discourse after the Second World War was triggered in part by the investigation of National Socialist (NS) language (Klemperer, 1975/1947); it was essential to understand and explain the roles and importance of language and communication in totalitarian regimes and their propaganda. Utz Maas was the first linguist to subject the everyday linguistic practice of National Socialism to an in-depth analysis: he used NS texts to exemplify his approach of *Lesweisenanalyse* (Maas, 1984, 1989a, 1989b).

His historical 'argumentation analysis', based on the theories of Michel Foucault, demonstrates how in complex ways discourse is determined by society, i.e. in what may be termed 'a social practice'. In his analysis of language practices during the National Socialist regime between 1932 and 1938, he showed how the discursive practices of society in Germany were impacted by the National Socialist (NS) discourse characterized by social–revolutionist undertones. NS discourse had superseded almost all forms of language (practices), a fact that made it difficult for an individual who did not want to cherish the tradition of an unworldly Romanticism to use language in a critical–reflective way. Discourse is basically understood as the result of *collusion*: the conditions of the political, social and linguistic practice impose themselves practically 'behind the back of the subjects', while the actors do not understand 'the game' (see also Bourdieu's 'violènce symbolique'). Discourse analysis identifies the rules which make a text into a fascist text. In the same way as grammar characterizes the structure of sentences, discourse rules characterize utterances/texts that are acceptable within a certain practice. The focus is not on 'National Socialist language' per se, but the aim is rather to record and analyse the spectrum of linguistic relations based on a number of texts dealing with various spheres of life. These texts represent a complicated network of similarities, which overlap and intersect. Therefore, it is also important to do justice to the 'polyphony' of texts resulting from the fact that societal contradictions are inscribed into texts (see also the concept of 'entextualization' as employed by Blommaert, 2005). Texts from diverse social and political contexts (cooking recipes, local municipal provisions on agriculture, texts by NS politicians, but also by critics of this ideology, who are ultimately involved in the dominant discourse) are analysed in a representative sample (see Wodak and de Cillia, 2006, for details and an extensive overview of the field of language and politics).

The study of political institutions and everyday life and decision-making in organizations has become a major new focus of CDA. Krzyżanowski and Oberhuber (2007), for example, have analysed the European Convention in much detail. The focus on discursive dimensions of transnational political organizations also led to the elaboration of discursively constructed visions/conceptions of social and political order in Europe/the EU. Wodak (2009) focuses on the everyday lives of MEPs and other politicians because – as she argues – *depoliticization* is linked to 'the democracy deficit' and the huge dissatisfaction about the strong ritualization of politics and the snapshots provided by media which condense complex political processes into iconic images (Triandafyllidou et al., 2009). Such studies allow insight into 'politics as a profession' and into the complexity of political decision-making. If the media, however, allow us to venture *backstage*, this usually happens in the context of the sex and corruption scandals of politicians. (Hence, in the above-mentioned ethnographic studies, 'backstage' access opens the door to understanding 'the doing of politics'.)

Much CDA research in the domain of politics centres on right wing populist rhetoric on many occasions, as right wing populist rhetoric is becoming more and more hegemonic in many European countries (see 'Haiderization' – Krzyżanowski and Wodak, 2008; Pelinka and Wodak, 2002; Richardson and Wodak, 2008; Rydgren, 2005; Wodak and Pelinka, 2002). This research is triggered by the rising dominance and hegemony of this kind of rhetoric and its apt use of indirect strategies to address multiple audiences (see Reisigl and Wodak, this volume). The latter research also develops new methodologies for CDA: the use of ethnography, focus groups and narrative interviews, combined with more traditional data sources such as newspapers and political speeches (Wodak and Krzyżanowski, 2008).

Research on politics from a historical perspective also co-triggered CDA from the very beginning. The study for which the Discourse-Historical Approach (DHA) was actually developed, for instance, first attempted to trace in detail the constitution of an antisemitic stereotyped image, or *Feindbild*, as it emerged in public discourse in the 1986 Austrian presidential campaign of Kurt Waldheim (Gruber, 1991; Mitten, 1992; Wodak et al., 1990). In order to be able to study the discourse about the 'Waldheim Affair', 'context' was unravelled into various dimensions.

The DHA has been further elaborated in a number of more recent studies, for example, in a study on racist discrimination against immigrants from Romania and in a study on the discourse about nation and national identity in Austria (Kovàcs and Wodak, 2003; Wodak et al., 1999) and in the European Union (Muntigl et al., 2000; Wodak and Van Dijk, 2000). The 1999 study was concerned with the analysis of the relationships between the discursive construction of national sameness and the discursive construction of difference leading to the political and social exclusion of specific out-groups. The findings suggest that discourses about nations and national identities rely on at least four types of discursive macro-strategies. These are:

- constructive strategies (aiming at the construction of national identities)
- justificatory strategies (aiming at the conservation and reproduction of national identities or narratives of identity)
- transformative strategies (aiming at the change of national identities)
- destructive strategies (aiming at the dismantling of national identities).

More recently, much research has focused on commemorative events which manifest hegemonic ways of dealing with traumatic pasts in various societies

(Anthonissen and Blommaert, 2007; Blommaert, 2005; de Cillia and Wodak, 2008; Ensink and Sauer, 2003; Heer et al., 2008; Le, 2006; Martin and Wodak, 2003; Reisigl, 2007; Wodak and de Cillia, 2007). In most of these studies, media, school books, speeches at national days and the like are analysed to illustrate the myths which are constructed to provide new, 'sanitized' narratives which cover up ruptures, war crimes and conflicts which have occurred in the past. For example, Heer et al. (2008) describe in detail the huge scandal and crisis when the two exhibitions on war crimes committed by the German *Wehrmacht* during the Second World War were opened to viewers, in 1995 and 2001. A carefully constructed and protected myth was destroyed by these exhibitions – the myth that the *Wehrmacht* soldiers had been innocent whereas the SS and other units had been the sole perpetrators.

Differences and similarities – beyond the social dimension

The differences between CDA and other DA, pragmatic and sociolinguistic approaches may be most clearly established with regard to the general principles of CDA. Firstly, the nature of the problems with which CDA is concerned differs from all those approaches which do not explicitly express their research interest. In general, CDA asks different research questions, and some CDA scholars play an advocatory role for socially discriminated groups. Looking at the CDA contributions collected in this reader, it also becomes evident that the line drawn between social scientific research which ought to be intelligible, and political argumentation sometimes gets blurred.

Specifically, we distinguish between approaches which proceed deductively and such that choose a more inductive perspective. Linked to this distinction is the choice of objects under investigation: more deductively oriented theories which also propose a closed theoretical framework are more likely to illustrate their assumptions with a few examples which seem to fit their claims (e.g. the dialectical–relational approach and socio-cognitive approach in this volume). More inductively oriented approaches usually stay at the 'meso level' and select problems where they attempt to discover new insights through in-depth case studies and ample data collection (for example, DHA, social actors approach, corpus linguistics approach, dispositive analysis, in this volume). Of course, all approaches moreover proceed abductively, i.e. oscillate between theory and data analysis in retroductive ways. However, on a continuum, we are able to distinguish obvious priorities in choosing entry points and themes (see Figure 1.1).

Related to the choice of more 'macro-' or 'meso-topics' (such as 'globalization' or 'knowledge' versus 'un/employment' or 'right wing populism'), we encounter differences in the evaluation of the chosen topics and objects under investigation. Macro-topics are relatively non-controversial in the respective

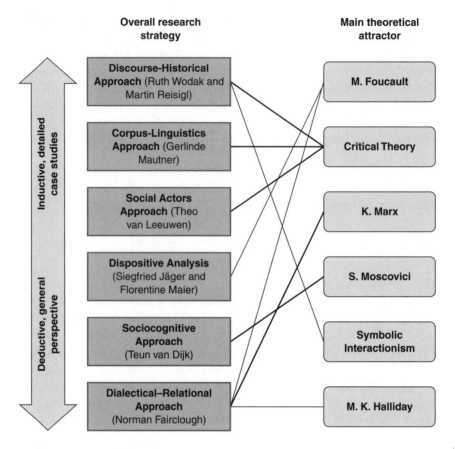

FIGURE 1.1   *Overall research strategies and theoretical background*

national or international academic contexts; some meso-topics, however, can touch on the very core of the respective national community to which the researcher belongs. For example, research on concrete antisemitic, xenophobic and racist occurrences is much more controversial in certain academic and national contexts and regarded as 'unpatriotic' or hostile than many macro-themes – this explains grave problems which critical scholars have encountered when venturing into such seemingly tabooed fields (see Heer et al., 2008).

In any case, related to the object of investigation, it remains a fact that CDA follows a different and critical approach to problems, since it endeavours to reveal power relations that are frequently obfuscated and hidden, and then to derive results which are also of practical relevance.

Furthermore, one important characteristic arises from the assumption that all discourses are historical and can therefore only be understood with reference to their context. Therefore, these approaches refer to such extralinguistic factors as culture, society and ideology in intricate ways, depending on their concepts of context and their research methodologies and ways of data collection. Hence, the notion of context is crucial for CDA, since this explicitly includes social–psychological, political and ideological components and thereby postulates interdisciplinary procedures.

Interdisciplinarity is implemented in many different ways in the CDA approaches assembled in this volume: in some cases, interdisciplinarity is characteristic of the theoretical framework (dispositive approach, dialectical–relational approach, socio-cognitive approach); in other cases, interdisciplinarity also applies to the collection and analysis of data (social actors approach, DHA). Moreover, CDA uses the concepts of intertextuality and interdiscursivity; in sum, it may be concluded that CDA is open to a broad range of factors exerting an influence on texts.

A further difference between CDA and other DA approaches emerges with regard to the dialectic relationships between language and society. CDA does not take this relationship to be simply deterministic but invokes the concept of *mediation*. The dialectical–relational approach draws on Halliday's multifunctional linguistic theory (Halliday, 1985) and the concept of *orders of discourse* according to Foucault, while the discourse-historical approach and the socio-cognitive approach make use of theories of social cognition (e.g. Moscovici, 2000). This reflection on issues of mediation between language and social structure is absent from many other linguistic approaches, for example from conversation analysis. This is somewhat related to the level of social aggregation: though CDA concentrates on notions like ideology or power, scholars focus on different units of analysis – the way in which individuals mentally perceive, or the way social structures determine discourse (see Figure 1.2). In simplified terms, we can distinguish between more cognitive–socio-psychological and more macro-sociological–structural approaches – although, admittedly, this is a rough distinction.

A further characteristic of CDA is that most researchers integrate linguistic categories into their analyses – but to a different extent and with a different focus and intensity. CDA does not necessarily include a broad range of linguistic categories in each single analysis; one might get the impression that only a few linguistic devices are central to CDA studies. For instance, many CDA scholars consistently use *social actor analysis* by focusing upon pronouns, attributes and the verbal mode, time and tense; Hallidayan transitivity analysis and the analysis of argumentative *topoi* are also used frequently by other social scientists because these concepts seem to be quite easy to apply without much linguistic background knowledge. Exceptions always prove the generalization: Reisigl and Wodak (this volume) and Van Dijk (this volume) illustrate how a broad range of macro and micro linguistic, pragmatic and argumentative features can be operationalized and integrated in the analysis of specific texts (Figure 1.2).

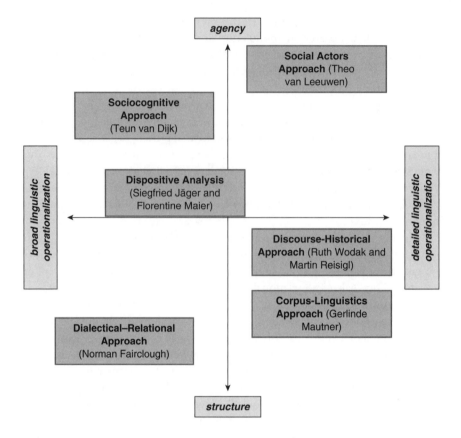

FIGURE 1.2   *Linguistic depth of field and level of aggregation*

In principle, we may assume that linguistic categories such as *deixis* and pro-nouns can be analysed in any linguistic methodology, but they are salient for CDA. Explicitly or implicitly, CDA distinguishes between the linguistic surface and some kind of deep structure; for instance, the dialectical–relational approach speaks of form and texture at the textual level, the discourse-historical approach of forms of linguistic realization.

As for the methods and procedures used for interpretation, CDA generally views them as hermeneutic, although this characteristic is not completely evident in the positioning of every author. Hermeneutics can be understood as the method of grasping and interpreting meanings. The *hermeneutic circle* – i.e. the meaning of one part can only be understood in the context of the whole, but this in turn is only accessible from its components – indicates the problem of the intelligibility of the hermeneutic interpretation. Therefore, hermeneutic interpretation requires detailed documentation. However, the specifics of the hermeneutic interpretation process are not made completely transparent by many CDA-orientated studies.[6] If a crude distinction has to be made between 'text-extending' and 'text-reducing' methods of analysis, then CDA, on account of its concentration of very clear formal properties and the associated compression of texts during analysis, may be characterized as 'text-reducing'. These findings contradict the mainly hermeneutic impetus of most CDA approaches.

Methodology

CDA in all its various forms understands itself to be strongly based in theory. To which theories do the different approaches refer? Here we encounter a variety of theories, ranging from theories on society and power in Michel Foucault's tradition and theories of social cognition and grammar, to individual concepts that draw on larger theoretical traditions. As a first step, this section aims to systematize these different theoretical influences (see Figure 1.1).

Moreover, this section is devoted to the problem of the operationalization of theoretical concepts. The primary issue here is how the various approaches of CDA are able to 'translate' their theoretical claims into instruments and methods of analysis. In particular, the emphasis is on *mediation* between 'grand theories' as applied to larger society, and concrete instances of social interaction which result in texts. In addition to what can be described primarily as   hermeneutics, one finds interpretative perspectives with differing emphases, among them even quantitative procedures (see Mautner, this volume).

Particularly worthy of discussion is the way in which sampling is conducted in CDA. Most studies analyse 'typical texts'. What is typical in which social situation, and for which aspect of a social problem, however, frequently remains vague.

The links between theory and discourse in CDA can be described in terms of the model for theoretical and methodological research procedures illustrated in Figure 1.3 (see below).

Theoretical grounding and objectives

Among the different positions within CDA presented in this book, there is neither any guiding theoretical viewpoint that is used coherently within CDA, nor do the CDA protagonists proceed consistently from the area of theory to the field of discourse and text, and back to theory (see Figure 1.1).

Within the CDA approaches presented here, all the theoretical levels of sociological and socio-psychological theory can be discovered (the concept of different theoretical levels is in the tradition of Merton, 1967: 39–72):

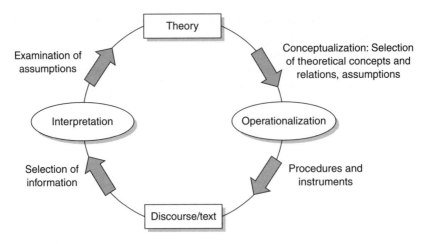

FIGURE 1.3   *Empirical research as a circular process*

- **Epistemology**, i.e. theories which provide models of the conditions, contingencies and limitations of human perception in general, and scientific perception in particular.
- **General social theories**, often called 'grand theories', try to conceptualize the complex relations between social structure and social action and thus link micro- and macro-sociological phenomena. Within this level, one can distinguish between the more structuralist and the more individualist approaches. To put it very simply, the former provide top-down explanations (structure>action), whereas the latter prefer bottom-up explanations (action>structure). Many modern theories try to reconcile these positions and imply some kind of circularity between social action and social structure.
- **Middle-range theories** focus either upon specific social phenomena (e.g. conflict, cognition, social networks) or on specific subsystems of society (e.g. economy, politics, religion).
- **Micro-sociological theories** try to explain social interaction, for example the resolution of the double contingency problem (Parsons and Shils, 1951: 3–29) or the reconstruction of everyday procedures which members of a society use to create their own social order (i.e. ethnomethodology).
- **Socio-psychological theories** concentrate upon the social conditions of emotion and cognition and, compared to microsociology, prefer causal explanations to a hermeneutic interpretation of meaning.
- **Discourse theories** aim at the conceptualization of discourse as a social phenomenon and try to explain its genesis and its structure.
- **Linguistic theories**, e.g. theories of argumentation, of grammar, of rhetoric, describe the patterns specific to language systems and verbal communication.

As all these theoretical levels can be found in CDA, in the following, we present a short overview of the theoretical positions and methodological objectives of CDA approaches.

Among the approaches assembled in this reader, **Dispositive Analysis** (**DA** – Siegfried Jäger and Florentine Maier in this volume) is closest to the origin of the notion of discourse, i.e. to Michel Foucault's structuralist explanations of discursive phenomena. However, it detects a blind spot in Foucault's theory, namely the mediation between subject and object, between discursive and non-discursive practices (activities) on the one hand and manifestations (objects) on the other. Here, DA strategically inserts Aleksej Leont'ev's (e.g. 1982) activity theory. Thus, the social actor becomes the link between discourse and reality. The epistemological position is based upon Ernesto Laclau's social constructivism, which denies any societal reality outside of the discursive. In that way, Dispositive Analysis introduces a dualism of discourse and social reality.

As all CDA approaches accept that discourse, understood as language use, is but one manifestation of social action (Chilton, 2005b: 20), DA is forced to argue against the Foucauldian notion of discourse which also includes non-linguistic elements. DA therefore applies Jürgen Link's notion of discourse as 'an institutionalized way of talking that regulates and reinforces action and thereby exerts power' (Link, 1983: 60). Furthermore, Foucault's concept of the 'dispositive' frames both discursive and nondiscursive practices and materializations. DA thus explicitly aims at the analysis of discourses and dispositives.

The **Sociocognitive Approach** (**SCA** – Teun van Dijk in this volume) is situated on the socio-psychological dimension of the CDA field. The approach draws on social representation theory (e.g. Moscovici, 2000). Discourse is seen as a communicative event, including conversational interaction and written text, as well as associated gestures, facework, typographical layout, images and any other 'semiotic' or multi-media dimension of signification. Van Dijk relies on socio-cognitive theory and understands linguistics in a broad 'structural–functional' sense. He argues that CDA should be based on a sound theory of context. Within this claim, the theory of social representations plays a major role.

Social actors involved in discourse do not only use their individual experiences and strategies, they rely upon collective frames of perceptions, i.e. *social representations*. These socially shared perceptions form the link between the social system and the individual cognitive system, and perform the translation, homogenization and coordination between external requirements and subjective experience. Thus, the approach refers to the 'link' which Chilton (2005a) detects as missing. This assumption is not new: already in the first half of the 20th century, Émile Durkheim (e.g. 1933) pointed to the significance of collective ideas in constructing social order. Serge Moscovici (1982) coined the notion of social representations as a bulk of concepts, opinions, attitudes, evaluations, images and explanations which result from daily life and are sustained by communication. Social representations are shared among members of a social group, which was already stated by Émile Durkheim: 'The ideas of man … are not personal and are not restricted to me; I share them, to a large degree, with all the men who belong to the same social group that I do. Because they are held in common, concepts are the supreme instrument of all intellectual exchange' (cited in Bellah, 1973: 52). Thus, they form a core element of the individual's social identity (Wagner, 1994: 132). Social representations are always bound to specific social groups. They are dynamic constructs and subject to permanent change. Together, they constitute a hierarchical order of mutual dependency (Duveen and Lloyd, 1990). SCA introduces the concept of *context models*, i.e. mental representations of the structures of the communicative situation that are salient for a participant. These context models control the 'pragmatic' part of discourse, whereas event models control the 'semantic' part. Three forms of social representations are relevant in this context:

1. knowledge (personal, group, cultural)
2. attitudes (not in the social psychology understanding)
3. ideologies.

Discourses take place within society, and can only be understood in the interplay of social situation, action, actor and societal structures.

The **Discourse-Historical Approach (DHA)** explicitly tries to establish a theory of discourse by linking *fields of action* (Girnth, 1996), *genres*, *discourses* and *texts*. Although DHA is aligned to critical theory, 'grand theories' play a minor role compared with the discourse model and the emphasis on historical analysis: context is understood as mainly historical. Thus far, the DHA consistently agrees with Mouzelis's (1995) pessimistic diagnosis of social research. DHA consequently follows his recommendations: not to get lost in theoretical labyrinths, not to invest too much in the operationalization of inoperationalizable 'grand theories' – but rather to develop conceptual tools adequate for specific social problems. The DHA focuses on the field of politics, where it develops conceptual frameworks for political discourse. Reisigl and Wodak try to fit linguistic theories into their model of discourse. They make extensive use of argumentation theory in the example presented in this volume. That does not necessarily imply that the concepts resulting from argumentation theory are adequate for other research questions.

As the **Corpus Linguistics Approach** (**CLA** – Gerlinde Mautner in this volume) is a quantitative, linguistic extension of CDA, it provides additional linguistic devices for thorough analysis – and can be applied against the backdrop of CDA approaches.

The **Social Actors Approach** (**SAA** – Theo van Leeuwen in this volume) refers to a broad scope of sociological and linguistic theories, especially to those explaining the role of action to establish social structure: representation is ultimately based on practice, on that which people do – it is the primacy of practice which constitutes the theoretical core of SAA. Therefore, SAA introduces sources from Malinowski to Parsons, and from Bernstein to Bourdieu. This idea of individual actors permanently constituting and reproducing social structure is linked with a Foucauldian notion of discourse, somewhat similar to DA and DRA.

The **Dialectical–Relational Approach** (**DRA** – Norman Fairclough in this volume) takes a rather grand-theory-oriented position: Fairclough focuses upon social conflict in the Marxian tradition and tries to detect its linguistic manifestations in discourses, in specific elements of dominance, difference and resistance. According to DRA, every social practice has a semiotic element. Productive activity, the means of production, social relations, social identities, cultural values, consciousness and semiosis are dialectically related elements of social practice. He understands CDA as the analysis of the dialectical relationships between semiosis (including language) and other elements of social practices. These semiotic aspects of social practice are responsible for the constitution of genres and styles. The semiotic aspect of social order is called the *order of discourse*. His approach to CDA oscillates between a focus on structure and a focus on action. CDA should pursue emancipatory objectives, and should be focused upon the problems confronting what can loosely be referred to as the 'losers' within particular forms of social life. DRA draws upon a specific linguistic theory – Systemic Functional Linguistics (Halliday, 1985) – which analyses language as shaped (even in its grammar) by the social functions it has come to serve.

Gathering data

We concluded above that CDA does not constitute a well-defined empirical methodology but rather a bulk of approaches with theoretical similarities and research questions of a specific kind. But there is no CDA way of gathering data, either. Some authors do not even mention sampling, while other scholars strongly rely on traditions based outside the sociolinguistic field.[7] In any case, similar to Grounded Theory (Glaser and Strauss, 1967), data collection is not considered to be a specific phase that must be completed before analysis begins: it is a matter of finding indicators for particular concepts, expanding concepts into categories and, on the basis of these results, collecting further data (*theoretical sampling*). In this procedure, data collection is never completely excluded, and new questions always arise which can only be dealt with if more data are collected or earlier data are re-examined (Strauss, 1987; Strauss and Corbin, 1990).

Most of the approaches to CDA do not explicitly recommend sampling procedures. Obviously, CLA specifically refers to large corpora of text. DA, SCA, SAA and DRA mainly rely on existing texts, such as mass media communication or documents. This is also true for DHA, though it additionally postulates that studies should incorporate fieldwork and ethnography if possible to explore the object under investigation as a precondition for any further analysis and theorizing. The focus on already existing texts implies specific strengths, in particular it provides non-reactive data (Webb et al., 1966), and certain weaknesses concerning the research questions which have to be operationalized.

Operationalization and analysis

CDA places its methodology in the hermeneutic rather than in the analytical–deductive tradition. In any case, the linguistic character of CDA becomes evident, because in contrast to other approaches of text and discourse analysis (e.g. Content Analysis, Grounded Theory, Conversation Analysis; see Titscher et al., 2000), CDA strongly relies on linguistic categories. This does not mean, of course, that topics and contents play no role, but the core operationalizations depend on linguistic concepts such as actors, mode, time, tense, argumentation and so on. Nevertheless, an exhaustive list of linguistic devices cannot be given, for their selection depends mainly on the specific research questions.

DA distinguishes between a more content-oriented phase of (1) structure analysis and a more linguistically oriented phase of (2) fine analysis. Within *structure analysis*, the media and the general themes have to be characterized. Within the *fine analysis*, DA focuses upon context, text surface and rhetorical means. Exemplary linguistic indicators are figurativeness, vocabulary and argumentation types. DA takes into account both qualitative and quantitative aspects of these features. DA analyses:

- the kind and form of argumentation
- certain argumentation strategies
- the intrinsic logic and composition of texts
- implicit implicateurs and insinuations
- the collective symbolism or 'figurativeness', symbolism, metaphors and so on, both in language and in design (statistics, photographs, pictures, caricatures, etc.)
- idioms, sayings, clichés, vocabulary and style
- actors (persons, pronominal structure)
- references, for example, to (the) science(s)
- the particulars of the sources of knowledge, etc.

SCA generally argues that a complete discourse analysis of a large corpus of text or talk is totally impossible. If the focus of research is on the ways in which some speakers or writers exercise power in or by their discourse, research focuses on those properties that can vary as a function of social power. SCA therefore suggests the following linguistic indicators:

- stress and intonation
- word order
- lexical style
- coherence
- local semantic moves such as disclaimers
- topic choice

- speech acts
- schematic organization
- rhetorical figures
- syntactic structures
- propositional structures
- turn-takings
- repairs
- hesitation.

SCA assumes that most of these are exemplary forms of interaction which are in principle susceptible to speaker control, but are in practice mostly not consciously controlled. Other categories, such as the form of words and many structures of sentences, are grammatically obligatory and contextually invariant and hence are usually not subject to speaker control and social power. SCA further suggests six steps of analysis:

1. The analysis of *semantic macrostructures*: topics and macropropositions.
2. The analysis of *local meanings*, where the many forms of implicit or indirect meanings, such as implications, presuppositions, allusions, vagueness, omissions and polarizations, are especially interesting.
3. The analysis of *'subtle' formal structures*: here, most of the linguistic markers mentioned are analysed.
4. The analysis of *global and local discourse forms* or formats.
5. The analysis of *specific linguistic realizations*, e.g. hyperbole, litotes.
6. The analysis of *context*.

DHA unfolds a four-step strategy of analysis: after (1) having established the specific *contents* or *topics* of a specific discourse (e.g. with racist, antisemitic, nationalist or ethnicist ingredients), (2) the *discursive strategies* (including argumentation strategies) are investigated. Then (3), the *linguistic means* (as types) and the specific, context-dependent *linguistic realizations* (as tokens) of the discriminatory stereotypes are examined (4).

In these studies, DHA focuses on the following discursive strategies:

- *Referential strategy or strategy of nomination*, where the salient linguistic devices are membership categorization (Sacks, 1992), metaphors, metonymies and synecdoches.
- *Strategies of predication* which appear in evaluative attributions of positive or negative traits and implicit or explicit predicates.
- *Strategies of argumentation* which are reflected in certain *topoi* (i.e. used to justify political inclusion or exclusion).
- *Strategies of perspectivization, framing or discourse representation* use specific means of reporting, description, narration or the quotation of events and utterances.
- *Strategies of intensification and mitigation* intensify or mitigate the illocutionary force of utterances (Ng and Bradac, 1993).

This methodology aims to be abductive, because the categories of analysis are first developed in accordance with the research questions, and a constant movement back and forth between theory and empirical data is suggested. The historical context is always analysed and integrated into the interpretation, although there is no clear procedure for this task.

CLA adds a quantitative methodology to CDA: large corpora are analysed by means of concordance software, thus providing frequency lists and specific measures of statistical significance. Therefore, CLA applies a rather deductive methodology in selecting specific words which are relevant for analysis, but also offers concordance lines as a basis for further (qualitative) interpretation.

In a very general sense, SAA describes and explains social practices by identifying seven core elements. Firstly, it tries to identify (1) actions within given texts; then it analyses (2) performance modes and denotes (3) actors which apply (4) specific presentation styles of their actions. Social practices which are constituted by these actions take place in (5) specific times and (6) spaces, and actors require (7) specific resources. Some of these elements of social practice are eligible, while some are deleted, i.e. are not represented in a specific discourse. Some are substituted; some reactions and motives are added to the representation of social practices.

DRA suggests a stepwise procedure in preparation for analysis. Like DHA, it prefers a pragmatic, problem-oriented approach, where the first step is to identify and describe the social problem which should be analysed. DRA stages of analysis are as follows:

1. Focus upon a specific social problem which has a semiotic aspect, go outside the text and describe the problem, and identify its semiotic dimension.
2. Identify the dominant styles, genres and discourses constituting this semiotic dimension.
3. Consider the range of difference and diversity in styles, genres and discourses within this dimension.
4. Identify the resistance against the colonialization processes executed by the dominant styles, genres and discourses.

After these preparatory steps, which also help to select the material, DRA suggests (1) a *structural analysis* of the context, and then (2) an *interactional analysis*, which focuses on such well-known linguistic features as:

- agents
- time
- tense
- modality
- syntax

and finally (3) an *analysis of interdiscursivity*, which tries to compare the dominant and resistant strands of discourse.

Above, we have only been able to give a brief overview of the core procedures applied in the different approaches to CDA. Finally, it should be pointed out that, although there is no consistent CDA methodology, some features are common to most CDA approaches: (1) they are problem-oriented and not focused on specific linguistic items, yet linguistic expertise is obligatory for the selection of the items relevant to specific research objectives; (2) theory as well as methodology is eclectic, both of which are integrated to be able to understand the social problems under investigation.

Criteria for assessing quality

It seems to be beyond controversy that qualitative social research also needs concepts and criteria to assess the quality of its findings. It is also indisputable that the classical concepts of validity, reliability and objectivity used in quantitative research cannot be applied in unmodified ways. 'The real issue is how our research can be both intellectually challenging and rigorous and critical' (Silverman, 1993: 144); Silverman also provides a detailed discussion of these concepts and a reformulation for qualitative research. Within CDA, there is little specific discussion about quality criteria.

DA at least mentions the classical criteria of representativeness, reliability and validity. Beyond it, DA suggests 'completeness' as a criterion suited for CDA: the results of a study will be 'complete' if new data and the analysis of new linguistic devices reveal no new findings. SCA suggests accessibility as a criterion which takes into account the practical targets of CDA: findings should at least be accessible and readable for the social groups under investigation.

DHA suggests triangulation procedures to ensure validity – '... which is appropriate whatever one's theoretical orientation or use of quantitative or qualitative data' (Silverman, 1993: 156).[8] DHA's triangulatory approach is mainly *theoretical* and based on the concept of context which takes into account four levels: (1) the immediate language- or text-internal co-text; (2) the intertextual and interdiscursive relationship between utterances, texts, genres and discourses; (3) the extralinguistic (social) level, which is called the 'context of situation' and is explained by middle-range theories; and (4) the broader sociopolitical and historical contexts. Permanent switching between these levels and evaluating the findings from these different perspectives should minimize the risk of being biased. Beyond it, DHA suggests methodical triangulation by using multimethodical designs on the basis of a variety of empirical data as well as background information.

Triangulation among different types of data, participants' definition of relevance and problem-based analysis to establish the significance of the sites of engagement and mediated actions under investigation are suited to bring the analyses back to participants: to uncover divergences and contradictions between one's own analysis of the mediated actions one is studying and those of participants.

Nevertheless, rigorous 'objectivity' cannot be reached by means of discourse analysis, for each 'technology' of research must itself be examined as potentially embedding the beliefs and ideologies of the analysts and therefore guiding the analysis towards the analysts' preconceptions.

Summary and criticism

The goal of this chapter was to provide a summary of CDA approaches, their similarities and differences. One of CDA's volitional characteristics is its diversity. Nevertheless, a few salient cornerstones can be noticed within this diversity:

- Concerning its theoretical background, CDA works eclectically in many aspects. The whole range between grand theories and linguistic theories is evoked, although each approach emphasizes different levels.
- There is no accepted canon of data collection, but many CDA approaches work with existing data, i.e. texts not specifically produced for the respective research projects.
- Operationalization and analysis are problem-oriented and imply linguistic expertise.

The most evident similarity is a shared interest in social processes of power, hierarchy-building, exclusion and subordination. In the tradition of critical theory, CDA aims to shed light on the discursive aspects of societal disparities and inequalities. CDA frequently detects the linguistic means used by the privileged to stabilize or even to intensify inequalities in society. This entails careful systematic analysis, self-reflection at every point of one's research and distance from the data which are being investigated. Description and interpretation should be kept apart, thus enabling transparency and retroduction of the respective analysis. Of course, not all of these recommendations are consistently followed, and they cannot always be implemented in detail because of time pressures and similar structural constraints. Therefore, some critics will continue to state that CDA constantly sits on the fence between social research and political argumentation (Wodak, 2006a), while others will accuse some CDA studies of being too linguistic or not linguistic enough. In our view, such criticism keeps a field alive because it necessarily stimulates more self-reflection and encourages new questions, new responses and new thoughts.

Notes

1   This chapter is based on long and extensive discussions with friends, colleagues and co-researchers as well as students. Ruth Wodak would like to thank Teun van Dijk, Paul Chilton, Theo van Leeuwen, John Richardson, Jay Lemke and Michael Billig, as well as all her co-researchers and (former) students. Finally, we would like to thank the many colleagues we have not been able to mention here.

2 See Anthonissen, 2001; Blommaert and Bulcaen, 2000; Fairclough and Wodak, 1997; Reisigl and Wodak, 2001; Titscher et al., 2000; Weiss and Wodak, 2003; Wodak and Meyer, 2001; Wodak and Pelinka, 2002, etc.

3 See *Language and Power* by Norman Fairclough (1989/1991), *Language, Power and Ideology* by Ruth Wodak (1989) and *Prejudice in Discourse* by Teun van Dijk (1984).

4 The Erasmus network 1995 consisted of a cooperation between Siegfried Jäger, Duisburg, Per Linell, Linköping, Norman Fairclough, Lancaster, Teun van Dijk, Amsterdam, Gunther Kress, London, Theo van Leeuwen, London, and Ruth Wodak, Vienna.

5 Unfortunately, we have to neglect much research here which could certainly also be categorized as critical, such as feminist CDA (see Lazar, 2005), critical ethnographic approaches (see Blommaert, 2005), research situated between sociolinguistics, literacy research and CDA (see Tricento, 2005), etc. We have to refer readers to the many publications and overview essays in the field.

6 The question of whether it is possible to make hermeneutic processes transparent and intelligible at all remains undecided, although some authors (Oevermann et al., 1979) have developed a hermeneutically orientated method with well-defined procedures and rules.

7 A general survey on sampling and the selection of texts is given by Titscher et al. (2000).

8 An early proponent of the method of triangulation is Norman Denzin (1970). For further discussion of criteria for assessing interpretive validity in qualitative research, see, for example, Altheide and Johnson (1994); Morse et al. (2002).

2

Theoretical and Methodological Aspects of Foucauldian Critical Discourse Analysis and Dispositive Analysis

Siegfried Jäger and Florentine Maier

Introduction

This article aims to give a concise introduction to the methodology of analysing discourses and dispositives, building on the theoretical insights of Michel Foucault. The article is mainly aimed towards novices to this approach.[1]

Critical discourse analysis (CDA) based on Michel Foucault's discourse theory centres on the following questions:

- What is valid knowledge at a certain place and a certain time?
- How does this knowledge arise and how is it passed on?
- What functions does it have for constituting subjects?
- What consequences does it have for the overall shaping and development of society?

'Knowledge' refers to all kinds of contents that make up a human consciousness, or in other words, all kinds of meanings that people use to interpret and shape their environment. People derive this knowledge from the discursive surroundings into which they are born and in which they are enmeshed throughout their lives. Knowledge is therefore conditional, i.e. its validity depends on people's location in history, geography, class relations and so on.

Discourse analysis and its extension, dispositive analysis, aim to identify the knowledges contained in discourses and dispositives, and how these knowledges are firmly connected to power relations in power/knowledge complexes. Discourse and dispositive analysis subject these workings of power/knowledge to critique. All sorts of knowledge can be subjected to analysis. This, for example, includes everyday knowledge transmitted through everyday communication, scientific knowledge from the natural as well as the cultural sciences, knowledge transmitted by the media, by schools and so on.

To provide an overview of the methodology for critically analysing discourses and dispositives, we first need to establish the foundations of Foucauldian discourse theory on which critical discourse and dispositive analysis build. A brief outline of this theoretical background is given in the ensuing section on the foundations of discourse theory. The third section (From discourse to dispositive) then introduces the concept of the dispositive. Dispositives can be understood as the synthesis of discursive practices (i.e. speaking and thinking on the basis of knowledge), non-discursive practices (i.e. acting on the basis of knowledge) and materializations (i.e. the material products of acting on the basis of knowledge). In the final section, practical methodological guidelines for analysing discourses and dispositives are provided.

Foundations of discourse theory

One of the most fruitful approaches to Foucauldian discourse analysis in the cultural sciences has been developed by literary and cultural scientist Jürgen Link and his team at the University of Dortmund. Their work, on which we build here, focuses on the analysis of current discourses and their power effects, on uncovering the linguistic and iconographic means – in particular, the collective symbolism – by which discourses work, and on the function of discourse to legitimize and secure dominance in bourgeois-capitalist modern society (see Link, 1982).

The concept of discourse

According to Link, a **discourse** can be defined as 'an institutionalized way of talking that regulates and reinforces action and thereby exerts power' (Link, 1983: 60, author's own translation). This definition can be illustrated by the image of discourse as a flow of knowledge throughout time. Different discourses are intimately entangled with each other and together form the giant milling mass of overall societal discourse. This milling mass of discourse is growing constantly and exuberantly.

Discourses are not only mere expressions of social practice, but also serve particular ends, namely the exercise of power. The concept of power, in the Foucauldian sense, refers to 'a whole series of particular mechanisms, definable and defined, that seem capable of inducing behaviours or discourses' (Foucault, 1996: 394). Discourses exercise power in a society because they institutionalize and regulate ways of talking, thinking and acting.

Aims of critical discourse analysis

CDA aims to disentangle the giant milling mass of discourse, to chart what is said and can be said in a given society at a given time with regard to its qualitative spectrum (What is said? How is it said?), and to uncover the techniques through which discursive limits are extended or narrowed down.

Last but not least, and to live up to its name, CDA aims to question and criticize discourses. CDA does so in two ways.

Firstly, CDA reveals the contradictions within and between discourses, the limits of what can be said and done, and the means by which discourse makes particular statements seem rational and beyond all doubt, even though they are only valid at a certain time and place.

Secondly, the critical discourse analyst needs to be clear about the fact that her critique is not situated outside discourse – as this would contradict the fundamental assumptions of discourse analysis. The analyst can – and has to – take a stand. She can invoke values, norms, the constitution, universal human rights and so on. But when doing so, she must never forget that these values, norms, laws and rights have been discursively constructed too. This kind of critique is not ideological, because unlike ideology it does not make claims to absolute truth. A critical discourse analyst needs to be clear about the fact that her position is also the result of discursive processes. With this outlook, she can enter discursive arguments, where she may defend and possibly modify her position. Foucauldian CDA here clearly differs from orthodox Marxist positions, which stipulate that social existence determines consciousness (as discussed under the terms of false consciousness and the fetishism of commodities in Marx, 1992/1867). Foucault understands this relationship rather the other way around and emphasizes the materiality of discourse (cf. Jäger, 2008; Link, 1996).

The question of how the production of discourses and the temporarily and spatially contingent knowledge they contain are connected to mechanisms and institutions of power has been central for Foucault (as he states in the introduction to the German version of *The History of Sexuality* – see Foucault, 1983: 8). To clarify the connections between discourses and power, it is necessary to first examine how discourses and reality are connected to each other. The following section examines this connection between discourse and reality. We then examine how discourses relate to power.

Discourses and reality

Discourses do not merely reflect reality. Rather, discourses not only shape but even enable (social) reality. Without discourses, there would be no (social) reality. Discourses can thus be understood as material reality *sui generis*. They are not a second-class material reality, not 'less material' than 'real' reality, not passive media into which reality is imprinted. Discourses are fully valid material realities among others (Link, 1992). Therefore, discourse cannot be reduced to a notion of 'false consciousness' or a 'distorted view of reality', as is done by some orthodox Marxist approaches to 'ideology critique'. Discourse is a material reality of its own. It is neither 'much ado about nothing', nor a distortion, nor a lie about reality. This characterization of discourse as material reality implies that discourse theory is a materialist theory. Contrary to a common misconception, probably based on the fact that discourse analysis deals with language, discourse theory is not an idealist theory. Discourse theory deals with material realities, not with 'mere' ideas. Discourses may be conceptualized as societal means of production. Discourses are not 'mere ideology'; they produce subjects and reality.

Discourses determine reality, though of course always via intervening active subjects in their social contexts as co-producers and co-agents of discourses. The subjects are able to do this *because* they are entangled into discourse and therefore have knowledge at their disposal. Discourse analysis is therefore not only about the retrospective analysis of allocations of meaning, but also about the analysis of the ongoing production of reality through discourse, conveyed by active subjects.

Discourses and power

Based on the above outline of the connection between discourses and reality, we can now examine the connections between discourses and power. On the one hand, there is the power of discourse. On the other hand, there is also something like the power over discourse.

The *power of discourse* lies in the fact that discourses delineate a range of 'positive' statements, which are sayable. This means that they simultaneously inhibit a range of other statements, which are not sayable (cf. Link and Link-Heer, 1990). As flows of knowledge through time, discourses determine the way in which a society interprets reality and organizes further discursive and non-discursive practices (i.e. further talking, thinking and acting). To put it more precisely, we can distinguish two effects of discourse. Firstly, discourses form individual and mass consciousness and thereby constitute individual and collective subjects. Secondly, since consciousness determines action, discourses determine action. This human action creates materializations. Discourses thus guide the individual and collective creation of reality.

From a discourse-theoretical point of view, it is thus not the subject who makes the discourses, but the discourses that make the subject (which may be irritating for those attached to the idea of the uniqueness of the individual). The subject is of interest not as an actor, but as a product of discourses. As Foucault argues:

> One has to dispense with the constituent subject, to get rid of the subject itself, that's to say, to arrive at an analysis which can account for the constitution of the subject within a historical framework. And this is what I would call genealogy, that is, a form

of history which can account for the constitution of knowledges, discourses, domains of objects etc. without having to make reference to a subject which is either transcendental in relation to the field of events or runs in its empty sameness throughout the course of history. (Foucault, 1980a: 117)

Foucauldian discourse theory, though often wrongly accused of so doing, does not deny the subject. It aims to analyse the constitution of the subject in its historical and social context from a diachronic (i.e. longitudinal) and synchronic (i.e. cross-sectional) perspective: who was conceived of as a subject at a particular point in time? How, and how come? For example, unlike in the past, women and children in Western society usually have subject status today. In modern management, in contrast to traditional bureaucracy, employees are depicted as subjects. They are 'empowered', with all the responsibilities that involves. The subject status of foetuses and apes is something that is hotly debated. Asylum seekers and criminals are often denied a subject status, for example when they are portrayed as maniacs, dogs or viruses (these are collective symbols – see the section on collective symbols). In a nutshell, Foucauldian discourse theory contests the existence of an autonomous subject, but that does not mean that it is against the subject. The active individual is fully involved when it comes to realizing power relations in practice. The individual thinks, plans, constructs, interacts and fabricates. The individual also faces the problem of having to prevail, to assert himself, to find his place in society.

When analysing the power effects of discourse, it is important to distinguish between the effects of a text and the effects of a discourse. A single text has minimal effects, which are hardly noticeable and almost impossible to prove. In contrast, a discourse, with its recurring contents, symbols and strategies, leads to the emergence and solidification of 'knowledge' and therefore has sustained effects. What is important is not the single text, the single film, the single photograph and so on, but the constant repetition of statements. The philologist Victor Klemperer recognized this mechanism as early as the 1930s, when he observed the language of the Nazis. In his analysis of the language of the Third Reich (Klemperer, 2000/2006), he contends that fascist language works like the continuous administration of small doses of arsenic, which unfold their poisonous effect only over the long term.

With regard to *power over discourse*, different individuals and groups have different chances of influence. However, none of them can simply defy dominant discourse, and none of them alone has full control over discourse. Discourses are supra-individual. Everybody is co-producing discourse, but no single individual or group controls discourse or has precisely intended its final result. Discourses take on a life of their own as they evolve. They transport more knowledge than the single subject is aware of. In Foucault's words, '[p]eople know what they do; they frequently know why they do what they do; but what they don't know is what what [sic] they do does' (personal communication, quoted in Dreyfus and Rabinow, 1982: 187). The power effects of discourses should therefore not necessarily be interpreted as the conscious and manipulative intent of some individual or group. There may be a difference between a speaker's reasons for using a particular discourse, and the social consequences of doing so (Burr, 2003: 61).

It should be kept in mind, however, that in the long run, powerful politicians and other groups can accomplish changes in discourse. For example, the Basic Constitutional Law that governs the right of asylum in Germany was tightened after over ten years of intensive political and media lobbying. In a similar way, the stance towards deployments abroad of the German armed forces was changed in a long process. Examples like these show that certain groups and individuals have more power over discourse than others, for example because they have privileged access to the media or greater financial resources. Exclusions inherent to the structure of discourse can thus be amplified by institutional conditions.

This section can therefore be summarized as follows: *discourses exert power because they transport knowledge on which collective and individual consciousness feeds. This knowledge is the basis for individual and collective, discursive and non-discursive action, which in turn shapes reality.*

From discourse to dispositive

Since knowledge is the basis for acting, we can analyse not only discursive practices, but also non-discursive practices and materializations, as well as their relationships with each other. Building on Foucault, we call the interplay between discursive practices, non-discursive practices and materializations a dispositive. In this section, this interplay is examined.

As human beings, we assign meanings to reality. This is how we bring reality into existence. Of course, this does not mean that human beings are the creators of the raw matter of material reality. But people shape and use these raw materials. The assignment of meanings includes very tangible physical acts, such as when a tree is sawn into boards, or when boards are joined into a table. People moreover learn the conventions of assigned meanings through language, which helps them to interpret reality in the way it has previously been interpreted by others. For example, people learn that a certain object is called a 'table', and by so doing, they simultaneously learn what a table is good for. (Different cultures have different objects, which makes translations from one language into another difficult.) Dispositive analysis examines how such assignments of meaning create reality. (In contrast, some other disciplines such as the natural sciences and medicine examine material reality as an objective, natural or biological given.)

Consciousness does not passively reflect reality, but actively takes hold of it. This works through discourses, which provide the knowledge for shaping reality. If a discourse withdraws from the reality that has been built on it, or to put it more precisely, if people withdraw from that discourse, this part of reality becomes meaningless in the truest sense of the word. It returns to a blank state. If the knowledge assigned to a particular part of reality changes, this part of reality turns into a different thing. For example, tramps may move into an abandoned bank and turn it into their flop. A steel mill may be closed down and may be turned into an amusement park. In these examples, original meanings are withdrawn and new meanings are assigned.

Foucault's views on the relationship between discursive and non-discursive realities have been somewhat ambiguous. In the remainder of this section, we will first provide an overview of Foucault's conception of this relationship. Then we will propose a different understanding, which builds on Foucault, but at the same time goes beyond his ideas.

Foucault writes in his *Archaeology of Knowledge* that discourses can be treated as 'practices that systematically form the objects of which they speak' (Foucault, 2002: 54). But Foucault also sees that non-discursive practices play a decisive role in forming objects. He talks about 'discursive relations' in this regard. He states that discursive relations are

> in a sense, at the limit of discourse: they offer it objects of which it can speak, or rather [...], they determine the group of relations that discourse must establish in order to speak of this or that object, in order to deal with them, name them, analyse them, classify them, explain them, etc. (Foucault, 2002: 50f.)

With this statement, Foucault circumnavigates the problem of the relationship between discourse and reality without really solving it. It remains unclear what he actually means by 'objects'. Presumably, he does not mean materializations but themes, theories, statements or other purely discursive 'objects'.

This circumnavigating becomes most apparent in his attempt to define the dispositive. In a conversation with several psychoanalysts in 1977, he defined the dispositive as follows:

> What I'm trying to pick out with this term is, firstly, a thoroughly heterogeneous ensemble consisting of discourses, institutions, architectural forms, regulatory decisions, laws, administrative measures, scientific statements, philosophical, moral and philanthropic propositions – in short, the said as much as the unsaid. Such are the elements of the [dispositive]. The [dispositive] itself is the system of relations that can be established between these elements. (Foucault, 1980b: 194)

He further differentiates:

> [... B]etween these elements, whether discursive or non-discursive, there is a sort of interplay of shifts of position and modifications of function which can also vary very widely. (ibid.: 195)

He states that by the term 'dispositive', he understands:

> [...] a sort of – shall we say – formation which has as its major function at a given historical moment that of responding to an *urgent need* [*urgence*]. The [dispositive] thus has a dominant strategic function. (ibid.)

He mentions the example of the control of madness, of mental illness, and later of neurosis which served the function of assimilating a floating population that would otherwise be burdensome for an economy (ibid.: 195).

In the further course of the conversation, the psychoanalysts begin to nit-pick his distinction between the discursive and the non-discursive. It seems that Foucault is in a tight spot here; the psychoanalysts drive him into a corner. It is noticeable that his interview partners are getting on his nerves; he is becoming impatient, even annoyed. He answers them:

> Yes, if you like, but it doesn't much matter for my notion of the [dispositive] to be able to say that this is discursive and that isn't. If you take Gabriel's architectural plan for the Military School together with the actual construction of the School, how is one to say what is discursive and what is institutional? That would only interest me if the building didn't conform with the plan. But I don't think it's very important to be able to make that distinction, given that my problem isn't a linguistic one. (ibid.: 198)

Foucault thereby liberates himself – and us – from a linguistics that is not based on thought and consciousness. He subordinates language and also linguistics to thought and knowledge. Thereby he basically turns linguistics into a sub-discipline of the cultural sciences, which deal with the conditions and results of meaningful human activities. Human activities are meaningful because they are based on thought and consciousness.

After his archaeological endeavours that aimed to reconstruct the development of knowledge from a purely materialistic perspective, Foucault arrived at the conviction that talk/text/discourse alone is not what makes the world tick. He invented the dispositive to permit a better analysis of historic and current reality. With regard to the concept of the dispositive, the question about the relationship between discourse and dispositive, as well as between discourse and reality, is of fundamental importance.

As is evident from the above quotes, Foucault clearly assumes a co-existence of discourse and objects. They are related elements of the dispositive. The dispositive as a whole comprises the net that is spun between these elements and connects them. However, Foucault is unable to tell us what concrete, or to put it very concisely, what empirical relationship connects discourses and objects. The reason for this problem is that while he is interested in the nature of the relationship between these heterogeneous elements, he assumes a dualism of discourses and material reality. Foucault did not see discourses and material reality as interrelated and unable to exist on their own. According to him, the dispositive assembles various elements that are connected to each other, and these connections are what constitute the dispositive (see also Balke, 1998; Deleuze, 1988). Foucault apparently understands these connections as follows: an urgent need emerges and an existing dispositive becomes precarious. The need for action arises, and society or its hegemonic forces, confronted with the urgent need, gather all the elements they can get hold of to deal with it. These may be speeches, people, knives, cannons, organizations and so on. By these means, they mend the 'leak', the urgent need that has arisen (see Balke, 1998; Deleuze, 1988).

The elements of the dispositive are connected by the common purpose they serve, namely the purpose of dealing with an urgent need. No other 'inner bond' between these elements is apparent in Foucault's understanding of the dispositive.

In what follows, we propose a different understanding of the bond between the elements of a dispositive. This bond exists in the form of non-discursive practices (in other words, human actions), which connect the subject and the object, symbolic reality and material reality. In Foucault's definition of the dispositive, non-discursive practices are not mentioned explicitly. The ensuing arguments draw on the activity theory developed by Leontjev (Leont'ev [sic], 1978), which is based on Lev Vygotsky's book *Thought and Language* (Vygotsky, 1986). Activity theory is essentially an approach to the critique of ideology, which for the purpose in hand is here given a discourse-theoretical turn.

As mentioned above, human beings are able to assign meaning to objects. What is more, only by being assigned a meaning does the object turn into an object. For example, I can assign the meaning 'table' to a piece of wood that I find in the woods. I can eat my bread from it and put my mug on it. An object that is not assigned any meaning is not an object. It is totally nondescript, invisible, even nonexistent. I don't see it because I overlook it. For example, I don't see the bird that the forester sees ('forester syndrome'). I may see a red spot, and I may think 'there is a red spot.' It will have the meaning of a red spot for me. It is beyond my knowledge whether it is a bird, a flower or the recently dyed hair of Lothar Matthäus, who is going for a walk because he was injured playing in the last football match and therefore cannot train today. Of course, a friend can tell me: 'Look, that is Lothar Matthäus, and he used to be captain of the German national team.' Then I may say: 'Yes, okay, I know him', or 'no, that was definitely a bird or a flower.'

The point is that all meaningful reality exists for us because we make it meaningful for us, or because our ancestors and neighbours assigned meaning to it, and this meaning is still valid for us. It is like King Midas with his gold: everything he touched turned into gold. Similarly, everything that human beings assign meaning to becomes a particular kind of reality, according to the meaning it was assigned. Ernesto Laclau expressed this connection elegantly:

> By 'discursive' I do not mean that which refers to 'text' narrowly defined, but to the ensemble of the phenomena in and through which social production of meaning takes place, an ensemble which constitutes a society as such. The discursive is not, therefore, being conceived as a level nor even as a dimension of the social, but rather as being co-extensive with the social as such. This means that the discursive does not constitute a superstructure (since it is the very condition of all social practice) or, more precisely, that all social practice constitutes itself as such insofar as it produces meaning. Because there is nothing specifically social which is constituted outside the discursive, it is clear that the non-discursive is not opposed to the discursive as if it were a matter of two separate levels. History and society are an infinite text. (Laclau, 1980: 87)

The question is: why, when, how and under what conditions do I assign meaning to objects? How is the 'gap' between discourse and reality closed? According to Leontjev's activity theory, meaning is assigned to an object if I derive a motive from a particular need and therefore aim to achieve a particular aim, for which I use actions and raw materials. In other words, meaning is assigned to an object through work. The products thus created can be articles of daily use, but also new thoughts and plans, which again may give rise to new activities and products. It seems strange that Foucault, who had a background in psychology, did not know activity theory, which is based on the materialistic psychology of the early 1930s. Maybe he rejected it because he found that it centred too much on the subject. Yet the approach is fruitful because it deals with the connection of subject and object, society and objective reality, through human activity. Foucault also overlooks the fact that the materializations of work are part of reality. People create these through their non-discursive practices, as they build houses, benches, banks and so on, which exist only as long as they are embedded into discourses. For example, a bank, as an element of the dispositive of capital, stops functioning as a bank if it is no longer supported by discourse. It becomes meaningless, reduced to nothing but raw matter (which, if called this way, again takes on a certain meaning). Alternatively, it may be 'discursified anew' into another object. Tramps may sleep in the former bank and thereby assign another meaning to it, turning it into their flop. Foucault also sees this and writes:

> [I]t is not the objects that remain constant, nor the domain that they form; it is not even their point of emergence or their mode of characterization; but the relation between the surfaces on which they appear, on which they can be delimited, on which they can be analysed and specified. (Foucault, 2002: 52)

Or to put it more simply: if the discourse changes, the object does not only change its meaning, it turns into a different object. It loses its previous identity. This may happen abruptly or as the result of a long process that impalpably but thoroughly changes everything.

Foucault does not want to define objects with 'reference to the ground, the foundation of things' (ibid.: 53), but to define objects 'by relating them to the body of rules that enable them to form as objects of a discourse and thus constitute the conditions of their historical appearance' (ibid.). However, he gets stuck at this point because he does not conceptualize subject and object, society and discourse, as connected by activity, i.e. by non-discursive practices. Discursive practices remain verbal for him, strictly separated from non-discursive practices. With this separation of intellectual activity and (unintellectual?) physical activity, he shows himself as a product of his times and his origins, where the bourgeoisie highly valued mental work and believed manual work to be completely unintellectual. Foucault knows that the signs do more than designate things, and he states that '[i]t is this more that renders them irreducible to the language (langue) and to speech' (ibid.: 54). He wants to 'reveal and describe' (ibid.) this 'more', but does not succeed fully. He is not really able to grasp this 'more'. In this chapter, we argue that this 'more' is the knowledge that enables the transformation of verbally articulated knowledge into material objects: knowledge about statics, materials, tools, routines and the like that enters every kind of physical work. However, it is rarely verbalized, or even cannot be verbalized (i.e. tacit knowledge). For example, a steelworker at a blast furnace sees when the steel is ready or what ingredients are still missing. However, it may be impossible to teach this knowledge to somebody else just through verbalization. One may have to watch and try for oneself. In a way, the knowledge is in the practices.

We may therefore say that reality is meaningful, that reality exists in the way it does, only insofar as it is assigned meaning by people, who are themselves entangled into and constituted by discourses. If people no longer assign the same meaning to an object, the object changes or loses its meaning. This meaning may then at most be reconstructed as a former meaning that has mixed with other meanings or has ceased to be valid. Even if we just watch the night sky and see constellations of stars there, we see them as a result of a discourse. We see the constellations because we have learnt to see them. To assign meaning is not a noncommittal, 'merely symbolic' act. To assign meaning is to animate whatever one comes across, to re-shape and change. For example, from the collective symbolism used with regard to immigrants, it is apparent that many people have learnt to assign negative meanings to immigrants, and now actually perceive them as floods that need to be held back, or even as lice or pigs that should be crushed or slaughtered.

Bernhard Waldenfels (1991) confirms this criticism of Foucault, which at the same time is inspired by Foucault. He writes that it is:

> unclear how [Foucault] draws the line between discursive and non-discursive practices and how he bridges this line. It even remains unclear if this line is drawn at all. I think that in a way, Foucault drove himself into a blind alley when he first conceptualized the formations of the order of history as orders of knowledge (epistemes), and then conceptualized them as orders of speech (discourses), instead of assuming an order that is shared by all behavioural registers of people, i.e. by their speech and actions (!) but also their gazes, their bodily conventions, their erotic relationships, their technical handlings, their economic and political decisions, their expression in art and religion, etc. It is not clear why any of these areas should not have the functionality that Foucault developed based on speech alone. (Waldenfels, 1991: 291, author's own translation)

Waldenfels notes that Foucault himself crossed this border at several points. In the *Archaeology of Knowledge*, Foucault (2002) mentions the discourse of the painter, who 'speaks' without words. Foucault also mentions political discourse, where for example an unexpected revolution may take place, which cannot be traced back to a revolutionary situation or a revolutionary conscience. From a superficial point of view, this unexpected revolution is not based on knowledge, while on closer inspection, it is very much based on knowledge. As often happened, Foucault preferred to do *bricolage*[2] here (cf. Waldenfels, 1991: 291).

In this text, we continue the *bricolage*, pick up Foucault's toolbox of theoretical and practical instruments, and develop his ideas further. So far, we have done so in two regards. Firstly, Foucault's notion of discourse, which is too bound to the verbal, is shifted one step 'backwards', namely into human thinking and knowledge, or in other words, into consciousness. This is where the contents of thought (including emotions and perceptions) are located, which are the basis for shaping reality through work.

Secondly, and by the same token, activity theory is made available for discourse theory. Activity theory explains how subjects and objects are connected to each other. Foucault mainly saw discourse as *somehow* connected to reality. Drawing on Leontjev, we identify the subject as the missing link that connects discourses to material reality. Subjects do this in all their activities. The way in which those activities become effective has not been intended in exactly this way by any individual or single group. Nevertheless, it is human consciousness and physical strength that shape reality. Everything in human consciousness is discursive, i.e. constituted by knowledge. Moreover, subjects continuously draw on tacit knowledge. Tacit knowledge is passed on in non-discursive practices and materializations, and the researcher can aim to reconstruct tacit knowledge from both of them.

To summarize the problems discussed in this section, many of the difficulties in analysing dispositives stem from an insufficient conceptualization of discursive practices, non-discursive practices and materializations (see also Bublitz, 1999: 82–115). Many of these problems can be solved by drawing on Leontjev's and others' understanding of materializations and non-discursive practices as realizations of discourse, i.e. knowledge (for further discussion see, for example, Jäger, 2001a). The following section provides some ideas on how discourses and dispositives can be analysed systematically.

Methods for analysing discourses and dispositives

To recapitulate briefly our initial definition, a discourse can be characterized as 'an institutionalized way of talking that regulates and reinforces action and thereby exerts power' (Link, 1983: 60, author's own translation), as illustrated by the image of a flow of knowledge throughout time (see Jäger, 2004). Together, all discourses form the giant milling mass of overall societal discourse.

The theoretical considerations introduced in the early sections of this chapter are the basis for the development of concepts and methods that facilitate analysis. A range of these concepts and methods is outlined in this section. The scope of this chapter does not allow for detailed methodological justifications of each of these concepts and methods, but such explanations can be found in the book on methods of CDA by Jäger (2004).

Methods of CDA also include linguistic concepts (e.g. figurativeness, vocabulary, pronominal structure, argumentation) which can be used to examine the more subtle workings of texts. However, these linguistic instruments are not described in detail here, as good explanations can be found in works on style and grammar. Linguistic concepts fill only one slot in the 'toolbox' of discourse analysis. Depending on the research question and subject matter, various other tools can be added to the toolbox. In any case, certain methods are part of a standard repertoire. These are described in the remainder of this section, putting special emphasis on discourse theory and activity theory as outlined above.

The structure of discourse

The following suggestions on terminology aim to provide some help in making the structure of discourses more transparent and amenable to analysis.

Special discourses and interdiscourse
A basic distinction can be drawn between special discourses and interdiscourse. Special discourses are discourses in the sciences, while interdiscourse refers to all non-scientific discourses. Elements of special discourses continuously feed into interdiscourse.

Discourse strands
In general societal discourse, a great variety of topics arise. Flows of discourse that centre on a common topic are called discourse strands. Each discourse strand comprises several sub-topics, which again can be summarized into groups of sub-topics.

The concept of 'discourse strands' is similar to the one of 'discourses'. The difference is that 'discourse' is the more abstract concept, located at the level of statements (*énoncés*). 'Discourse strands', in contrast, are conceived of at the level of concrete utterances (*énonciations*) or performances located on the surface of texts (cf. Foucault, 2002).

Every discourse strand has a diachronic and a synchronic dimension. A synchronic analysis of a discourse strand examines the finite spectrum of what is said and sayable at a particular point in time. A synchronic analysis can cut through a discourse strand at various points in time, for example at particular discursive events. By comparing these synchronic cuts, it provides insights into the changes and continuities of discourse strands over time.

In a way, a synchronic cut through a discourse strand is always also a diachronic one. This is because each topic has a genesis, a historical a priori. When analysing a topic, the analyst has to keep an eye on its history. To identify the knowledge of a society on a topic, the analyst has to reconstruct the genesis of this topic. Foucault has undertaken several attempts to do so, not only with regard to the sciences, but also with regard to everyday life and institutions (e.g. the hospital, the prison).

Discursive limits and techniques for extending them or narrowing them down

Each discourse delineates a range of statements that are sayable and thereby inhibits a range of other statements, which are not sayable (cf. Link and Link-Heer, 1990). The borders to what is not sayable are called discursive limits.

Through the use of certain rhetorical strategies, discursive limits can be extended or narrowed down. Such strategies for example include direct prescriptions, relativizations, defamations, allusions and implicatures. Discourse analysis examines these strategies in their own right, and also uses them as analytic clues to identify discursive limits: if 'tricks' are used, this is an indicator that certain statements cannot be said directly without risking negative sanctions.

Discourse fragments

Each discourse strand consists of a multitude of elements that are traditionally called texts. We prefer the term 'discourse fragment', because one text may touch on various topics and thus contain various discourse fragments. A discourse fragment therefore refers to a text or part of a text that deals with a particular topic (for example, the topic of immigration). Or to put it the other way around, various discourse fragments on the same topic form a discourse strand.

Entanglements of discourse strands

A text usually refers to various topics and therefore to various discourse strands. In other words, it usually contains fragments from various discourse strands. These discourse strands are usually entangled with each other. An entanglement of discourse strands can take the form of one text addressing various topics to equal degrees, or of one text addressing mainly one topic and referring to other topics only in passing.

A statement where several discourses are entangled is called a **discursive knot**. For example, in the statement 'integrating immigrants into our society costs a lot of money', the discourse strand of immigration is entangled with the discourse strand of the economy. In the statement 'in [insert any Islamic country here], they still live in a patriarchal society', the discourse strand of immigration is entangled with the discourse strand of women.

Two discourse strands can be entangled more or less intensively. For example, in everyday discourse in Germany, the discourse strand of immigration is intensively entangled with the discourse strand of women, as sexist attitudes and behaviours are attributed to immigrants (see Jäger, 1996).

Collective symbols

An important means of linking up discourse strands is the use of collective symbols. Collective symbols are 'cultural stereotypes', also called 'topoi', which are handed down and used collectively (Drews et al., 1985: 265). They are known to all members of a society. They provide the repertoire of images from which we construct a picture of reality for ourselves. Through collective symbols we interpret reality, and have reality interpreted for us, especially by the media.

An important technique for connecting collective symbols is **catachreses** (also called image fractures). Catachreses establish connections between statements, link up spheres of experience, bridge contradictions and increase plausibility. Thereby, catachreses amplify the power of discourse. An example of a catachresis is the statement 'the locomotive of progress can be slowed down by floods of immigrants'. Here, the symbols of the locomotive (meaning progress) and floods (meaning a threat from the outside) are derived from different sources of images. The first one is taken from traffic and the second from nature. With a catachresis, the images are connected.

Discourse planes and sectors

Different discourse strands operate on different discourse planes, such as the sciences, politics, the media, education, everyday life, business, administration and so forth. These discourse planes can be characterized as social locations from which speaking takes place.

Discourse planes influence each other and relate to each other. For example, on the media plane, discourse fragments from scientific specialist discourse or political discourse are taken up. The media also take up everyday discourse, bundle it, bring it to the point, or – especially in the case of the yellow press – spice it up with sensational and populist claims. In this way, the media regulate everyday thinking and exert a considerable influence on what is and what can be done in politics and everyday life. For example, the larger-than-life image of Jörg Haider would hardly have come about without the help of media reports that normalized right-wing populism.

A discourse plane consists of various sectors. For example, women's magazines, TV news broadcasts and newspapers are different sectors of the discourse plane of the media.

A discourse plane is tightly interwoven in itself. For example, on the discourse plane of the media, leading media may also repeat and build on contents that have already been brought up in other media. It is therefore all the more justified to talk about *the* media discourse plane, which – especially with regard to the dominant media in a society – can be considered as integrated in its major aspects.

Discursive events and discursive context

All events are rooted in discourse. However, an event only counts as a discursive event if it appears on the discourse planes of politics and the media intensively, extensively and for a prolonged period of time.

A major reason why it is important to identify discursive events is that they influence the development of discourse. For example, the Three Mile Island nuclear accident near Harrisburg was comparable to the one in Chernobyl. But while the Three Mile Island accident was covered up for years, the Chernobyl accident was a major media event and influenced global politics. Whether an event, such as a nuclear accident, becomes a discursive event or not depends on the power constellations at work in politics and the media.

Discourse analysis can examine whether an event becomes a discursive event or not. If it becomes a discursive event, it influences the further development of discourse: the Chernobyl disaster contributed to a changing policy towards nuclear power in Germany. Germany is now, albeit hesitantly, going to phase out nuclear power. Environmentalist discourse, which had been developing for some time, could hardly have achieved this on its own. At the same time, a discursive event like the Chernobyl disaster can influence the whole discourse about new technologies, for example by drawing attention to the need to develop alternative energy sources. Another example for a discursive event is the success of the FPÖ (Freedom Party of Austria) in the 1999 Austrian National Parliamentary Elections, and the FPÖ's ensuing participation in government. While the FPÖ's success in the elections attracted considerable media coverage, the ensuing participation of the FPÖ (and indirectly Jörg Haider) in government triggered a far greater worldwide response, and became a discursive mega event that kept the European and US press in suspense for months. It had an effect on the discourses of the extreme right in countries in Europe and beyond.

Another reason why the identification of discursive events is important for the analysis of discourse strands is that they outline the discursive context that a discourse strand relates to. For example, a synchronic (i.e. cross-sectional) analysis of a discourse strand can be enriched with diachronic (i.e. longitudinal) elements by adding a chronicle of the discursive events belonging to it. Such historic references can be very helpful for synchronic analyses of discourse strands (as, for example, demonstrated by Caborn, 1999).

Discourse positions

A discourse position describes the ideological position from which subjects, including individuals, groups and institutions, participate in and evaluate discourse. Also, the media take up discourse positions, which become evident in their reporting. (As noted above, subject status is nothing natural and obvious, but something that in itself needs to be established through discourse.)

Subjects develop a discourse position because they are enmeshed in various discourses. They are exposed to discourses and work them into a specific ideological position or worldview in the course of their life. This relationship also works the other way around. Discursive positions contribute to and reproduce the discursive enmeshments of subjects (Jäger, 1996: 47).

Discourse positions can be identified through discourse analysis. But a rough outline of discourse positions is also part of people's everyday knowledge. People know roughly which politicians and newspapers tend towards the left, the right or the centre. Everyday self-descriptions of one's discourse position, however, should be taken with a grain of salt. For example, newspapers often describe themselves as 'independent' and 'impartial', while from a discourse-theoretical perspective, this is an impossibility.

The discourse positions of subjects may vary widely. For example, with regard to the discourse strand of the economy, many subjects take up a neo-liberal discourse position and favour privatization, free trade, low taxes, fiscal policy discipline and so on. Others, in contrast, reject neo-liberalism and take up Keynesianism or something even more unorthodox as their discourse position.

Discourse positions are homogeneous only in their core and become diffuse with regard to less central issues. For example, subjects who embrace the hegemonic discourse position of neo-liberalism agree that it is in principle right and important to reduce the nation's budget deficit. They do not question the current economic system. However, they may have differing views on the *best way* to reduce the budget deficit.

Within a dominant discourse, discourse positions are fairly homogeneous, which itself is already an effect of dominant discourse. Dissenting discourse positions often belong to complete counter-discourses (e.g. a fundamental questioning of the current economic system may not arise from economic discourse, but from ecology or ethics). However, these counter-discourses can pick up arguments from dominant discourse and subvert their meaning. For example, some people interpret the widespread saying that 'time is money' with an anti-capitalist twist, as when saying 'If time was money, I'd already be rich.'

Overall societal discourse and global discourse

All the entangled discourse strands in a society together form the overall societal discourse. A society is never totally homogeneous but consists of different subcultures. In Germany, since reunification in 1989, overall societal discourse has become ideologically more homogeneous, and it seems unlikely that this is going to change easily (Teubert, 1999).

The overall societal discourse of a society, in turn, is part of global discourse. Even though global discourse is very heterogeneous, it is probably safe to say that global discourse has also become more homogeneous and has switched from a confrontation of the West against communism to a confrontation of the West against the Islamic World.

Overall societal discourse is a very complex network. Discourse analysis aims to disentangle this net. The usual procedure is to first identify single discourse strands on single discourse planes (for example, the discourse strand of immigration on the discourse plane of the media). Subsequently, analyses of this discourse strand on further discourse planes, such as politics or everyday communication, can be added. At the end of such analyses, the question is usually how the different discourse planes of a discourse strand relate to each other. For example, one may examine whether and how the political discourse plane is linked to the discourse planes of the media and everyday communication, whether and how the media discourse plane influences the discourse plane of everyday communication, and so on.

The history, present, and future of discourse strands

Discourse strands have a history, a present and a future. In order to identify the changes, ruptures, ebbings and recurrences of a discourse strand, it is necessary to analyse longer periods of time. To put it into Foucault's words, an 'archaeology of knowledge' or a 'genealogy' is needed. On the basis of such an analysis, even prognoses about discourse can be undertaken. These can take the form of scenarios based on different future discursive events.

Of course, an analysis of the history, present and future of overall societal or even global discourse is an enormous endeavour and can only be tackled in the form of many single projects. Such single projects, however, are extremely helpful because they create reliable knowledge about certain sub-zones of overall societal discourse. This scientific knowledge can be the basis for a change of everyday, political and media knowledge, and can change behaviours and policies. Work on the discursive plane of science can thus influence the further development of a particular discourse strand.

On the completeness of discourse analyses

A discourse analysis fully captures the qualitative range of what can be said and how it is said in one or more discourse strands. It is complete if further analysis leads to no further new findings. Social scientists who mainly work with large amounts of quantitative data will be surprised to learn that in discourse analysis, a relatively small amount of qualitative data suffices to reach this point. The arguments and contents that can be read or heard about a particular topic (e.g. immigration) at a particular time in a particular social location are amazingly limited (often in both senses of the word). With regard to methodology, this means that the analyst continues to analyse new materials until he notices that arguments begin to repeat themselves. If this is the case, completeness (in the sense of theoretical saturation) has been achieved.

While qualitative analysis is the bedrock of discourse analysis, quantitative analyses can also be interesting. The analyst can examine with what frequency particular statements occur. In this way, focal issues in discourse strands, or statements that have the character of slogans and are therefore accompanied by a bulk of judgements and prejudices, can be identified. If a statement occurs very frequently, it has sustained effects and strongly solidifies a particular knowledge. In diachronic analysis, frequencies can also be used to identify trends. However, for the explanatory power of a discourse analysis, the qualitative aspect is of greater importance than the quantitative.

A little toolbox for discourse analysis

In this section, a brief summary of our toolbox for discourse analysis is presented. As noted above, within the scope of this chapter, we cannot provide detailed methodological justifications for each of the tools, but these can be found in the volume by Jäger (2004). In our own research projects, we use short handouts like the following as memory aids or checklists when first dealing with materials.

This outline deals with the practical procedures for subjecting empirically obtained materials to discourse analysis. In an actual project, these elements are supplemented with a clarification of the theoretical foundations and methodology used. The tools presented in the remainder of this section are discussed using the example of a hypothetical research project on the discourse strand of stem cell research in newspapers, or to put it more concisely, in the newspaper sector of the discourse plane of the media.

Choosing a subject matter

The first step in a discourse analysis project is usually to choose a subject matter. In the project report (usually in the introduction), a rationale for the project and its subject matter has to be given.

It needs to be kept in mind that the relationship between a phenomenon of interest and particular discourse strands is often not straightforward because a phenomenon may permeate many discourse strands. For example, in a research project that aims to examine how racism permeates the media, the researcher has to decide which discourse strand(s) to focus on. To make the choice, the researcher has to have an initial concept of racism in mind. (This concept may be developed further in the course of the analysis.) Theoretical concepts are always debatable, and the researcher needs to clarify and justify which concept he is working with.[3] Equipped with this concept, the researcher can think about promising discourse strands where racism may be found. In the case of racism, it is, for example, the discourse strand of immigration, refugees and asylum-seeking. Of course, the discourse strand of immigration could also be interpreted in the light of other research interests. To choose a subject matter means to choose a phenomenon of interest and a discourse strand which will be examined. This discourse strand delineates the scope of materials for analysis.

Choosing a discourse plane and a sector and characterizing them

Typically, it will be necessary, at least initially, to confine the analysis to one discourse plane (for example, the media). When examining a discourse plane, analysis may cover one or several sectors of this plane (for example, the sector of newspapers). The choice of sector needs to be justified. For example, a sector may be exemplary for how an issue is dealt with in the media, or a sector may not have previously been examined in any research project. In the latter case, of course, a review of previous research should summarize the findings from an analysis of other sectors.

In some cases, it may be possible to examine several discourse planes at once. The analysis of interactions of several discourse planes in the regulation of mass consciousness is extremely interesting, but also very time-consuming. To achieve this task, it is necessary to base the analysis on well-justified examples of sectors of these discourse planes and instances of their interaction. The task becomes even more complex if entanglements of discourse strands are also considered.

Accessing and preparing the materials

As a next step, the concrete corpus for analysis needs to be delineated. For example, when analysing newspapers, the particular newspapers and the time periods under consideration need to be decided on. Again, these choices have to be justified.

As a preparation for analysis, a general characterization of the newspaper(s) in question needs to be provided: what is their political orientation, who are their readers, what is their circulation, and so on?

Stem cell research is a topic that continually crops up in newspapers but is often not treated very extensively. In this case, it makes sense to use different newspapers from the period of a whole year, because even if the newspapers are read very carefully, the whole qualitative variety of the discourse strand becomes apparent only in those materials that cover a longer period of time.

In contrast, a project that examines the portrayal of women in pop songs could probably rely on a few exemplary songs (though this would have to be demonstrated in the particular project).

Analysis

The following sequence of steps can be modified and does not have to be adhered to dogmatically. The steps usually have to be gone through several times. In these cycles of analysis, connections between different levels of analysis are discovered, interpretations are developed and weak arguments are discarded.

A structural analysis of the discourse strand

The detailed steps for a structural analysis of a discourse strand are as follows:

1. A list of all articles of relevance for the discourse strand is compiled. This list should include bibliographical information, notes about topics covered in the article, the literary genre, any special characteristics and the section in which the article appears.
2. Structural analysis should roughly capture the characteristics of articles on particular aspects of interest, such as any illustrations, the layout, the use of collective symbols, the argumentation, the vocabulary and so on, and identify which forms are typical for the newspaper. This outline will be needed later to identify typical articles for the detailed analysis (see the next subsection).
3. A discourse strand encompasses various sub-topics. These are first identified and then summarized into groups. For example, in the case of the discourse

strand of stem cell research, sub-topics may be summarized into groups such as the 'legal implications of stem cell research', the 'benefits of stem cell research', the 'technical procedures of stem cell research', the 'ethical problems of stem cell research', the 'costs of stem cell research' and so on. The development of groups of sub-topics is an iterative process, which should lead to a good compromise between parsimony and discriminatory power.

4.   The next step is to examine with what frequency particular groups of sub-topics appear. Which ones are focused on and which ones are neglected? Are there any sub-topics that are conspicuous by their absence?

5.   If the analysis is diachronic, it will also examine how sub-topics are distributed over the course of time. Are some sub-topics particularly frequent at particular times? How does this relate to discursive events?

6.   Discursive entanglements are then identified. For example, the discourse strand of stem cell research is entangled with the discourse strands of ethics, business and medicine.

The findings from these steps of analysis are combined and interpreted together. Thereby, a characterization of the newspaper's discourse position begins to emerge. For example, does the newspaper perceive stem cell research positively or negatively?

The structural analysis of a discourse strand can and should already yield ideas for the ensuing detailed analysis of typical discourse fragments (see the next subsection) and for the final synoptic analysis (see the subsection on synoptic analysis). These ideas should be written down immediately and marked accordingly.

Detailed analysis of typical discourse fragments

To identify the fine detail within the newspaper's discourse position and to assess the effects of this discourse on readers, certain discourse fragments are subjected to detailed analysis. Discourse fragments that are typical of the particular newspaper are selected for this purpose. Criteria for typicality are, for example, typical illustrations, typical use of collective symbols, typical argumentation, typical vocabulary and so on. The typical forms of these aspects have been identified in the preceding structural analysis.

To select typical discourse fragments, the researcher can proceed in several steps and rate the articles according to defined criteria. To ensure that the selection is intersubjectively plausible, several researchers can engage in this rating. The articles that score highest on typicality are then subjected to detailed analysis. If time restraints require it, detailed analysis may also be confined to one article only.

If structural analysis has shown that the discourse strand is very heterogeneous, and if no single homogeneous discourse position can be discerned, the researcher can also address several typicalities, i.e. several kinds of 'typical' articles.

The procedures for selecting typical articles should be systematic and transparent, but not mechanical. What is an appropriate procedure depends on the concrete research project and the discourse strand in question.

The detailed analysis of typical discourse fragments should cover the following aspects:

1. Context

    - Why was this article selected? Why is this article typical?
    - Who is the author? What is her position and status within the newspaper? What are her special areas of coverage, and so on?
    - What was the occasion for the article?
    - In which section of the newspaper does the article appear?

2. Surface of the text

    - What is the layout like? What kinds of pictures or graphs accompany the text?
    - What are the headings and subheadings?
    - How is the article structured into units of meaning?
    - What topics are touched upon in the article? (In other words, what discourse strands is the article a fragment of?)
    - How do these topics relate to each other and overlap (entanglements of discourse strands)?

3. Rhetorical means

    - What kind and form of argumentation does the article follow? What argumentation strategy is used?
    - What logic underlies the composition of the article?
    - What implications and allusions does the article contain?
    - What collective symbolism is used (linguistic and graphic, involving, for example, statistics, photographs, pictures, caricatures, etc.)?
    - What idioms, sayings and clichés are used?
    - What are the vocabulary and style?
    - What actors are mentioned, and how are they portrayed (persons, pronouns used)?
    - What references are made (e.g. references to science, information about the sources of knowledge used)?

4. Content and ideological statements

    - What concept of humankind does the article presuppose and convey?
    - What concept of society does the article presuppose and convey?
    - What concept of (for example) technology does the article presuppose and convey?
    - What perspective regarding the future does the article give?

5. Other peculiarities of the article
6. Discourse position and overall message of the article.

In analysing each of these aspects, the researcher has to ask herself what this peculiarity of the article means, what it implies. For example, what does it mean that a particular image accompanies this text? What effect does this image create? Each of these interpretations remains open to revisions. At the end of the detailed analysis, the interpretations of single aspects are combined into a total interpretation of the article.

Usually, the interpretations of the single aspects fit together like the pieces of a jigsaw puzzle and form a unitary picture. If one aspect stands out, it is often due to special circumstances, such as when a photo or a headline has not been provided by the author but by the editor, who had other purposes in mind, such as spicing up the article. Such discrepancies also provide important insights into the newspaper's discourse position.

Together with the findings from structural analysis, the findings from detailed analysis form the basis for synoptic analysis.

Synoptic analysis

In synoptic analysis, a final assessment of the newspaper's discourse position is made. For this purpose, the findings from structural analysis and detailed analysis are interpreted in relation and comparison to each other.

In conclusion, it needs to be emphasized that CDA is not a rigid formula that can be followed mechanically to produce results. Depending on the research question and the type of materials used, different procedures are appropriate. The researcher has to keep this in mind when developing her analytical strategy. In doing so, she needs to be flexible and imaginative. Therefore, in a way, the best way to learn CDA is to do CDA. An article like the present one only provides initial insights into the wide range of possibilities. We therefore close our 'little toolbox' with one more quotation from Foucault, talking about methodology:

> If you want an image, think of a network of scaffolding that functions as a point of relay between a project being concluded and a new one. Thus I don't construct a general method of definitive value for myself or for others. What I write does not prescribe anything, neither to myself nor to others. At most, its character is instrumental and visionary or dream-like. (Foucault, 1991: 29)

Initial thoughts on analysing dispositives

Discourses do not exist independently; they are elements of dispositives. A dispositive, as outlined above, is the constantly evolving synthesis of knowledge that is built into language, action and materializations. The concept of the dispositive can be visualized as a triangle, or rather a rotating circle, with three transit points:

- discursive practices (language and thought)
- non-discursive practices (action)
- materializations (which are created through non-discursive practices).

Dispositives

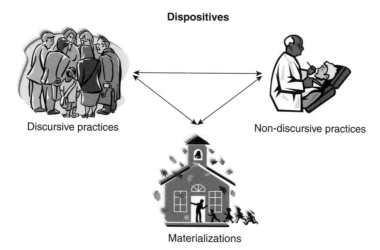

Discursive practices   Non-discursive practices

Materializations

FIGURE 2.1   *Dispositives*

The visibility of materializations is upheld through discursive and non-discursive practices. Figure 2.1, which is a graphic simplification of the concept, summarizes this relationship.

Though a dispositive has certain durability, it is also subject to historical changes and is constantly influenced by other dispositives. A synchronic analysis serves to identify the current state of a dispositive. A particular discursive practice, non-discursive practice or materialization can be relevant for various dispositives. For example, the dispositive of 'traffic' encompasses streets, cars, traffic jams, drivers, traffic signs and so on. But 'traffic' is also an economic problem that creates costs and affects business. 'Traffic' is therefore embedded into the economic dispositive. The economic dispositive, in turn, is embedded into the political dispositive. In a society, dispositives overlap and are entangled with each other. These entanglements may be what unifies a society.

A dispositive analysis has to include the following steps:

1. Reconstructing the knowledge that is built into discursive practices (through discourse analysis, as described above). This analysis is the basis for the further steps in a dispositive analysis. It already creates an awareness of important aspects of the dispositive, such as uncharted territories in discourse, significant materializations and so on.
2. Reconstructing the knowledge that is built into non-discursive practices.
3. Reconstructing the knowledge that is built into materialization, and the non-discursive practices that have created these materializations.

Reconstructing this knowledge usually results in texts. A dispositive analysis thus translates non-discursive and materialized knowledge into discursive knowledge.

A dispositive analysis should also consider the form in which the examined knowledge occurs: is the knowledge manifestly apparent? Or is it implicit, for example hidden in implicatures? Into what arguments is the knowledge packed? And so on. It should be noted again that the concept of knowledge is here a very broad one, including not only cognitions but also emotions. Knowledge includes all the contents that make up a human consciousness.

Since the analysis of discursive elements of a dispositive has already been discussed extensively above, the remainder of this section will focus on reconstructing the knowledge that is built into non-discursive practices and materializations.

Knowledge in non-discursive practices

Non-discursive practices, i.e. actions, can be observed and described. For a dispositive analysis, the task is to reconstruct the knowledge that enables and accompanies these practices.

For example, the analyst can observe a man who crosses a street and walks into a bakery, where he buys a loaf of bread. The analyst's task is now to find out what this man knows and wants. The man knows that he has to go to a certain place to be able to buy bread. He knows that for this purpose he has to dress in a certain way (e.g. put on shoes and a coat). He knows that when crossing a road, he has to pay attention to the traffic and observe the traffic rules. Moreover, he knows that the bakery is located in a particular place, or how to look for a bakery. He knows that in a bakery he can buy bread, and that he needs money for that. The simple act of buying bread is thus already based on a considerable amount of knowledge, and this analysis only gives a small hint of it.

The following is a more complex example. Suppose the analyst observes a man who has dug a hole at the side of a road, and is now standing in this hole and manipulating a large pipe. To reconstruct the knowledge built into this practice, the analyst has to share this knowledge and understand what the man is doing. Suppose that to a large extent she is lacking this knowledge.

There are basically three things she can do to gain an understanding of what the man is doing.

Firstly, the researcher can of course draw on existing texts. For example, she can consult previous research, but also more mundane documents such as practitioners' literature, instruction sheets, or field manuals.

Secondly, the analyst can ask the man what he is doing. In research methodology, this is called an ethnographic interview (see, for example, Spradley, 1979). When the researcher asks the man what he is doing, the man may answer: 'I am repairing a burst pipe.' With this information, she already understands better what he is doing. Next, she may ask him: 'Why are you doing that?' He may answer something like: 'Because the pipe has burst', or 'That's my job', or 'I need to earn money somehow', and so on. The knowledge built into his activity is thus fairly complex and can be followed up to the economic practice of dependent wage labour.

A large part of knowledge is only available to people in their practices (tacit knowledge), and people cannot easily explicate it in talk. In other words, people will know more than they can tell. As a third option, the researcher can therefore rely on participant observation (see, for example, Agar, 2002; Emerson et al., 1995; Hammersley and Atkinson, 2007; Spradley, 1980) to learn about this implicit knowledge and make it explicit in her research. In the extreme case, the researcher may herself learn to dig holes and mend burst pipes (a fascinating example of such work is Wacquant's [2004] study of boxing).

Knowledge in materializations

When an analyst observes an object, such as a house, a church or a bicycle, obviously he cannot ask this object about its knowledge directly. However, there are indirect ways of reconstructing the knowledge built into materializations. Methodological guidelines for doing so can, for example, be found in multimodal discourse analysis (Van Leeuwen, 2005) and artefact analysis (Froschauer, 2002; Lueger, 2004; for an example of empirical work that combines multimodal discourse analysis and artefact analysis, see Maier, forthcoming).

To analyse materializations, the researcher has to rely on his own and his fellow researchers' background knowledge. In addition, he should aim to extend this knowledge by drawing on the pertinent literature, and by questioning users, producers and other persons who are experts on the materialization in question.

Artefact analysis, as developed by Lueger (2004) and Froschauer (2002), suggests that one of the first steps in analysing a materialization is to deconstruct the materialization by dividing it into its constituent parts and transcribing it into a field protocol. The material object is thus transformed into a text. Here, another problem arises, which incidentally also applies to the field notes and observation protocols produced in the participant observation of non-discursive practices. The field protocols written by the researcher are not neutral. Like any text, they pursue particular interests, and in the ideal case, this interest should be to answer the research question.

In some cases, the researcher may even be able to draw on previous research that has already discursified the materialization in question as, for example, Caborn (1999, 2006) has done with regard to state architecture in Berlin.

It should be emphasized again that the meaning of a materialization is not fixed. The knowledge built into a materialization today may be different from the knowledge it contained in the past. 'Legends' might have formed around it, and meanings may have changed. Moreover, a materialization may have different meanings for members of different cultures (as well as cultures understood in the broad sense of the term). A good case in point is the Aztec crown of feathers, which is exhibited in the Anthropological Museum in Vienna. In pre-Columbian times, it was a ritual headdress, worn by priests or even by the Aztec emperor Montezuma. For the Spanish conquistador Hernán Cortés, it was a treasure which he stole. The Habsburg emperors bought it as an exotic curiosity. In today's Anthropological Museum, it is an exhibit of scientific value. For today's descendants of the Aztecs, the crown is a symbol of their cultural identity and stands for the blossoming and ensuing destruction of their culture. They argue that the crown was stolen from them, and that the Museum should return it. For Austrian politicians and diplomats, the crown has thus become a cause for political dissonance with Mexico (for an in-depth analysis of the transformations of exhibits in anthropological museums, see Döring and Hirschauer, 1997).

As the example of the feather crown shows, each of the meanings assigned to a materialization is tightly related to power relations (e.g. whether the crown is a ritual item, a scientific exhibit, or a symbol of collective identity). In the materialization as such, these power relations are invisible, and the task of the analyst is to bring them out into the open. The analyst can only do this if he considers historical contexts (this touches on the issue of historical discourse and dispositive analysis, which is currently revolutionizing historical theory; see, for example, Sarasin, 2003).

As these initial thoughts on methods for analysing dispositives indicate, the task of a dispositive analysis is very complex. It encompasses the analysis of knowledge in discursive and non-discursive practices as well as in materializations. An example of such an analysis is Michel Foucault's (1979) book *Discipline and Punish*. Also, Victor Klemperer's (2001) *Diary of the Nazi Years* can be read as a dispositive analysis. Both authors provided no explicit information on their methodology. They applied their methodology implicitly, or as Foucault calls it, in the form of *bricolage*. They analysed discourse, assembled knowledge, consulted statistics, deconstructed them critically, drew conclusions, added their own opinions, and so on.

The thoughts on dispositive analysis presented in this chapter do not provide a recipe or schema. However, they do give some ideas on how to approach dispositive analysis. A central part of dispositive analysis is the discourse analysis of texts. Moreover, dispositive analysis comprises the analysis of non-discursive practices, for which methods developed in ethnography, such as ethnographic interviews and participant observation, provide important means. A final component is the analysis of materializations, which can draw on methods such as multimodal discourse analysis and artefact analysis. An explicit methodology for combining these approaches has yet to be developed. Such an endeavour can probably only be achieved in connection with concrete research projects. It would therefore be desirable for such projects to devote some space and time to explicit reasoning about methodology. This would promote the development of dispositive analysis, and would contribute to bridging the existing gaps between discourse analysis and other methods of empirical social research.

Notes

1   We therefore keep the discussion of theoretical background as short as possible and do not present previous empirical research projects at great length. To readers particularly interested in these aspects, we recommend the works by Siegfried Jäger (2001b, 2004) and by Margarete and Siegfried Jäger (2007).

2   This French term literally means 'tinkering', 'fiddling', creative 'do-it-yourself', making use of any resources that happen to be at hand

3   For example, a definition of racism that is generally justifiable and well-accepted in the sciences encompasses the following three elements: (1) One or several people are for biological or cultural reasons constructed as an ethnic group or even a race. (2) This group is evaluated (negatively or positively, e.g. when blacks are assumed to be superior jazz musicians). (3) The construction and evaluation take place from a position of power (which in discourse analysis is obvious, since discourse is per se 'powerful').

3

Critical Discourse Studies: A Sociocognitive Approach[1]

Teun A. van Dijk

Terminology and definitions

Although critical approaches to discourse are commonly known as Critical Discourse Analysis (CDA), I prefer to speak of Critical Discourse Studies (CDS). This more general term suggests that such a critical approach not only involves critical *analysis*, but also critical *theory*, as well as critical *applications*. The designation CDS may also avoid the widespread misconception that a critical approach is a *method* of discourse analysis.

For the same reason, I favour the term Discourse Studies (DS), rather than Discourse Analysis, to designate a multidisciplinary field of scholarly activities that are obviously not limited to the *analysis* of text and talk. Moreover, as a *discipline*, DS has many types and methods of analysis: it is not 'a' method among others within the humanities and the social sciences.

CDS is not a method, but rather a critical *perspective, position* or *attitude* within the discipline of multidisciplinary Discourse Studies. Critical research makes use of a large number of methods, both from Discourse Studies itself, as well as from the humanities, psychology and the social sciences.

The critical approach of CDS characterizes scholars rather than their methods: CDS scholars are sociopolitically committed to social equality and justice. They also show this in their scientific research, for instance by the formulation of specific goals, the selection and construction of theories, the use and development of methods of analysis and especially in the application of such research in the study of important social problems and political issues.

CDS scholars are typically interested in the way discourse (re)produces social *domination*, that is, the *power abuse* of one group over others, and how dominated groups may discursively *resist* such abuse.

CDS is not just any social or political research, as is the case in all the social and political sciences, but is premised on the fact that some forms of text and talk may be *unjust*. One of the tasks of CDS is to formulate the norms that define such 'discursive injustice'. CDS aims to expose and help to combat such injustice. It is *problem-oriented* rather than discipline- or theory-oriented. Such a research policy presupposes an *ethical* assessment, implying that discourse as social interaction may be *illegitimate* according to some fundamental *norms*, for instance those of international human and social rights. At the same time, critical analysis should be aware of the fact that such norms and rights change historically, and that some definitions of 'international' may well mean 'Western'. As a criterion, we thus call any discourse unjust if it violates the internationally recognized human rights of people and contributes to social inequality. Typical examples are discourses that ultimately (re)produce inequalities of gender, race or class.

Finally, socially committed research should be carried out in close collaboration and solidarity with those who need it most, such as various dominated groups in society. This also means, not least for students, that CDS research and especially its practical applications should be accessible, and avoid an esoteric style. In that and many other senses, CDS researchers are profoundly aware of the role of scholarly activities in society.

What are Critical Discourse Studies (CDS)?

Although it is virtually impossible to briefly and adequately define a type of scholarly investigation, critical studies of discourse typically have the following properties:

- They aim to analyse, and thus to contribute to the understanding and the solution of, serious social problems, especially those that are caused or exacerbated by public text and talk, such as various forms of social power abuse (domination) and their resulting social inequality.

- This analysis is conducted within a normative perspective, defined in terms of international human rights, that allows a critical assessment of abusive, discursive practices as well as guidelines for practical intervention and resistance against illegitimate domination.
- The analysis specifically takes into account the interests, the expertise and the resistance of those groups that are the victims of discursive injustice and its consequences.

The discourse–cognition–society triangle

It is within this framework that I propose to formulate and illustrate some of the principles I try to observe when doing CDS. Given my multidisciplinary orientation, the overall label I sometimes use for my approach is that of 'sociocognitive' discourse analysis. Although I dislike labels (because they are reductionist and because I have many times changed my area and perspective of research), I have few quarrels with this one, especially since it emphasizes that – unlike many of my colleagues in CDS and various interactionist approaches – I value the fundamental importance of the study of *cognition* (and not only that of society) in the critical analysis of discourse, communication and interaction.

This means, among other things, that I am also interested in the study of mental representations and the processes of language users when they produce and comprehend discourse and participate in verbal interaction, as well as in the knowledge, ideologies and other beliefs shared by social groups. At the same time, such an approach examines the ways in which such cognitive phenomena are related to the structures of discourse, verbal interaction, communicative events and situations, as well as societal structures, such as those of domination and social inequality, as mentioned above.

What is 'cognition'?

As is the case for other fundamental notions, 'cognition' is a notion that is jointly defined by all the disciplines currently integrated under the label 'cognitive science', such as psychology, linguistics, philosophy and logic as well as the brain sciences. Some typical cognitive notions used here are, for instance:

- **Mind,** defined, for example, as a central function of the human brain.
- **Cognition** as the set of functions of the mind, such as thought, perception and representation.
- **Memory**: Short Term (Working) Memory (STM) and Long Term Memory (LTM).
- **Episodic** (personal, autobiographic) **Memory** (EM) and **Semantic** (sociocultural, shared) **Memory** – as part of LTM.

- Semantic **Mental Models** (represented in EM) as the subjective representations of the events and situations observed, participated in or referred to by discourse.
- **Goals** as mental models of the situations to be realized by action.
- Pragmatic **Context Models**: specific mental models of subjective representations (definitions) of the relevant properties of communicative situations, controlling discourse processing and adapting discourse to the social environment so that it is situationally appropriate.
- **Knowledge** and its organization: shared, sociocultural **beliefs** that are certified by the (knowledge) criteria or standards of a (knowledge) community.
- **Ideology** as the shared, fundamental and axiomatic beliefs of specific social groups (socialism, neoliberalism, feminism, (anti)racism, pacifism, etc.).
- **Attitudes** as the socially shared, ideologically based opinions (normative beliefs) about specific social issues having given rise to debate or struggle (abortion, divorce, euthanasia, immigration, etc.).
- **Cognitive processes** such as the production and comprehension of discourse/ interaction on the basis of specific mental models, controlled by context models, and based on knowledge and ideologies.

The label of the 'sociocognitive' approach does not mean that I think that CDS should be *limited* to the social and cognitive study of discourse, or to some combination of these dimensions. It only means that (at present) I am personally most interested in the fascinating sociocognitive interface of discourse, that is, the relations between mind, discursive interaction and society. For instance, in my work on racism (Van Dijk, 1984, 1987, 1991, 1993a, 2005, 2007b), and in my research on ideology (Van Dijk, 1998) and context (Van Dijk, 2008a, 2009), I have shown that these are *both* mental *and* social phenomena. It goes without saying, however, that the complex, 'real-world' problems CDS deals with also need a historical, cultural, socio-economic, philosophical, logical or neurological approach, among others, depending on what one wants to know (see, for instance, the various approaches represented in Van Dijk, 1997, 2007a).

Given the verbal–symbolic nature of discourse, explicit CDS of course also needs a solid 'linguistic' basis, where 'linguistic' is understood in a broad sense. Whatever cognitive and social dimensions of discourse CDS deals with, it always needs to account for at least some of the detailed structures, strategies and functions of *text* or *talk*. These may include grammatical, pragmatic, interactional, stylistic, rhetorical, semiotic, narrative, argumentative or similar forms and meanings of the verbal, paraverbal and multimodal structures of communicative events.

Having emphasized the necessity of a broad, diverse, multidisciplinary and problem-oriented CDS, I thus limit my own endeavours to the domain defined by the discourse–cognition–society triangle.

In a more or less informal way, we may view the combined cognitive and social dimensions of the triangle as defining the relevant (local and global) *context* of discourse. Indeed, the sociopolitical and problem-oriented objectives of

CDS especially need sophisticated theorization of the intricate relationships between text and context. We shall see that adequate discourse analysis at the same time requires detailed cognitive and social analysis, and vice versa, and that it is only the *integration* of these accounts that may reach descriptive, explanatory and especially critical adequacy in the study of social problems.

It should be emphasized that context, as I define it, is not simply some kind of social environment, situation or structure – such as the social 'variables' of gender, age or 'race' in classical sociolinguistics. Rather, a context is a subjective mental representation, a dynamic online model, of the participants about the for–them–now relative properties of the communicative situation. I call such a representation a *context model* (Van Dijk, 2008a, 2009). It is this mental 'definition of the situation' that controls the adequate adaptation of discourse production and comprehension to their social environment. This is just one of the ways in which cognition, society and discourse are deeply and mutually integrated in interaction.

Within the theoretical framework of the discourse–cognition–society triangle, context models mediate between discourse structures and social structures at all levels of analysis. This means that 'society' is understood here as a complex configuration of situational structures at the local level (participants and their identities, roles and relationships engaging in spatiotemporally and institutionally situated, goal-direction interaction), on the one hand, and societal structures (organizations, groups, classes, etc. and their properties and – e.g. power – relations), on the other hand. This side of the triangle also includes the cultural and historical dimensions of interaction and social structure, that is, their cultural variation as well as their historical specificity and change. It is also at this side of the triangle that we locate the consequences of discursive injustice, for instance in the form of social inequality.

Finally, it should be stressed that the use of the triangle is merely an analytical metaphor representing the major dimensions of critical analysis. It should *not* be interpreted as suggesting that cognition and discourse are *outside* society. On the contrary, human beings as language users and as members of groups and communities, as well as their mental representations and discourses, are obviously an inherent part of society. It is also within social structure that language users interpret, represent, reproduce or change social structures such as social inequality and injustice.

What is 'discourse'?

Discourse analysts are often asked to define the concept of 'discourse'. Such a definition would have to consist of the whole discipline of discourse studies, in the same way as linguistics provides the many dimensions of the definition of 'language'. In my view, it hardly makes sense to define fundamental notions such as 'discourse', 'language', 'cognition', 'interaction', 'power' or 'society'. To understand these notions, we need whole theories or disciplines of the objects or phenomena we are dealing with. Thus, discourse is a multidimensional social phenomenon. It is at the same time a linguistic (verbal, grammatical) object (meaningful sequences or words or sentences), an action (such as an assertion or a threat), a form of social interaction (like a conversation), a social practice (such as a lecture), a mental representation (a meaning, a mental model, an opinion, knowledge), an interactional or communicative event or activity (like a parliamentary debate), a cultural product (like a telenovela) or even an economic commodity that is being sold and bought (like a novel). In other words, a more or less complete 'definition' of the notion of discourse would involve many dimensions and consists of many other fundamental notions that need definition, that is, theory, such as meaning, interaction and cognition.

The example: the defense of capitalism

After a discussion of some of the general notions of CDS, I shall now be more specific about the kind of discourse structures to be attended to in such a critical approach. At the same time, I shall illustrate and further develop the theoretical notions introduced above by analysing some properties of a specific example: a text – 'A Petition Against the Persecution of Microsoft' of the Center for the Moral Defense of Capitalism (now called Center for the Advancement of Capitalism) – downloaded from the internet in 2001 (www.moraldefense.com) (text no longer available on the website in 2008). This petition criticizes the US government for its legal battle against Microsoft, and asks readers to sign it.

I have chosen this text as an example because of the widely perceived socioeconomic problem that vast international corporations may abuse their power in order to dominate the market and hence limit the freedom of choice of consumers.

Context

Of the communicative situation of this, we do not know much more than that the text was found on the internet in 2000, and that it was produced by the *Center for the Moral Defense of Capitalism,* whose very name suggests a neoliberal, conservative think tank. A new internet search in December 2007 presented the following definition of the goals of the Center:

> The Center for the Advancement of Capitalism is dedicated to advancing individual rights and economic freedom through Ayn Rand's philosophy of Objectivism. (www.moraldefense.com)

This means that readers who know this Center may already have a more detailed context model of the communicative situation than other readers (such as information about the ideological background, identity and goals of the Center), and can interpret the text in that light. Intended recipients are people who use the web and understand English. A further aspect of the communicative situation is the assumed *previous knowledge* about legal actions against Microsoft because of its abuse of market power (a near monopoly, because of the pervasive use of Windows as an operating system for PCs) to couple other programs (such as its web browser Explorer) to this operating system. In other words, the context analysis focuses on Setting (Time, Place), Participants and their properties and relations, as well as on their Goals, the Knowledge presupposed by the participants, and the Ideology of the participants.

Topics: semantic macrostructures

I often advocate beginning Critical Analysis (CrA) with an analysis of semantic macrostructures, that is, with a study of global meanings, topics or themes. These are what discourses are (globally) about; they are mostly intentional and consciously controlled by the speaker; they embody the (subjectively) most important information of a discourse, express the overall 'content' of mental models of events (see below), and perhaps most importantly, they represent the meaning or information most readers will memorize best of a discourse. Discursively, topics or themes are characteristically expressed in titles, abstracts, summaries and announcements.

For contextual reasons, we select topics as a significant structure to study because they are usually controlled by powerful speakers, because they influence many other structures of a discourse (such as its global coherence), and because they have the most obvious effects on the (memory and consequent actions of) recipients and hence on the process of reproduction that underlies social power and dominance (for details, see Van Dijk and Kintsch, 1983).

> In our sample text, the title, 'A Petition Against the Persecution of Microsoft' expresses not only part of the topic ('the persecution of Microsoft'), but also the self-categorization of the text genre ('petition'). Theoretically and psychologically, topics or macrostructures are derived from a text by inference – through a process of information reduction that is being practised especially in text summarization. Thus, we may 'summarize' this text by, for example, the following macropropositions:
>
> M1   The freedom of enterprise is under attack by antitrust laws.
> M2   Successful businessmen are being represented as tyrants.
> M3   The suit against Microsoft is an example of this M1 and M2.
> M4   Government should not limit the freedom of the market.
> M5   Microsoft has the right to do what it wants with its products.
> M6   Innovators should not be punished.
> M7   We call that the case against Microsoft be dismissed.

In a further reduction, one can summarize these macropropositions with the overall macroproposition (topic): 'The US government is requested to stop its judicial persecution of the innovator Microsoft.'

We see that these various topics/macropropositions indeed represent very high level, sometimes abstract, principles. In this case, these propositions are more or less a direct expression of some tenets of a classical capitalist ideology about the freedom of enterprise. In other words, the macropropositions express the general ideological principles of the freedom of the market, and then apply these to the special case of Microsoft. We shall see later that this distinction reflects the difference between socially shared representations, on the one hand, and more personal mental models, on the other.

Local meanings

Next, a CrA may focus on local meanings, such as the meaning of words (a study that also may be called lexical, depending on one's perspective), the structures and nature of propositions, and coherence and other relations between propositions, such as implications, presuppositions, levels of description, degrees of granularity and so on.

The reasons to give priority to semantic analysis in CrA are mostly contextual: local meanings are a function of the selection made by speakers/writers in their mental models of events or their more general knowledge and ideologies. At the same time, they are the kind of information that (under the overall control of global topics) most directly influences the mental models, and hence the opinions and attitudes of recipients. Together with the topics, these meanings are best recalled and reproduced by recipients, and hence may have the most obvious social consequences.

As is the case for many variable structures of discourse, local meanings may also be *controlled by context models*. That is, not all local meanings are equally appropriate in communicative situations, as we know from the general distinction between formal, casual and popular discourse styles, as well as from social and cultural taboos. Indeed, most institutional text and talk is contextually constrained by the specific aims and norms of institutional interaction and organization.

Theoretically, this means that the generation of meanings based on mental models of events talked about is controlled by the various categories and contents of context models. One obvious controlling mechanism is that the mutual *knowledge* as indexed by the context model requires that speakers ongoingly in principle only assert what the recipients do not already know, as we also know from the appropriateness conditions of the speech act of an assertion. Other constraints are defined for specific kinds of *participants* and their identities, roles and relationship: there are often limitations of 'content' or meaning for specific categories of speakers, and this is especially so in institutional situations.

At this local semantic level, we may for instance examine the choice of the word 'per-secution' in the title of our sample text, a choice that has various implications that express the ideological perspective of the author (The Center for the Moral Defense of Capitalism): the action of the government is defined in negative terms, implying a form of morally or legally reprehensible harassment or force, or abuse of power. At the same time, the choice of this word implies that Microsoft is the victim of this aggression. In more general terms, lexical selection here shows the familiar form of negative other-presentation, and positive self-presentation as an organization taking the defence of the victims. As part of the main macroproposition, the choice of the concept of 'persecution' also contributes to the organization of the local meanings in the rest of the text. In more cognitive terms, this means that the choice of this word may influence the formation of the macronodes of the mental model of the readers of this text.

Similarly relevant is the repeated use of the word 'rights' in the first paragraph, typ-ically associated with 'individual' and 'freedom', all profoundly ideological concepts related to the constitution and prevailing ideology of the United States. In order to be able to qualify the legal action of the government in the starkly negative terms of a 'persecution', it needs to be shown that the rights of individuals are being violated, and what these rights are. The emphasis on rights has several other functions, such as associating Us and Our position with something good and legitimate, and thus preparing the negative evaluation of the US Government when it violates these rights. Apart from polarizing the mental model being construed here, this paragraph at the same time functions as an important premise in the overall argumentation of this text.

For CDS, especially interesting in such a local semantic analysis is the study of the many forms of implicit or indirect meanings, such as implications, presuppositions, allusions, vagueness and so on. Again, such meanings are related to underlying beliefs, but not openly, directly or precisely asserted for various contextual reasons, including the well-known ideological objective to de-emphasize Our bad things and Their good things.

In our sample text, there are many propositions that are implied or presupposed, but not explicitly asserted. When the authors say that antitrust legislation comes 'under the guise of "protecting the public"', the expression 'under the guise' and the quotes imply that it is not true (or merely alleged) that antitrust laws protect the public. Note also that in the second paragraph, as well as throughout the text, many expressions have ideological presuppositions, such as:

- competitors are envious of successful business men
- officials are power-hungry
- the business world has creative geniuses
- business empires are hard-won.

Apart from further emphasizing the polarization between Government and Business, the local meanings of the text thus create another polarization between envious competitors and brilliant creators in the business. Notice also that the lexical choice and metaphors further emphasize these polarizations: envious, power-hungry, hard-won, control, regulators, and breaking to pieces, etc. are the negative concepts associated with Them, the government (and some business people), whereas We and those we protect are associated with success, creative geniuses and by litotes with 'crime' and 'tyrant'. Again, such words not only contribute to the overall polarization of the conceptual structure of the text, but also to the formation of a biased, polarized model of the events, where the Actors are neatly differentiated between the Good and the Bad.

The first two paragraphs are formulated in general terms, and apply to rights and their violation, as well as to the antitrust laws. The third paragraph begins with the functional move of Specification or Example: what has been said so far specifically applies to the case of Microsoft. Theoretically, this means that the first paragraphs are rather expressions of (general) social representations, such as attitudes and ideologies, whereas the third paragraph describes the current case, Microsoft, and thus sets up the more specific mental model based on these general social representations. Given the ideological slant of the first paragraphs, there is little doubt that this model, as expressed by the Center, is also ideologically biased, and we may expect that the general polarization constructed before will be applied here, as is indeed the case. Notice also that conceptual polarization is often implemented in the text by various forms of hyperboles, as we have already seen in the lexical choice of 'crime', 'tyrants' and 'geniuses'. Such hyperboles may even come close to outright lies, for instance when it is asserted that Bill Gates has been deprived of his right to control his own company.

The use of 'his', 'businessmen' and 'the men who have made this country great' suggests that men, especially or exclusively and no women, are involved in business and its success. Thus, apart from expressing a starkly conservative neo-liberal ideology, the Center also professes a sexist ideology by verbally excluding women, thus contributing to a more overall conservative meta-ideology that also controls the nationalist ideology expressed in the characteristic form of US self-glorification (the 'greatness' of this country).

Finally, among the many other semantic properties of this text, we should also mention the importance of what is being left out in the text. Thus, it is suggested that the success of Microsoft is based on the principle of better products for a lower price, but of course not the well-known practice of the forced bundling of products (like Windows and its internet browser). Nearly trivially then, we may formulate the general rule that the negative properties of Us (or those we defend) are either omitted or downgraded in the text. Note that, theoretically, omission is only a relevant property of a discourse when it can be shown that the omitted information is part of the mental model (the Center no doubt knows about the illegal practices of Microsoft), or of more general, shared knowledge that is needed or may be used to produce or understand a text. In this case, the mental model of a critical reader may of course be different from that persuasively expressed by the Center.

We now have a first impression of the theoretically based practical guidelines on which discourse structures to study among many hundreds. Of course, this is only an example. The point is that such a choice is twice context-bound: first, by our own (scholarly) aims, our research problems, and the expectations of our readers, as well as the social relevance of our research project. Second, by the relevance of specific discourse structures studied in their own context, such as the aims and beliefs of the speaker or the recipients, the social roles, positions and relations of participants, institutional constraints and so on.

The relevance of subtle 'formal' structures

Besides or instead of the semantic structures just mentioned, we may be more interested in those structures of text or talk that are usually less consciously controlled or controllable by the speakers, such as intonation, syntactic structures, propositional structures, and rhetorical figures, as well as the many properties of spontaneous talk, such as turn-taking, repairs, pauses, hesitation, and so on.

These various 'forms' generally do not directly express the underlying meanings and hence beliefs, but rather signal the 'pragmatic' properties of a communicative event, such as the intention, current mood or emotions of speakers, their perspective on the events talked about, their opinions of co-participants, and interactional concerns especially such as positive self-presentation and impression formation. Thus, men may well be able to hide their negative opinions of women, or white people of black people, but indirectly their evaluations, position or face, and hence their identity, may be signalled by subtle structural or formal characteristics of talk or the non-verbal properties of communicative events (gestures, face work, body position, distance, and so on).

> At both the global and local levels, our sample text also has several formal properties that enhance the general underlying topic and argumentation. Indeed, as we have seen, the very argumentative structure of this petition is one of the global, formal properties that organizes this text: the general premises, expressed in the first two paragraphs, focus on constitutional rights on the one hand, and the alleged violation of such rights by the antitrust laws on the other. Both are then applied to the more particular premise that Microsoft is the victim of this violation. In the same way, several of the meanings in these and other paragraphs have specific argumentative functions, such as the reference to the Declaration of Independence as an authoritative and hence credible set of principles by which the government's duties are evaluated.
>
> Similarly, the discourse may enhance its effectiveness by various rhetorical moves, of which hyperboles have already been mentioned ('geniuses', etc.). There is also the use of the opposite of what is being meant, for instance in irony or litotes (such as the Microsoft 'crime' of being successful).
>
> Indeed, the very structure of polarization of this kind of ideological discourse not only has a semantic property, but also formal properties, such as the rhetorical contrast expressed in the fourth paragraph: here, the government's views that the 'free' market imposes 'force', and that 'control' is 'freedom', are criticized as an inversion of reality as the Center sees it, and it does so by a construction of a contrast.
>
> Finally, in the same way that the semantic and rhetorical polarizations of this text express and help construct biased models of the case against Microsoft, its formal style is a marker of its genre: the official petition. This formal style begins with the paraphrase of the Declaration of Independence, but is also lexically expressed in the Center's own petition, as in the repeated 'We hold that …', 'not by anyone's permission, but by absolute right', etc., signalling something like a Declaration of the Free Market.

One conclusion of this discussion of the criteria applied in the choice of the discourse structures studied in CDS projects is that any 'method' or 'approach' that limits itself to some genre or dimension of discourse only can by definition only provide a very partial analysis. Trivially, grammarians usually study grammar, conversation analysts conversations, and narratologists stories and their structures. Now, if some CDS researcher, for the double contextual reasons explained above, precisely needs to study some aspects of grammar, conversation or narration, it is obviously in these more specific areas of research that one looks for relevant structures. But as soon as the 'critical' aims of the research project require a broader approach, those scholars who limit themselves to the study of a single genre or types of structure are often unable to fully deploy their expertise. Hence also my oft-repeated criticism of the exclusive membership of one school, approach or scholarly sect, and my plea for diversity, flexibility and multidisciplinarity as general criteria for CDS. This obviously first of all applies to CDS and critical scholars themselves! Indeed, there are many ways to do interesting and relevant discourse analysis, and we also need to develop the more general theories, concepts and methods that may (also) be used in critical analysis. Indeed, few of the general notions used so far in our analysis were developed within critical studies.

Relating text and context: context models

It has been assumed above that the relation between discourse and society is not direct, but needs to be *mediated* by so-called *context models* (Van Dijk, 2008a, 2009). That is, social structures − organizations, groups, gender, race, etc. − are phenomena that cannot be directly linked to the mental processes of discourse production and understanding, as was previously the case in traditional sociolinguistics.

Hence, we need a mediating *cognitive* device that is able to *represent* the relevant structures of the social situation, both locally (micro) as well as globally (macro), and that at the same time is able to *control* discourse, the mental processes of production and comprehension and its situated *variation*.

Context models, defined as specific mental models, represented in episodic memory, do just that. They make sure that language users adapt their discourse to the social environment, so that it is socially *appropriate*.

Given more or less the same 'content' or 'information' as specified in the (semantic) mental model of things talked about, context models are needed to appropriately formulate more or less the 'same' content in different communicative situations. This means that context models define the *genre* as well as the *style* of text and talk.

As summarized above, context models are organized by a relatively simple *schema* consisting of fundamental *categories*, such as:

- a spatiotemporal setting
- participants

    o identities, roles, relationships
    o goals
    o knowledge
    o ideologies

- the ongoing social action.

Context models are dynamic and are ongoingly adapted to the communicative situation, if only because the knowledge of the recipients is constantly changing as a result of the very discourse itself.

Since context models control all the variable aspects of discourse (intonation, syntax, lexicon, etc.), they need to be kept activated at least in the background of working memory – and hence cannot be too complex or voluminous (and represent dozens or hundreds of aspects of the current communicative situation).

It goes without saying that context models as a crucial interface between discourse and society also play a fundamental role in critical discourse studies, which are premised on the detailed analysis of some of these discourse–society relationships, such as those of power and domination.

> In our example of a petition, the context defining the communicative event is rather obvious. The overall societal domain for this text is that of business or the market, and the overall actions are those of advocating the freedom of enterprise, and protecting business against government interference. The local setting of the communicative event is the internet. The communicative role of the participant is that of speaker/writer, author and originator, the interactional role that of a defender of Microsoft and as an opponent of the government, whereas the socio-economic role is that of an organization advocating the freedom of the market. The other participant, the addressee, is explicitly referred to in the beginning of the text as 'Fellow Americans', thus pragmatically trying to emphasize the unity of the 'we' group for which this Center claims to be the defender. It is interesting that although the proposal for the petition is directed at 'Fellow Americans', the proposed petition itself is addressed to the relevant final destinataries: the judge, the Senate Judiciary Committee, the Attorney General and the President of the United States.
>
> The current communicative action is that of publishing a text on the internet persuading readers to sign a petitition. This action is being performed through the speech acts of accusing the government, and defending Microsoft. The (complex) mental structures defining the cognitive dimension of the context consist of the various ideologies analysed above, as well as the more specific attitudes and opinions (about the legal action of the government against Microsoft) we have found expressed throughout the text. Although expressing group co-membership in addressing 'Fellow Americans', the persuasive structure of the text presupposes that not all Americans may have the same opinion about the practices of Microsoft. Finally, the text is meaningful for its readers only because it presupposes a vast amount

of common ground and commonsense knowledge, such as about the Declaration of Independence, Microsoft, antitrust laws and so on, as well as specific (model-based) knowledge about the current court case against Microsoft.

The important point is that throughout, the text adapts to this subjectively construed context model of the current communicative situation, for example, as follows:

- The meanings of the text are all understandable within the broader framework of the three semantic domains of business, justice and goverment.
- The genre and speech act of the petition is one form of implementing the overall defence of the free market, which is the global aim of the Center.
- The action of the government is defined as a violation of Our rights, and hence is a sufficient condition for the success of the current genre and speech act of a petition.
- The overall topic semantically realizes the reason for the speech act and genre of this specific petition: Microsoft's rights have been violated.
- The argumentative structure is organized in such a way as to optimally sustain the communicative function of this text as a form of persuasion.
- The polarization of the opinions at all levels of the text expresses the attitudes and the ideology of the Center, and tries to influence those of the readers – and final destinataries.
- Lexical choice is appropriate for the genre of a formal, public petition.
- The text presupposes existent general knowledge about what business, laws, governments, etc. are, as well as specific knowledge about the process against Microsoft. However, it does not express or presuppose knowledge that debilitates its defence (e.g. about the illegal practices of Microsoft).

For any kind of CDS research that links text with some social situation, it is important to realize that whatever the broader social or political situation, it may not 'reach' or impact on discourse simply because a speaker may find it irrelevant and further ignores the relevant information in the construction of the context model. Also, the changes that speakers apply in their discourses, for example, because of politeness or other forms of persuasion, need to be taken into account.

We see that the notion of subjective context models theoretically implies the important criterion of *relevance*, namely that only those properties of communicative situation are construed as forming part of the context, if they are (now) relevant for the participant. Note that relevance is not absolute or (only) socially determined, but is relative to the current knowledge, goals, wishes, interests and personal experiences of the current speaker or recipient at each moment of a communicative event.

Discourse semantics: event models

Crucial to any theory of discourse is its semantics, which provides a theory of discourse meaning and interpretation. Traditionally, a linguistic semantics is formulated in terms of abstract meanings: concepts, propositions and their mutual relations. Thus, local coherence of discourse is defined as constraints on relations between propositions, on the one hand, and on the relations between the referents ('facts' of some mental model) of such propositions, on the other hand. For instance, a sequence of propositions may be said to be coherent if the facts (states of affairs, events, actions, etc.) referred to by these propositions are related, for instance by relations of causality or more generally by relations of conditionality (such as enabling). We may call this *referential* or *extensional coherence*. On the other hand, coherence may also be established by intensional (meaning) relations among the propositions themselves, for instance when a proposition Q is a Generalization, Specification, Example, Illustration, etc. of a previous proposition P. Since Q is defined here in terms of its function relative to P, we may call this *functional coherence*.

As suggested, such an account is rather abstract, and appears to have little empirical relevance: this is not the way language users go about producing and understanding meaningful discourse. Instead of an abstract theory of meaning, therefore, we may define meaning and interpretation in cognitive terms, that is, in terms of mental operations and representations.

Such an approach also solves a major problem of the more formal account, namely the nature of reference: notions that define referential coherence, such as referents, facts and causal relations between facts, are not defined in linguistic (grammatical) semantics. A cognitive approach to discourse meaning not only may solve that problem, but at the same time accounts for the subjectivity of coherence: discourses are not coherent in the abstract, but are coherent for language users, and according to their intentions, interpretations or understandings.

Thus, discourses are not so much coherent because their propositions refer to related 'objective' facts in some possible world, but rather to the episodes (events and situations) as interpreted, defined and (seen to be) related by language users. We have seen above that such subjective interpretations are represented in episodic memory as *mental models* of events and situations. We may now simply say that a discourse is coherent if language users are able to construct a mental model for it. We may call these models *event models* in order to account for the fact that they subjectively represent the events the discourse refers to. Whereas context models, as discussed above, are pragmatic, event models are *semantic*.

Since context models are a specific kind of event model (namely a model of communicative events), event models have more or less the same structure organized by a *schema* with *categories* such as Setting, Participants and Actions/Events – and their respective subcategories and properties.

Thus, in the analysis of our example, we have repeatedly seen how at all levels of the petition text, structures are geared not only to the adequate expression of the mental model of the (authors in the) Center for the Moral Defense of Capitalism, but also to the persuasive construction of a preferred model among the addressees. That is, this intended model features the macro-opinion that the US Government through its antitrust laws in general, and its case against Microsoft in particular, violates the basic principles of the freedom of the market. That is, the current mental model of the Microsoft case is a fairly direct instantiation of more general attitudes about antitrust legislation and their basic ideologies about the freedom of enterprise. The polarization between Us and Them, or between Business and Government, and its respective Good and Bad qualities, is thus a specification of more general opinions about ingroups and outgroups as we know them from the study of ideology (Van Dijk, 1998). In other words, the authors of the text not only try to adequately express their own model of the events, but formulate the text in such a way that the intended model be accepted by the readers. This is what persuasion is all about, and it may be obvious that without an account of mental model structures, such a verbal act and its concomitant verbal structures cannot be adequately described, let alone explained.

The notion of a mental model also explains another fundamental property of discourse meaning: its *incompleteness*. Semantically speaking, a discourse is like the tip of an iceberg: only some of the propositions needed to understand a discourse are actually expressed; most other propositions remain *implicit*, and must be inferred from the *explicit* propositions (given a body of world knowledge, to which we shall come back below). It is the model that provides these 'missing propositions'. Implicit or implied propositions of discourse are thus simply defined as those propositions that are part of the mental model for that discourse, but not present in its semantic representation. That is, for pragmatic reasons as defined by the context model of a discourse (including the beliefs attributed to the recipient by the speaker), only part of the propositions of a model need to be expressed – for instance, because the speaker believes that such information is irrelevant, because the recipient already knows these propositions, or because it may be inferred from other propositions. Hence, mental models at the same time provide an excellent definition of presuppositions, namely as those propositions of event models that are implied but not asserted by the discourse.

Besides discourse coherence and implications, the notion of event models provides a framework for many other, hitherto problematic, aspects of discourse and discourse processing, briefly summarized as follows:

- Event models are a crucial cognitive aspect of the *constructionist* way people view, understand, interpret and recall 'reality'. In other words, our personal *experiences*, as represented in episodic memory, consist of mental constructs: models.
- Event models are not only the result of discourse comprehension, but are also the basis of discourse *production*. Event models may be part of our planning of discourse ('what we want to say'). Thus, stories are contextually appropriate (relevant, interesting) formulations of underlying event models, for instance of personal experiences as stored in episodic memory.
- Event models are *subjective* (personal interpretations of events), but have a *social* basis, because they instantiate socially shared knowledge and possibly also group ideologies (see below). That is, context models explain how discourse

may be ideologically 'biased', namely when based on event models that instantiate ideological propositions.

- Event models account for the fact that different language users, members of different communities and of different social (e.g. ideological) groups, may have *different interpretations* of events, and at the same time, different interpretations of the same discourse. This implies that the *influence* of discourse on the minds of recipients may also be different.

Social cognition

CDS is not primarily interested in the subjective meanings or experiences of individual language users. Power, power abuse, dominance and their reproduction typically involve collectivities, such as groups, social movements, organizations and institutions (Van Dijk, 2008b).

Therefore, besides the fundamental interface of personal mental models that account for *specific* discourses, a cognitive approach also needs to account for *social cognition*, that is, the beliefs or *social representations* they share with others of their group or community. Knowledge, attitudes, values, norms and ideologies are different types of social representations.

These social representations also play a role in the construction of personal models, as we have seen in some detail in our brief analytical remarks about the Petition text. That is, socially shared knowledge and opinions may be 'instantiated' in such models. In other words, models are also the interface of the individual and the social, and explain how group beliefs may affect personal beliefs and thus be expressed in discourse. Ethnic or gender prejudice, which are typically defined for social groups, thus also appear as an (instantiated) property of individual discourses. And conversely, if the personal mental model of social events of an influential person is shared by others of a group or community, mental models may be generalized and abstracted from to form social representations such as knowledge, attitudes and ideologies. This is of course precisely the aim of the Petition text.

It is one of the aims of CDS research to analyse specific discourses in this broader, social framework, for instance by trying to infer (sometimes quite indirectly) which shared social representations are being expressed or presupposed by discourse. Thus, critical discourse studies of racism, sexism or classism need to relate properties of discourse with these underlying, socially shared, representations, which group members use as a resource to talk about (members) of other groups. *Outgroup derogation* and *ingroup celebration* are the social–psychological strategies typically defining this kind of chauvinist discourse.

Ideology

Dominance, defined as power abuse, is often based on, and legitimated by ideologies, that is, by the fundamental social beliefs that organize and control the social representations of groups and their members. Many forms of CDS research require such an ideological analysis, especially because ideologies are typically expressed and reproduced by discourse.

It is important to stress here that the cognitive framework sketched above suggests that *there is no direct link between discourse and ideology*. The basic beliefs of an ideology (for instance, about the equality of women and men in a feminist ideology) organize specific attitudes, that is, the socially shared opinions of a group (for instance, about abortion, sexual harassment or equal pay), which in turn may influence specific event models (about specific participants and actions), which finally may be related to discourse under the final control of context models. In other words, to 'read off' ideologies from discourse is not always possible, precisely because ideologies need to be very general and fairly abstract. Although we still ignore what the general structure of ideologies are (van Dijk, 1998), it may be assumed that they are organized by a *general schema* consisting of the basic categories that organize the self and other representations of a group and its members, such as:

- membership devices (who belongs to us?)
- typical acts (what do we do?)
- aims (why do we do it?)
- relations with other (opponent) groups
- resources, including access to public discourse.

Note that many of the features that were traditionally examined in the (critical or other) analysis of discourse are here accounted for in more explicit, separate theories of cognition. That is, meaningfulness, interpretation and understanding of text and context are described here in terms of specific mental representations, such as event models, context models and social representations. We are thus able not only to abstractly *describe* text and talk, but also to *explain* how real language users go about producing and understanding discourse, how their personal and socially shared beliefs affect discourse production and how these are in turn affected by discourse. No critical account of discourse is theoretically complete without such a cognitive interface.

Social situations

We shall be relatively brief about the third main component of our CDS approach: society. For obvious reasons, the social dimensions of CDS usually receive more attention from CDS researchers than its cognitive aspects, as is also shown in the other chapters in this book. Note though that our sociocognitive theory explains how social structures may affect (and be affected by) discourse structures via a theory of social cognition.

An account of the role of social structures in CDS requires an analysis of both micro (local) and macro (global) structures of society, that is, of individual social actors and their situated interactions, on the one hand, and of social groups, movements, organizations and institutions, as well as their relations, such as power and dominance, on the other hand.

Note that the micro–macro distinction is only analytic. In real life, social members may experience and interpret such structures at the same time: by 'locally' responding to a question from a student, which may be part of the somewhat more comprehensive social activity of giving a class, I at the same time may teach a course and reproduce the organization of this university as well as higher education – at increasingly 'higher', macro and abstract levels of analysis and (diminishing degrees of) awareness.

Unlike, for instance, therapists, CDS scholars are less interested in the account of specific discourses, interactions and situations – such as, indeed, the example analysed in this chapter. Rather, they focus on the more general ways specific discourses may be *instances* of more general discourse properties and how such discourse may contribute to social inequality, for instance by the formation of biased models and ultimately by the formation or confirmation of ideologies.

Micro vs. macro

As is the case for micro sociologists, discourse analysts deal primarily with text and talk, and hence with a typical 'micro' dimension of society. Indeed, it is generally assumed that society and its structures – as well as its structures of inequality – are 'locally' produced by its members. Yet, I additionally assume that *such local production in interaction is possible only if members have shared social representations such as knowledge and ideologies*. In that sense, 'local' social interaction is again 'enabled' by a macro dimension such as the social cognitions of collectivities. But then again, such a macro dimension is itself constructed cognitively by the mental representations of groups of individual social actors. We thus see how for CDS, the micro and macro dimensions of society, and their analysis, are multiply integrated, as is also embodied in the slo-gan that CDS is mainly interested in the *discursive* reproduction of the *social structure* of inequality. One of the reasons CDS research (critically) analyses specific discourses is the methodologically important fact that these are more directly analysable than abstract structures, and that abstract structures can only be inferred (as language users do) by studying special cases. Although the macrosocial dimensions of society (such as social inequality) will usually be the main reasons and aims of CDS, we can only observe and analyse such abstract structures in terms of how they are expressed or enacted locally in social practices in general, and in discourses in particular, that is, in specific situations.

As part of an analysis of social situations, let me briefly say a few words about two central categories of social situations: *action* and *actors*.

Discursive action as social–political action

In a similar way as the abstract meanings of discourse are intricately related to beliefs and other cognitive representations, the discursive acts accomplished in or by discourse can also hardly be separated from the social acts that define social situations: discourse is inherently part of both cognition and situations. Indeed, discursive acts are by definition also social acts. However, since not all social acts are discursive, we need more than just an analysis of speech acts, such as assertions, promises or threats, or typical discursive interactions such as turn-taking, interruptions, agreeing, or the opening and closing of a conversation. There are also a large number of social acts that are the conditions, consequences, or implications of discursive (verbal) interaction.

Thus, holding a speech in parliament may involve a sequence of speech acts such as assertions, questions, or accusations, as well as conversational moves and strategies such as responding to critique, agreeing with members of your own party, refusing to be interrupted, and many more. In this conversational aspect, parliamentary debates are not fundamentally different from other forms of public dialogue. However, what is typical and characteristic is that by such conversational moves, participants globally engage in legislation, government support or opposition, representation of the voters, and other global political actions. Similarly, by speaking negatively about refugees in order to persuade parliament to enact tough legislation against immigrants, this at the same time implies the social act of derogation and discrimination. Even quite local moves, such as denials in disclaimers ('I have nothing against blacks, but ...') may be part of a larger social–psychological strategy of positive self-presentation (ingroup celebration) and outgroup derogation which is so typical of contemporary racisms, especially of the elite.

In other words, in CDS, the action-analysis of text and talk is not limited to a study of typically discursive doings but also examines the ways in which discursive acts and structures are deployed in the enactment of broader social and political acts, especially those that are part of systems of dominance (or resistance against dominance).

The same is true for the embedding of discursive interaction in broader social and political acts, and the study of the social conditions and consequences of discourse. Thus, an immigration debate in parliament presupposes the global acts of immigration, and may globally result in keeping refugees out, and even more locally it may be a consequence of a political act of government, for instance a decision to close the borders for a specific group of refugees.

Actors

Similar remarks hold for the actors that define situations as participants in various roles, such as communicative roles (various kinds of 'producers' or 'recipients' of text or talk), social roles such as friends and enemies, occupational roles such as politicians, or political roles such as members of parliament or members of a party. Note that in the same way as an action may be defined at different levels, and thus relate discursive acts (such as denials) with social acts (such as discrimination), actors may also at the same time engage in various identities at the same time, although some identities or group affiliations will be stronger and more salient than others in a particular context. As we have emphasized before in the model theory of context, a relevant situational analysis of discourse does not abstractly examine all the possible identities of speakers or recipients, but only the locally relevant or more prominent ones, and how these affect or are affected by discourse.

Note that a local actor analysis of discourse situations at the same time involves an interface with societal structures: speakers act as members of various social groups, and we thus have an obvious link between the macrostructures of groups and the microstructures of interaction, namely via the relation of membership. A similar relationship was established in mental models, namely between personal beliefs and the socially shared beliefs of groups.

Societal structures

Local situations of interaction enact, manifest, or challenge global societal structures. Participants speak and listen as women, mothers, lawyers, party members, or company executives. Their actions, including their discursive actions, realize larger social acts and processes, such as legislation, education, discrimination and dominance, often within institutional frameworks such as parliaments, schools, families, or research institutes.

CDS is mainly interested in the role of discourse in the instantiation and reproduction of power and power abuse (dominance), and hence is particularly interested in the detailed study of the interface between the local and the global, between the structures of discourse and the structures of society. We have seen that such links are not direct, but need a cognitive and an interactional interface: social representations, including attitudes and ideologies, are often mediated by mental models in order to show up in discourse, and such discourse has social effects and functions only when it in turn contributes to the formation or confirmation of social attitudes and ideologies. White group dominance can only be 'implemented' when white group members actually engage in such derogating discourse as an instance of discrimination. Racism and sexism are thus not merely abstract systems of social inequality and dominance, but actually 'reach' down in the forms of everyday life, namely through the beliefs, actions and discourses of group members.

Similar remarks have been made in the analysis of our sample text. In order to fully understand and explain (the structures of) this text, we not only need to spell out its cognitive and contextual conditions and consequences, but also the broader societal structures on which such cognitions and contexts are ultimately based, and which at the same time they enable, sustain and reproduce. We have seen how throughout the text and at all levels, the negative opinion about the US Government in the Microsoft case is linked with the overall neo-liberal ideology of a free market, in which creative 'businessmen' are the heroes and the government (and its justice system) the enemies, against whose attacks the Center plays its specific role of 'defender' of capitalist values. That is, the ideology, as implemented in the mental models constructed for the Microsoft case and as more or less directly expressed in the text, needs to be linked to societal groups, organizations, structures and relationships of power. Indeed, the current text is in that respect just one of the myriad of (discursive and other) actions of the business community in its power struggle with the State. It is only at the highest level of societal analysis that we are able to fundamentally understand this text, its structures and functions.

It is this permanent bottom–up and top–down linkage of discourse and interaction with societal structures that forms one of the most typical characteristics of CDS. Discourse analysis is thus at the same time cognitive, social and political analysis, but focuses rather on the role discourses play, both locally and globally, in society and its structures.

The relevant relationships run both ways. Societal structures such as groups and institutions, as well as overall relations such as power or global societal acts such as legislation and education, provide the overall constraints on local actions and discourse. These constraints may be more or less strong, and run from strict norms and obligations (for instance, as formulated in law, such as the acts of judges or MPs), to more flexible or 'soft' norms, such as politeness norms.

These global constraints may affect such diverse discourse properties as interaction moves, who controls turn-taking or who opens a session, speech acts, topic choice, local coherence, lexical style or rhetorical figures. And conversely, these discourse structures may be 'heard as' (interpreted as, count as) actions that are instances or components of such very global societal or political acts as immigration policy or educational reform.

It is precisely in these macro–micro links that we encounter the crux for a critical discourse analysis. Merely observing and analysing social inequality at high levels of abstraction is an exercise for the social sciences – and a mere study of discourse grammar, semantics, speech acts or conversational moves, the general task of linguists, and discourse and conversation analysts. Social and political discourse analysis is specifically geared towards the detailed explanation of the relationship between the two along the lines sketched above.

FURTHER READING

Since the topics dealt with in this chapter would require a vast number of references, I have not made specific references in the text other than where I concretely refer to some of my earlier work, of which this chapter is a sample. Obviously, many of the notions dealt with in this chapter have been based on, or inspired by, the work of others. Thus, my ideas on CDS have been influenced by the many publications of the other scholars represented in this volume, and I may for the sake of space simply refer to their chapters for detailed references. For the other notions used in this chapter, see the following references and recommended readings:

- **Cognition, social cognition, memory, mental models, text processing**: Augoustinos and Walker (1995); Fiske and Taylor (1991); Graesser et al. (2003); Johnson-Laird (1983); Kintsch (1998); Moscovici (2000); Tulving (1983); Van Dijk and Kintsch (1983); Van Oostendorp and Goldman (1999).
- **Context**: Auer (1992); Duranti and Goodwin (1992); Gumperz (1982); Van Dijk (2008a, 2009).
- **Discourse and conversation structures**: Schiffrin et al. (2001); Ten Have (1999); van Dijk (1997; 2007a, 2007b).
- **Social situation analysis**: Argyle et al. (1981); Goffman (1970); Scherer and Giles (1979).
- **The analysis of social structure and its relations to discourse and cognition**: Alexander et al. (2004); Boden and Zimmerman (1991); Wuthnow (1989).
- **Discourse and ideology**: Van Dijk (1998).
- **Discourse and power**: Van Dijk (2008b).
- **Corporate and organizational discourse**: Grant et al. (2004).
- **Neoliberalism**: Rapley (2004).

Appendix

A Petition Against the Persecution of Microsoft

Sign the Petition – International Version (for non–US residents)
To: Members of Congress, Attorney General Janet Reno and President Bill Clinton.

Fellow Americans:

The Declaration of Independence proclaims that the government's fundamental purpose is to protect the rights of the individual, and that each individual has an inalienable right to the pursuit of happiness. Throughout America's history, this noble idea has protected the individual's right to pursue his own happiness by applying his energy to productive work, trading the products of his effort on a free market and rising as far as his abilities carry him.

Over the past century, however, this freedom has been under attack, and one notorious avenue of this attack has been the antitrust laws. Under the guise of 'protecting the public,' these laws have allowed envious competitors and power-hungry officials to attack successful businessmen for the crime of being successful. It has led to the ugly spectacle of the creative geniuses of the business world – the men who have made this country great – being branded as oppressive tyrants, whose hard-won business empires must be broken to pieces and subjected to the control of government regulators.

The Justice Department's current suit against Microsoft is the latest example of this trend. It is based on envy for the productive ability of Microsoft and its founder, Bill Gates. The result of this suit, if successful, will be to deprive Mr. Gates of his right to control his own company, and to deprive the company of its ownership and control of its own products.

The Justice Department's case – and indeed the entire edifice of antitrust law – is based on the bizarrely inverted notion that the productive actions of individuals in the free market can somehow constitute 'force,' while the coercive actions of government regulators can somehow secure 'freedom.'

The truth is that the only kind of 'monopoly' that can form in a free market is one based on offering better products at lower prices, since under a free market even monopolies must obey the law of supply and demand. Harmful, coercive monopolies are the result, not of the operation of the free market, but of government regulations, subsidies, and privileges which close off entry to competitors. No business can outlaw its competitors – only the government can.

We hold that Microsoft has a right to its own property; that it has the authority, therefore, to bundle its properties – including Windows 95 and Internet Explorer – in whatever combination it chooses, not by anyone's permission, but by absolute right. We hold that to abridge this right is to attack every innovator's right to the products of his effort, and to overthrow the foundations of a free market and of a free society.

We do not want to live in a country where achievement is resented and attacked, where every innovator and entrepreneur has to fear persecution from dictatorial regulators and judges, enforcing undefined laws at the bidding of jealous competitors. We realize that our lives and well-being depend on the existence of a free market, in which innovators and entrepreneurs are free to rise as far as their ability can carry them, without being held down by arbitrary and unjust government regulations.

As concerned citizens, we ask that the Justice Department's case against Microsoft be dismissed. We call for a national debate over the arbitrary and

unjust provisions of the antitrust laws and for an end to the practice of perse-
cuting businessmen for their success.

Note

1   This text is a new, shorter and partly rewritten version of the author's contribution
    to Wodak, R. and Meyer, M. (eds) (2002) *Methods of Critical Discourse Analysis*.
    London: Sage, pp. 95–120.

4

The Discourse-Historical Approach (DHA)

Martin Reisigl and Ruth Wodak

Introducing key concepts and terms

We start our chapter by introducing the notions of 'critique', 'ideology' and 'power'. These three concepts are constitutive for every approach in CDA, albeit frequently employed with different meanings. Therefore, it is important to clarify how they are conceptualized in the DHA. We then proceed with the delineation of other terms significant for our purposes, such as 'discourse', 'genre', 'text', 'recontextualization', 'intertextuality' and 'interdiscursivity'.

The second section summarizes some analytical tools and general principles of the DHA, while in the third section, we illustrate our methodology step by step by focusing on 'discourses about climate change'. In the final section, we refer to the strengths and limitations of the DHA and point to future challenges for the field.

'Critique', 'ideology' and 'power'

Three concepts figure indispensably in all variants of CDA: critique, power, and ideology.

'Critique' carries many different meanings: some adhere to the Frankfurt School, others to a notion of literary criticism, some to traditional Marxist notions. Adhering to a 'critical' stance should be understood as gaining distance from the data (despite the fact that critique is mostly 'situated critique'), embedding the data in the social context, clarifying the political positioning of discourse participants, and having a focus on continuous self-reflection while undertaking research. Moreover, the application of results is aspired to, be it in practical seminars for teachers, doctors and bureaucrats, in the writing of expert opinions or in the production of school books.

The DHA adheres to the socio-philosophical orientation of critical theory.[1] As such, it follows a concept of critique which integrates three related aspects (see Reisigl, 2003: 78–82; Reisigl and Wodak, 2001: 32–35 for extended discussions):

1. *Text* or *discourse-immanent critique* aims at discovering inconsistencies, self-contradictions, paradoxes and dilemmas in the text-internal or discourse-internal structures.
2. *Socio-diagnostic critique* is concerned with demystifying the − manifest or latent − persuasive or 'manipulative' character of discursive practices. Here, we make use of our contextual knowledge and draw on social theories as well as other theoretical models from various disciplines to interpret the discursive events.
3. Future-related *prospective critique* seeks to contribute to the improvement of communication (for example, by elaborating guidelines against sexist language use or by reducing 'language barriers' in hospitals, schools and so forth).

It follows from our understanding of critique that the DHA should make the object under investigation and the analyst's own position transparent and justify theoretically why certain interpretations and readings of discursive events seem more valid than others.

Thompson (1990) discusses the concept of ideology and its relationships to other concepts and especially to aspects of mass communication thoroughly. He points out that the notion of ideology has been given a range of functions and meanings since it first appeared in the late 18th century in France. For Thompson, ideology refers to social forms and processes within which, and by means of which, hegemonic symbolic forms circulate in the social world.

Ideology, for the DHA, is seen as an (often) one-sided perspective or world view composed of related mental representations, convictions, opinions, attitudes and evaluations, which is shared by members of a specific social group. Ideologies serve as an important means of establishing and maintaining unequal power relations through discourse: for example, by establishing hegemonic identity narratives, or by controlling the access to specific discourses or public spheres ('gate-keeping'). In addition, ideologies also function as a means of transforming power relations more or less radically. Thus, we take a particular interest in the ways in which linguistic and other semiotic practices mediate and reproduce ideology in a variety of social institutions. One of the aims of the DHA is to 'demystify' the hegemony of specific discourses by deciphering the ideologies that establish, perpetuate or fight dominance.

For the DHA, language is not powerful on its own − it is a means to gain and maintain power by the use 'powerful' people make of it. This explains why the DHA critically analyses the language use of those in power who have the means and opportunities to improve conditions.

'Power' relates to an asymmetric relationship among social actors who assume different social positions or belong to different social groups. Following Weber (1980: 28), we regard 'power' as the possibility of having one's own will within a social relationship against the will or interests of others. Some of the ways in which power is implemented are 'actional power' (physical force and violence), the control of people through threats or promises, an attachment to authority (the exertion of authority and submission to authority) and technical control through objects, such as means of production, means of transportation, weapons, and so on (see Popitz, 1992).

Power is legitimized or de-legitimized in discourses. Texts are often sites of social struggle in that they manifest traces of differing ideological fights for dominance and hegemony. Thus, we focus on the ways in which linguistic forms are used in various expressions and manipulations of power. Power is discursively exerted not only by grammatical forms, but also by a person's control of the social occasion by means of the genre of a text, or by the regulation of access to certain public spheres.

'Discourse', 'text', 'context'

By employing the DHA, we investigate multifaceted phenomena in our societies. This implies that the study of (oral, written, visual) language necessarily remains only a part of the whole enterprise – hence, our research must be interdisciplinary. Moreover, in order to analyse, understand and explain the complexity of the objects under investigation, we consider many different and accessible sources of data (in respect of external constraints such as time, funding, etc.) from various analytical perspectives. Thus, we follow the *principle of triangulation,* which implies taking a whole range of empirical observations, theories and methods as well as background information into account (see, for example, Heer et al., 2008; Wodak, 2007; Wodak et al., 1999). The specific choices depend on the specific problem – in this chapter, on controversies on climate change.

We consider 'discourse' to be:

- a cluster of context-dependent semiotic practices that are situated within specific fields of social action
- socially constituted and socially constitutive
- related to a macro-topic
- linked to the argumentation about validity claims such as truth and normative validity involving several social actors who have different points of view.

Thus, we regard (a) macro-topic-relatedness, (b) pluri-perspectivity and (c) argumentativity as constitutive elements of a discourse.[2]

The question of delimiting the borders of a 'discourse' and of differentiating it from other 'discourses' is intricate: the boundaries of a 'discourse', such as a discourse on global warming or climate change, are partly fluid. As an analytical construct, a 'discourse' always depends on the discourse analyst's perspective. As an object of investigation, a discourse is not a closed unit, but a dynamic semiotic entity that is open to reinterpretation and continuation.

Furthermore, we distinguish between 'discourse' and 'text': 'texts' are parts of discourses. They make speech acts durable over time and thus bridge two dilated speech situations, i.e. the situation of speech production and the situation of speech reception. In other words, texts – be they visualized and written or oral – objectify linguistic actions (Ehlich, 1983).

Texts can be assigned to *genres*. A 'genre' may be characterized as 'a socially ratified way of using language in connection with a particular type of social activity' (Fairclough, 1995a: 14). Consequently, a manifesto on combating global warming proposes certain rules and expectations according to social conventions, and has specific social purposes. A discourse on climate change is realized through a range of genres and texts, for example TV debates on the politics of a particular government on climate change, guidelines to reduce energy consumption, speeches or lectures by climatologists.

The DHA considers *intertextual* and *interdiscursive relationships* between utterances, texts, genres and discourses, as well as extra-linguistic social/sociological variables, the history of an organization or institution, and situational frames. While focusing on all these relationships, we explore how discourses, genres and texts change in relation to sociopolitical change.

Intertextuality means that texts are linked to other texts, both in the past and in the present. Such connections are established in different ways: through explicit reference to a topic or main actor; through references to the same events; by allusions or evocations; by the transfer of main arguments from one text to the next, and so on. The process of transferring given elements to new contexts is labelled *recontextualization*: if an element is taken out of a specific context, we observe the process of de-contextualization; if the respective element is then inserted into a new context, we witness the process of recontextualization. The element (partly) acquires a new meaning, since meanings are formed in use (see Wittgenstein, 1989). Recontextualization can, for instance, be observed when contrasting a political speech with the selective reporting of the speech in various newspapers. A journalist will select specific quotes which best fit the general purpose of the article (e.g. commentary). The quotations are thus de- and re-contextualized, i.e. newly framed. They can partly acquire new meanings in the specific context of press coverage.

Interdiscursivity signifies that discourses are linked to each other in various ways. If we conceive of 'discourse' as primarily topic-related (as 'discourse on x'), we will observe that a discourse on climate change frequently refers to topics or subtopics of other discourses, such as finances or health. Discourses are open and often hybrid; new sub-topics can be created at many points.

'Field of action' (Girnth, 1996) indicates a segment of social reality which constitutes a (partial) 'frame' of a discourse. Different fields of action are defined by different functions of discursive practices. For example, in the arena of *political action*, we differentiate among eight political functions as eight different fields (see Figure 4. 1). A 'discourse' about a specific topic can find its starting point within one field of action and proceed through another one. Discourses then 'spread' to different fields and relate to or overlap with other discourses.

We represent the relationship between fields of action, genres and macro-topics in the area of political action as follows (Figure 4.1):[3]

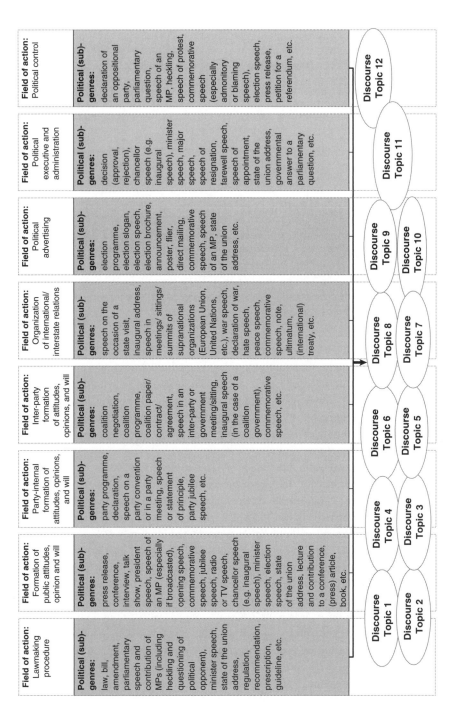

FIGURE 4. 1 *Fields of political action, political genres and discourse topics (see Reisigl, 2007: 34–35)*

Figure 4.2 further illustrates the interdiscursive and intertextual relationships between discourses, discourse topics, genres and texts.

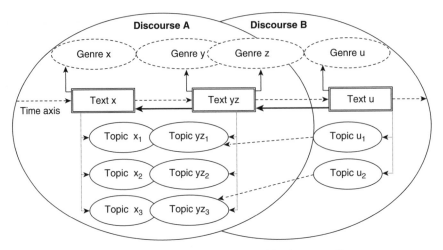

FIGURE 4.2   *Interdiscursive and intertextual relationships between discourses, discourse topics, genres and texts*

In this diagram, interdiscursivity is indicated by the two big overlapping ellipses. Intertextual relationships are represented by simple bold arrows. The assignment of texts to genres is signalled by simple arrows. The topics to which a text refers are indicated by small ellipses with simple dotted arrows; the topical intersection of different texts is indicated by the overlapping small ellipses. Finally, the specific intertextual relationship of the thematic reference of one text to another is indicated by simple broken arrows.

Several of these relationships can be illustrated with respect to our case study, if we choose three texts of the Czech president Václav Klaus, a fervid opponent of environmentalist warnings on the dangers related to global warming. On 16 March 2007, Klaus gave a speech entitled 'Innsbruck Speech: Three Threats of our Freedom' on the occasion of receiving an honorary doctorate by the University of Innsbruck (= text 1 that belongs to the 'epideictic genre' of speeches of gratitude). This speech is first and foremost a part of the 'discourse about freedom and liberalism' (= discourse A), but to a certain extent also of the 'discourse about climate change' (= discourse B), because climate change and environmentalism are important topics of the speech.

Three days later, on 19 March 2007, Klaus answered five questions from Republican politicians of the House of Representatives of the US Congress, in the Committee on Energy and Commerce, on issues of mankind's contribution to global warming and climate change. This rather formalized pseudo-dialogic text (= text 2) was realized as a written letter (dating from 19 March 2007) that was designated to answer the questions which were formulated in a letter (dating from 6 March 2007) signed by the Ranking Member of the Committee on Energy and Commerce, Joe Barton, and the Ranking

Member of the Subcommittee on Energy and Air Quality, J. Dennis Hastert. This letter shares several topics with text 1, relating to climate change, environmentalism and the threat of freedom, and is also part of various other discourses, for example the discourse on energy economy. Text 2, thus, is a somewhat hybrid genre, as it adopts features of both the (sub)genre of a written expert interview and the (sub)genre of a written letter which resembles the (sub)genre of parliamentary questions and answers.

On 14 June 2007, Václav Klaus published an article in the *Financial Times* entitled 'Freedom, not climate, is at risk'. This text (= text 3) is again part of both discourse A and discourse B. It picks up many of the topics of text 2 but, of course, manifests characteristics of another genre – the newspaper commentary. This text elicited many reactions and questions by readers, some of which were published in the newspaper on 21 June 2007, and also answered by Klaus (see www.klaus.cz/klaus2/asp/-default. asp?lang=EN&CatID=YJrRHRsP).

Our triangulatory approach is based on a concept of 'context' which takes into account four levels:

1. the immediate, language or text-internal co-text and co-discourse
2. the intertextual and interdiscursive relationship between utterances, texts, genres and discourses
3. the extralinguistic social variables and institutional frames of a specific 'context of situation'
4. the broader sociopolitical and historical context, which discursive practices are embedded in and related to.

In our analysis, we orient ourselves to all four dimensions of context in a recursive manner (see also Wodak, 2007, 2008a).

Some tools of analysis and principles of DHA

The DHA is three-dimensional: after (1) having identified the specific *contents* or *topics* of a specific discourse, (2) *discursive strategies* are investigated. Then (3), *linguistic means* (as types) and the specific, context-dependent *linguistic realizations* (as tokens) are examined.

There are several strategies which deserve special attention when analysing a specific discourse and related texts (see Step 5 below). Heuristically, we orient ourselves to five questions:

1. How are persons, objects, phenomena/events, processes and actions named and referred to linguistically?
2. What characteristics, qualities and features are attributed to social actors, objects, phenomena/events and processes?
3. What arguments are employed in the discourse in question?
4. From what perspective are these nominations, attributions and arguments expressed?
5. Are the respective utterances articulated overtly; are they intensified or mitigated?

According to these five questions, we elaborate five types of discursive strategies. By 'strategy', we generally mean a more or less intentional plan of practices (including discursive practices) adopted to achieve a particular social, political, psychological or linguistic goal. Discursive strategies are located at different levels of linguistic organization and complexity.[4]

TABLE 4.1   *A selection of discursive strategies*

Strategy	Objectives	Devices
nomination	discursive construction of social actors, objects/phenomena/ events and processes/ actions	• membership categorization devices, deictics, anthroponyms, etc. • tropes such as metaphors, metonymies and synecdoches (*pars pro toto, totum pro parte*) • verbs and nouns used to denote processes and actions, etc.
predication	discursive qualification of social actors, objects, phenomena, events/ processes and actions (more or less positively or negatively)	• stereotypical, evaluative attributions of negative or positive traits (e.g. in the form of adjectives, appositions, prepositional phrases, relative clauses, conjunctional clauses, infinitive clauses and participial clauses or groups) • explicit predicates or predicative nouns/adjectives/pronouns • collocations • explicit comparisons, similes, metaphors and other rhetorical figures (including metonymies, hyperboles, litotes, euphemisms) • allusions, evocations, presuppositions/implicatures, etc.
argumentation	justification and quest- ioning of claims of truth and normative rightness	• topoi (formal or more content-related) • fallacies
perspectivization, framing or discourse representation	positioning speaker's or writer's point of view and expressing involvement or distance	• deictics • direct, indirect or free indirect speech • quotation marks, discourse markers/ particles • metaphors • animating prosody, etc.
intensification, mitigation	modifying (intensifying or mitigating) the illocut- ionary force and thus the epistemic or deontic status of utterances	• diminutives or augmentatives • (modal) particles, tag questions, subjunctive, hesitations, vague expressions, etc. • hyperboles, litotes • indirect speech acts (e.g. question instead of assertion) • verbs of saying, feeling, thinking, etc.

The first study for which the DHA was developed analysed the constitution of antisemitic stereotyped images, as they emerged in public discourses in the 1986 Austrian presidential campaign of former UN general secretary Kurt Waldheim, who, for a long time, had kept secret his National Socialist past (Wodak et al., 1990).[5] Four salient characteristics of the DHA emerged in this research project: (1) interdisciplinary and particularly historical aims and interests; (2) team work; (3) triangulation as a methodological principle; and (4) an orientation towards application.

This interdisciplinary study combined linguistic analysis with historical and sociological approaches. Moreover, the researchers prepared and presented an exhibition about 'Post-war antisemitism' at the University of Vienna.

The DHA was further elaborated in a number of studies of, for example, racist discrimination against migrants from Romania and the discourse about nation and national identity in Austria (Matouschek et al., 1995; Reisigl, 2007; Wodak et al., 1999). The research centre 'Discourse, Politics, Identity' (DPI) in Vienna, established by the second author of this article (thanks to the Wittgenstein Prize awarded to her in 1996; see www.wittgenstein-club.at), allowed for a shift to comparative interdisciplinary and transnational projects relating to research on European identities and the European politics of memory (Heer et al., 2008; Kovács and Wodak, 2003; Muntigl et al., 2000).

Various principles characterizing the approach have evolved over time since the study on Austrian post-war antisemitism. Here, we summarize ten of the most important principles:

1. The approach is interdisciplinary. Interdisciplinarity involves theory, methods, methodology, research practice and practical application.
2. The approach is problem-oriented.
3. Various theories and methods are combined, wherever integration leads to an adequate understanding and explanation of the research object.
4. The research incorporates fieldwork and ethnography (study from 'inside'), where required for a thorough analysis and theorizing of the object under investigation.
5. The research necessarily moves recursively between theory and empirical data.
6. Numerous genres and public spaces as well as intertextual and interdiscursive relationships are studied.
7. The historical context is taken into account in interpreting texts and discourses. The historical orientation permits the reconstruction of how recontextualization functions as an important process linking texts and discourses intertextually and interdiscursively over time.
8. Categories and tools are not fixed once and for all. They must be elaborated for each analysis according to the specific problem under investigation.
9. 'Grand theories' often serve as a foundation. In the specific analyses, however, 'middle-range theories' frequently supply a better theoretical basis.
10. The application of results is an important target. Results should be made available to and applied by experts and be communicated to the public.

Approaching the analysis of 'discourses about climate change'

The DHA in eight steps

A thorough discourse-historical analysis ideally follows an eight-stage programme. Typically, the eight steps are implemented recursively:

1. **Activation and consultation of preceding theoretical knowledge** (i.e. recollection, reading and discussion of previous research).
2. **Systematic collection of data and context information** (depending on the research question, various discourses and discursive events, social fields as well as actors, semiotic media, genres and texts are focused on).
3. **Selection and preparation of data for specific analyses** (selection and downsizing of data according to relevant criteria, transcription of tape recordings, etc.).
4. **Specification of the research question and formulation of assumptions** (on the basis of a literature review and a first skimming of the data).
5. **Qualitative pilot analysis** (allows testing categories and first assumptions as well as the further specification of assumptions).
6. **Detailed case studies** (of a whole range of data, primarily qualitative, but in part also quantitative).
7. **Formulation of critique** (interpretation of results, taking into account the relevant context knowledge and referring to the three dimensions of critique).
8. **Application of the detailed analytical results** (if possible, the results might be applied or proposed for application).

This ideal-typical list is best realized in a big interdisciplinary project with enough resources of time, personnel and money. Depending on the funding, time and other constraints, smaller studies are, of course, useful and legitimate. Nevertheless, we believe that it makes sense to be aware of the overall research design, and thus to make explicit choices when devising one's own project such as a PhD thesis. In the latter case, one can certainly conduct only a few case studies and must restrict the range of the data collection (to very few genres). Sometimes, a pilot study can be extended to more comprehensive case studies, and, occasionally, case studies planned at the very beginning must be left for a follow-up project.

Because of space restrictions, we only elaborate on a few of the research stages (1, 2, 4 and especially 5) in this chapter. We have decided to focus on *argumentation analysis* in our pilot study, since other strategies such as nomination and predication strategies (which we also take into consideration) are subordinated under the persuasive aims of the text we want to analyse.

Analysing discourses on climate change and global warming

Step 1: Activation and consultation of preceding theoretical knowledge

The overarching research question on 'global warming' can be approached in various ways:

(a) What does 'climate change' mean according to the existing (scientific) literature?
(b) What does the relevant literature convey about the relationship between 'climate change' and modern societies, i.e. the influence of human beings on the global climate?

A first consultation of the relevant literature supplies us with the following answers:

(a) 'Climate change' in ordinary language use predominantly means 'global warming', although other meanings can also be detected: 'climate change' sometimes denotes 'global cooling towards a new ice age' and sometimes relates to a 'natural climatic variation which temporarily leads to a warming or cooling'. In scientific terms, 'climate change' refers to the change of the medial annual temperature, but also to various climatic alterations including precipitation change, sea-level rise, the increase of extreme weather events, ozone depletion and so on. A historical semantic reconstruction further reveals that the scientific and political meaning of the phrase has been extended more recently: whereas now '[i]t refers to any change in climate over time, whether due to natural variability or as a result of human activity', in the United Nations Framework Convention on Climate Change (UNFCCC) of 1992, 'climate change' had exclusively been related 'to a change of climate that is attributed directly or indirectly to human activity [...] in addition to natural climate variability' (Intergovernmental Panel on Climate Change (IPCC), 2007a, p. 1, downloaded from www.ipcc.ch/pdf/assessment-report/ar4/syr/ar4_syr_topic1.pdf on 9 February 2008).

(b) Most scientists consider the relationship between 'climate change' and modern societies to be a causal one in the sense that nature becomes more and more dependent on human civilization, global warming being the anthropogenic consequence of the greenhouse effect caused by the worldwide increase in the output of carbon dioxide and other greenhouse gases.[6]

After this first orientation, we are now able to formulate a more general discourse-related research question: what does 'climate change' mean in the specific public discourse we focus on and how are human influences on climate represented and discussed in this discourse?

Assumptions related to this question are that the discourse will comprise different and maybe contradicting interpretations of the 'nature' of climate change (of its existence, origins and consequences), of the relationship between climate and civilization, and of possible measures against climate change. If this should be the case, we assume that such differing discursive representations and positions make it difficult to achieve a political compromise as a basis for political decisions. Viewed from a historical perspective, we assume that the discourse (or some facets of the discourse) will have changed over time, depending on a range of factors to be identified in our analyses.

Step 2: Systematic collection of data and context information
Depending on what data are accessible (by observation, audio-visual recording, interview, research in archives) and on how much data can be analysed within the

respective research project, a range of empirical data could be collected, considering the following criteria:

- *specific political units* (e.g. region, nation state, international union) or 'language communities'
- *specific periods of time* relating to *important discursive events,* which are connected with the issue in question, for instance, climate summits or publications of reports issued by the IPCC and their discussion in public
- *specific social and especially political and scientific actors* (individual and 'collective' actors or organizations, for example, politicians with different party-political affiliations, environmentalists, climatologists, national and international councils on climate change, oil companies, car companies and so forth)
- *specific discourses* – in our case, discourses about climate change and particularly about global warming
- *specific fields of political action,* especially the formation of public attitudes, opinions and will (e.g. relating to media coverage), the management of international relations (e.g. relating to international summits and agreements), the fields of political control (e.g. relating to environmentalist actions), political advertising (e.g. relating to the promotion of the energy business), the inter-party formation of attitudes, opinions and will (e.g. relating to the inter-party coordination of environmental policy), the lawmaking procedure (e.g. relating to tax laws on carbon emissions), and *specific policy fields,* such as environmental policy, energy policy, economic policy, health policy or migration policy
- *specific semiotic media* and *genres* related to environmental policy (expert reports, election programmes, political debates inside and outside parliament, press articles, TV interviews and TV discussion, leaflets, car advertisements and popular scientific texts).

In the present case, we focus on one single *discourse fragment*: Václav Klaus's 'Answers to questions from the House of Representatives of the US Congress, Committee on Energy and Commerce, on the issue of mankind's contribution to global warming and climate change' (19 March 2007; www.klaus.cz/klaus2/asp/default.-asp?lang=EN&CatID=YJrRHRsP). We chose this text because it is rather brief, easily accessible on the internet, has been published in several languages (thus guaranteeing a remarkable communicative scope), and because it relates both to Europe and the United States. In Step 5, we will have a closer look at this text.

Step 3: Selection and preparation of data for specific analyses
When preparing the corpus for analysis, the collected data are downsized according to specific criteria such as frequency, representativity, (proto)typicality, intertextual or interdiscursive scope/influence, salience, uniqueness and redundancy. If it proves necessary, oral data have to be transcribed according to the conventions determined by the research question. As we now focus on a single text example, there is no need to continue the discussion of this step.

Step 4: Specification of the research question and formulation of assumptions

The research question could now be specified with regard to the question of whether:

- global warming is perceived as being undisputed by the discourse participants or not
- climate change is seen as a natural process or as co-caused by human beings.

Moreover, the research question has to consider opposing political accusations of abuse and manipulation, and alternative appeals for action (see, for instance, Al Gore, 2007, p. 268 ff. in contrast to Klaus, 2007: 79, 95, 97 ff.). Hence, a possible point of departure for the further elaboration of our research question could be the analysis of controversial positions. As critical discourse analysts, we describe and assess such contradictory positions and their persuasive character on the basis of principles of rational argumentation and with regard to underlying manipulative strategies.

A second point of departure could be the analysis of media coverage and of the relationship between the reporting of scientific statements about global warming and the media recipients' knowledge. Allan Bell (1994) has already focused on such issues two decades ago. In his case study of the discourse about climate change in New Zealand, he analysed the relationship between the media coverage of scientific explanations and laypersons' understanding of this coverage. Bell's research, which led to the insight that the knowledge about climate change is greater among the socially advantaged than among socially disadvantaged media users (Bell, 1994: 59), could be compared with today's situation. The DHA pays special attention to such diachronic comparisons.

On the basis of all these concerns, our research question could be divided into the following detailed questions:

- What social (political, scientific, environmentalist, media) actors participate in the specific discourse on climate change? What scientific, political, environmentalist and other positions are adopted in the different fields of political action relating to the discourse? (*We assume that different actors pursue different and often conflicting interests.*)
- What role do scientists play in the triangle of science, policy/politics and the mass-mediated public sphere? How do they 'translate' their expert knowledge for laypeople? How reliable are statements of scientists as epistemic and deontic authorities? How are scientists 'controlled' in modern democratic societies? On the basis of what criteria do laypeople judge scientific statements? (*Here, we assume that scientists play an important role as experts both in processes of political decision-making and in the formation of public attitudes, opinions and will.*)
- What role do the mass media play in the 'translation' of expert knowledge for laypeople? How are the media controlled in democratic societies? Is it difficult to

understand mass-media texts on climate change? (*We assume that the media play a crucial role in the formation of public attitudes, opinions and will as well as in the field of political control.*)

- What validity claims of truth and normative rightness are explicitly made or presupposed in the discourse in question? How are these claims related to party-political and – in a wider sense – ideological alignments? (*We assume that different discourse participants will make different and often contradicting, ideology-dependent claims on climate change.*)

- What are the main topics of the discourse? How is the influence of human beings on the global climate represented and discussed? In more linguistic terms: what descriptions, explanations, argumentations and narratives about the genesis, diagnosis, prognosis and avoidance of climate change are presented or reported in order to support the validity claims in question? What semiotic (especially linguistic and visual) means are employed to persuade recipients? What contradictions are constructed in the discourse? (*Here, a basic assumption is that we will not find a single and homogeneous depiction, but a wide range of differing representations and argumentations.*)

- What aspects of the discourse change over time? What are the reasons for change? (*This question presupposes that there is a diachronic change involving partial continuities and new developments.*)

- What other discourses does the discourse intersect with and relate to? (*We assume that the discourse in question has interdiscursive links with other discourses.*)

Of course, we cannot respond to any of these questions exhaustively in this chapter. Only large-scale interdisciplinary research projects would be able to investigate the above-mentioned complexities adequately. Smaller projects and pilot studies will necessarily only focus on some of these aspects.

Step 5: Qualitative pilot analysis

Our pilot study seeks to improve and differentiate the analytical instruments and to elaborate the assumptions mentioned above. Accordingly, we restrict this qualitative pilot investigation to one single text (which resembles the parliamentary genre of 'question time') from a prominent Czech politician (President Václav Klaus) who participates very actively in the American, Czech and German debates on climate change and global warming from a strictly (neo-)liberal, anti-communist as well as anti-environmentalist point of view. The text is a hybrid mix of a written expert interview and the written version of parliamentary questions and answers. It is constructed as a formalized, quasi-dialogic question–answer sequence composed of five questions and the respective answers to representatives of the US Congress in the Committee on Energy and Commerce. The text was originally published in English, but was reproduced in Czech and German in Klaus's book: *Modrá, nikoli zelená planeta* (Czech) and *Blauer Planet in grünen Fesseln! Was ist bedroht: Klima oder Freiheit?* (German)[7.]

The questioners to whom Klaus is replying remain anonymous in the books. However, a closer look at the political and historical context shows that Klaus's text, from 19 March 2007, was submitted on 21 March 2007 by the Republican J. Dennis Hastert, Ranking Member of the Subcommittee on Energy and Air Quality, in the Hearing of the US House of Representatives on 'Perspectives on Climate' before the Subcommittee on Energy and Air Quality of the Committee on Energy and Commerce and the Subcommittee on Energy and the Environment of the Committee on Science and Technology. In the official protocol of the Hearing (p. 137, downloaded from frwebgate.access.gpo.gov/cgi-bin/getdoc.cgi?dbname=110_ house_hearings&docid=f:37579.pdf on 10 April 2008), we read that Klaus's text has the form of a 'letter'. On pages 141–146 of the protocol, we learn that Klaus's letter answers questions posed in another letter addressed to Klaus on 6 March 2007. This first letter was signed by the two Republicans Joe Barton and J. Dennis Hastert, who seem to be responsible for the five questions. The two conservatives invited the Czech president as well the political scientist and statistician Bjørn Lomborg from the Copenhagen Business School, as a counterpart to the Democrat and environmentalist Al Gore. Both Gore and Lomborg – the latter is often referred to by anti-environmentalists, because he criticizes Gore for exaggerating the possible consequences of global warming – were personally present and questioned at the Hearing on 21 March 2007, whereas Klaus's letter was only submitted and accepted, without any objection. In their letter, the two Republicans state the following reasons for inviting Klaus to respond to their questions:

> Over the past several decades, as an economist and political leader, you have developed an important perspective on the forces that effect individual freedom and economic progress and abundance, especially as you have helped to lead the Czech Republic out of the deadly stagnation of the former Soviet regime to become one of the fastest growing vibrant economies in Europe. You have also taken public positions regarding the climate change debate. We believe your perspective on the political, economic, and moral aspects of the climate change debate can be useful as we seek to assess the potential impacts of proposed US climate-related regulations on the economic well-being of its citizens and their ability to contribute to future economic vitality and innovation here and abroad.

The Republican Barton is well known as a vehement sceptic of the anthropogenic thesis on global warming. During the hearing, Barton attacked Gore for being 'totally wrong' (p. 24) with regard to the depiction of the causal relationship of the change of CO_2 levels and the increase in temperature. Thus, it is understandable why Barton invited the sceptic Klaus to tell the US Congress his viewpoint. In Table 4.2, the right column next to the text lists the themes ('T' stands for 'theme') contained in the five questions and Klaus's first answer (we list the themes only for the first question; readers may attempt to generate respective lists for the remaining questions). The third column points to plausible argumentation schemes (i.e. *topoi*) and fallacious argumentation schemes (i.e. *fallacies*).

TABLE 4.2 *Klaus's answers to questions from the House of Representatives of the US Congress (text, macrostructure/topics and argumentation)*

	Macro- and mesostructure: Turn-taking and discourse topics	Argumentation: Claims, topoi and fallacies
Václav Klaus, 19 March 2007	Date	
Answers to questions from the House of Representatives of the US Congress, Committee on Energy and Commerce, on the issue of mankind's contribution to global warming and climate change	Parliamentary (sub)genre	
Concerning mankind's contribution to climate change and in keeping with obligations towards the welfare of our citizens: what, in your view, should policymakers consider when addressing climate change?	**Question 1:** **Topic:** anthropogenic climate change **T:** policymakers 'obligations towards citizens' welfare	
The – so called – climate change and especially man-made climate change has become one of the most dangerous arguments aimed at distorting human efforts and public policies in the whole world.	**Answer 1 by Klaus:** **T:** anthropogenic climate change	*Claim 1:* Anthropogenic climate change as dangerous argument (topos or fallacies of threat of freedom)
My ambition is not to bring additional arguments to the scientific climatological debate about this phenomenon.	**T:** scientific climatological debate	
I am convinced, however, that up to now this scientific debate has not been deep and serious enough and has not provided sufficient basis for the policymakers' reaction.	**T:** policymakers' reaction	*Fallacy of superficiality and lack of scientific seriousness*
What I am really concerned about is the way the environmental topics have been misused by certain political pressure groups to attack fundamental principles underlying free society. It becomes evident that while discussing climate we are not witnessing a clash of views about the environment but a clash of views about human freedom.	**T:** misuse of environmental topics by political pressure groups **T:** attack on freedom and free society	*Topos or fallacy of abuse* *Topos or fallacy of danger for threat of freedom and free society*

TABLE 4.2 (Continued)

	Macro- and mesostructure: Turn-taking and discourse topics	Argumentation: Claims, topos and fallacies
As someone who lived under communism for most of my life I feel obliged to say that the biggest threat to freedom, democracy, the market economy and prosperity at the beginning of the 21st century is not communism or its various softer variants. Communism was replaced by the threat of ambitious environmentalism. This ideology preaches earth and nature and under the slogans of their protection – similarly to the old Marxists – wants to replace the free and spontaneous evolution of mankind by a sort of central (now global) planning of the whole world.	T: victim of communism T: threat of freedom, democracy market economy and prosperity by environmentalism T: environmentalist centralism similar to old Marxism	Fallacy of threat of freedom, democracy and market economy (formally; fallacy of comparison of communism and environmentalism [threat of centralism])
The environmentalists consider their ideas and arguments to be an undisputable truth and use sophisticated methods of media manipulation and PR campaigns to exert pressure on policymakers to achieve their goals. Their argumentation is based on the spreading of fear and panic by declaring the future of the world to be under serious threat. In such an atmosphere they continue pushing policymakers to adopt illiberal measures, impose arbitrary limits, regulations, prohibitions, and restrictions on everyday human activities and make people subject to omnipotent bureaucratic decision-making. To use the words of Friedrich Hayek, they try to stop free, spontaneous human action and replace it by their own, very doubtful human design.	T: belief in undisputable truth T: media manipulation T: pressure on policymakers T: spreading of fear and panic T: pressure on policymakers to adopt illiberal measures T: arbitrary restrictions of freedom	Topos or fallacy of abuse (of media manipulation) Topos or fallacy of pressure/compulsion Topos or fallacy of frightening Topos or fallacy of pressure/compulsion Topos or fallacy of threat combined with the topos or fallacy of authority ('Hayek')
The environmentalist paradigm of thinking is absolutely static.	T: static environmentalist thinking	

(Continued)

TABLE 4.2 (Continued)

	Macro- and mesostructure: Turn-taking and discourse topics	Argumentation: Claims, topos and fallacies
They neglect the fact that both nature and human society are in a process of permanent change, that there is and has been no ideal state of the world as regards natural conditions, climate, distribution of species on earth, etc. They neglect the fact that the climate has been changing fundamentally throughout the existence of our planet and that there are proofs of substantial climate fluctuations even in known and documented history. Their reasoning is based on historically short and incomplete observations and data series which cannot justify the catastrophic conclusions they draw. They neglect the complexity of factors that determine the evolution of the climate and blame contemporary mankind and the whole industrial civilization for being the decisive factors responsible for climate change and other environmental risks.	**T:** permanent change of nature (including climate) and society **T:** neglecting proofs of substantial climate fluctuations **T:** historically short and incomplete environmental observations **T:** unjustified catastrophic conclusions **T:** neglecting complexity of climatic factors **T:** human contribution to climate change	*Topos or fallacy of nature* *Topos or fallacy of simplifying complexity* *Topos or fallacy of history*
By concentrating on the human contribution to the climate change the environmentalists ask for immediate political action based on limiting economic growth, consumption, or human behavior they consider hazardous. They do not believe in the future economic expansion of the society, they ignore the technological progress the future generations will enjoy, and they ignore the proven fact that the higher the wealth of society is, the higher is the quality of the environment.	**T:** appeal to immediate political action **T:** environmentalist distrust in economic and technological development and in the direct relationship between wealth and the quality of the environment **T:** accusing industrial civilization for climate change	*Topos of technological progress*
The policymakers are pushed to follow this media-driven hysteria based on speculative and hard evidence lacking theories, and to adopt enormously costly programs which would waste scarce resources in order to stop the probably	**T:** pressure on policymakers by media-driven hysteria **T:** speculative evidence **T:** costly programmes **T:** waste of scarce resources	*Topos or fallacy of (pos.) consequences of wealth to environment* *Topos or fallacy of pressure* *Topos of costs* *Topos or fallacy of wasting*

TABLE 4.2   (Continued)

	Macro- and mesostructure: Turn-taking and discourse topics	Argumentation: Claims, topos and fallacies
unstoppable climate changes, caused not by human behavior but by various exogenous and endogenous natural processes (such as fluctuating solar activity).	T: unstoppable (natural) climatic processes	*Fallacy of nature*
My answer to your first question, i.e. what should policymakers consider when addressing climate change, is that policymakers	T: answer to the first question	***Claim 2:*** *Topos or fallacy of freedom*
should under all circumstances stick to the principles free society is based on, that they should not transfer the right to choose and decide from the people to any advocacy group claiming that it	T: sticking to principles of free society	
knows better than the rest of the people what is good for them. Policymakers should protect taxpayers' money and avoid wasting it on doubtful projects which cannot bring positive results.	T: protection of taxpayers' money and avoidance of wasting it T: doubtful projects	*Topos or fallacy of thrift* *Topos of uncertainty*
How should policies address the rate and consequences of climate change and to what extent should regulation of emissions of greenhouse gases be a focus of any such policies?	**Question 2:** T: speed and consequences of climate change T: extent of regulations of emissions of greenhouse gases	

(Continued)

TABLE 4.2   (Continued)

Macro- and mesostructure: Turn-taking and discourse topics	Argumentation: Claims, topos and fallacies
Answer 2 by Klaus	
Policies should realistically evaluate the potential our civilization has, as compared with the power of natural forces influencing climate. It is an evident waste of society's resources to try to combat an increase of solar activity or the movement of ocean currents. No government action can stop the world and nature from changing. **Therefore,** I disagree with plans such as the Kyoto Protocol or similar initiatives, which set arbitrary targets requiring enormous costs without realistic prospects for the success of these measures. If we accept global warming as a real phenomenon, I believe we should address it in an absolutely different way. Instead of hopeless attempts to fight it, we should prepare ourselves for its consequences. If the atmosphere warms up, the effects do not have to be predominantly negative. While some deserts may get larger and some ocean shores flooded, enormous parts of the earth – up until now empty because of their severe, cold climate – may become fertile areas able to accommodate millions of people. It is also important to realize that no planetary change comes overnight.	*Topos of realism* *Topos of nature* *Topos or fallacy of waste* *Topos or fallacy of nature* **Claim 3:** *Refusal of Kyoto Protocol or similar initiatives* *Top. or fall. of arbitrariness and* *Topos of costs and* *Topos or fall. of uncertainty of success* *Topos of realism* *Topos or fallacy of (pos.) consequences*
Therefore, I warn against adopting regulations based on the so-called precautionary principle which the environmentalists use to justify their recommendations, the clear benefit of which they are not able to prove. Responsible politics should take into account the opportunity costs of such proposals and be aware of the fact that the wasteful environmentalist policies are adopted to the detriment of other policies, thus neglecting many other important needs of millions of people all over the world. Each policy measure must be based on a cost-benefit analysis.	**Claim 4:** *Refusal of regulations based on precautionary principle* *Topos of time (slow change)* *Fallacy of uncertainty (lack of proof)* *Topos or fall. of responsibility* *Topos of costs* *Fallacy of waste* *Topos or fallacy of neglect of other needs*

TABLE 4.2 (Continued)

Macro- and mesostructure: Turn-taking and discourse topics	Argumentation: Claims, topos and fallacies
Mankind has already accumulated tragic experience with one very proud intellectual stream that claimed that it knew how to manage society better that spontaneous market forces. It was communism and it failed, leaving behind millions of victims. Now, a new-ism has emerged that claims to be able to manage even nature and, through it, people. This excessive human pride – just as the previous attempts – cannot but fail. The world is a complex and complicated system that cannot be organized according to an environmentalist human design, without repeating the tragic experience of wasting resources, suppressing people's freedom, and destroying the prosperity of the whole human society.	*Fallacy of history (experience of communism; formally a fallacy of comparison)* *Topos of complexity* *Topos or fallacy of negative consequence (waste, suppression and destruction of prosperity)*
My recommendation, **therefore**, is to pay attention to the thousands of small things that negatively influence the quality of the environment. And to protect and foster fundamental systemic factors without which the economy and society cannot operate efficiently – i.e. to guarantee human freedom and basic economic principles such as the free market, a functioning price system and clearly defined ownership rights. They motivate economic agents to behave rationally. Without them, no policies can protect either the citizens or the environment.	***Claim 5:*** *Attention to many small environmentally harmful things (instead of Kyoto Protocol or similar initiatives) and protection of freedom as well as free market etc.* *Topos or fallacy of freedom (motivating rational economy)*
Policymakers should resist environmentalist calls for new policies because there are too many uncertainties in scientific debates on climate change. It is impossible to control natural factors causing climate change. The negative impact of the proposed regulation on economic growth is to the detriment of all other possible risks, including the environmental ones.	*Fallacy of (scientific) uncertainty* *Topos or fallacy of nature* *Topos or fallacy of neg. consequences (on economy)*

(Continued)

TABLE 4.2 (Continued)

	Macro- and mesostructure: Turn-taking and discourse topics	Argumentation: Claims, topos and fallacies
What will be the effect on national economies, consumer well-being, job creation, and future innovation under various climate change policy scenarios that have come to your attention?	**Question 3:** T: effect of various climate change policy scenarios	
If the policymakers accept the maximalistic environmental demands, the effects on national economies will be devastating. It would stimulate some, very small parts of the economy while leaving a bigger part of it choked by artificial limits, regulations, and restrictions. The rate of growth would decline and the competitiveness of the firms on international markets would be seriously affected. It would have a negative impact on employment and job creation. Only rational policies, making spontaneous adjustments possible, can justify government intervention.	**Answer 3 by Klaus**	***Claim 6:*** *Topos or fallacy of negative consequence of maximalist environmental demands on national economies*
What impact and effectiveness will so-called cap-and-trade policies have upon the reduction of climate change threats and our ability to address these threats in the future?	**Question 4:** T: impact and effectiveness of 'cap-and-trade policies' on climate change threats	
Cap-and-trade policies are a technical tool to achieve pollution reduction goals by more market compatible means. They can help if the general idea behind the scheme is rational. I do not believe the whole idea to combat climate change by emission limits is rational and I, **therefore**, consider the technicalities of its eventual implementation to be of secondary importance.	**Answer 4 by Klaus**	*Topos of consequence of cap-and-trade policies* *Topos or fallacy of irrationality* ***Claim 7:*** *Topos or fallacy of secondariness (= priority of free market over cap-&-trade policies)*
What is the moral obligation of developed countries to the developing countries of the world? Should developed countries embark on large emissions reduction schemes while developing countries are allowed to continue to increase emissions unabated?	**Question 5:** T: moral obligation of developed countries to developing countries T: emission reduction and increase	

TABLE 4.2   (Continued)

Macro- and mesostructure: Turn-taking and discourse topics	Argumentation: Claims, topos and fallacies
Answer 5 by Klaus	Topos or fallacy of moral duty
The moral obligation of developed countries to the developing countries is to create such an environment which guarantees free exchange of goods, services, and capital flows, enables utilization of comparative advantages of individual countries and thus stimulates economic development of the less developed countries. Artificial administrative barriers, limits and regulations imposed by developed countries discriminate the developing world, affect its economic growth, and prolong poverty and underdevelopment. The environmentalist proposals are an exact example of such illiberal policies that are so harmful for the developing countries. They will not be able to cope with the limits and standards imposed on the world by irrational environmental policies, they will not be able to absorb new technological standards required by the anti-greenhouse religion, their products will have difficult access to the developed markets, and as a result the gap between them and the developed world will widen.	Topos or fallacy of free market combined with topos or fallacy of advantages/positive consequence on economy of developing countries

Topos or fallacy of neg. consequences of regulations on economy

Topos or fallacy of unsuccessfulness (of environmentalist proposals combined with topos or fallacy of irrationality)

Topos or fallacy of neg. consequences (gap) |
| It is an illusion to believe that severe anti-climate change policies could be limited to developed countries only. If the policies of the environmentalists are adopted by developed countries, sooner or later their ambitions to control and manage the whole planet will spread the emissions reduction requirements worldwide. The developing countries will be forced to accept irrational targets and limitations because 'earth is first' and their needs are secondary. The environmentalist argumentation gives ammunition to protectionists of all colors who try to eliminate competition coming from newly industrialized countries. **Therefore,** the moral obligation of the developed countries is not to introduce large emissions reduction schemes. | Topos or fallacy of neg. consequences (worldwide regulations = topos or fallacy of centralism)

Topos or fallacy of compulsion (as specific Topos or fallacy of consequence) combined with the Topos or fallacy of irrationality

Claim 8: Topos or fallacy of moral duty not to introduce large emissions reduction schemes |

Within argumentation theory, 'topoi' can be described as parts of argumentation which belong to the required premises. They are the formal or content-related warrants or 'conclusion rules' which connect the argument(s) with the conclusion, the claim. As such, they justify the transition from the argument(s) to the conclusion (Kienpointner, 1992: 194). Topoi are not always expressed explicitly, but can always be made explicit as conditional or causal paraphrases such as 'if x, then y' or 'y, because x' (for more details, see Reisigl and Wodak, 2001: 69–80).

Argumentation schemes are reasonable or fallacious. If the latter is the case, we label them *fallacies*. There are rules for rational disputes and constructive arguing which allow discerning reasonable topoi from fallacies (see the pragma-dialectical approach of van Eeemeren and Grootendorst, 1992). These rules include the freedom of arguing, the obligation to give reasons, the correct reference to the previous discourse by the antagonist, the obligation to 'matter-of-factness', the correct reference to implicit premises, the respect of shared starting points, the use of plausible arguments and schemes of argumentation, logical validity, the acceptance of the discussion's results, and the clarity of expression and correct interpretation. If these rules are flouted, fallacies occur. However, we must admit, it is not always easy to distinguish precisely without context knowledge whether an argumentation scheme has been employed as reasonable topos or as fallacy.

We analyse this text (see pp. 102–109) by focusing on three aspects according to the three dimensions of the DHA and the five strategies presented in Table 4.1:

1. First, we identify the main discourse topics of the text, extrapolating them from the themes (listed in the second column).
2. Then, we focus on the main nomination and predication strategies to be found in Klaus's answers.
3. Third, we focus on the argumentation and more specifically on the principal claims as well as on topoi and fallacies employed to justify these claims (listed in the third column).

We provide an overview of the basic analytical tools for the specific analysis of discourses about climate change by adapting the heuristic questions and strategies presented above in Table 4.3 on pp. 112–113 (the right column contains some examples of the text from Table 4.2).

Identifying the main discourse topics is based on generalizing the established list of themes from Table 4.2. Figure 4.3 presents the main discourse topics and the three fields of political action in which our text is primarily located.

The diagram represents the complex topical intersections in the text. It allows for a first impression of the fact that neo-liberal and policy-related topics dominate, whereas scientific topics are backgrounded by Klaus.

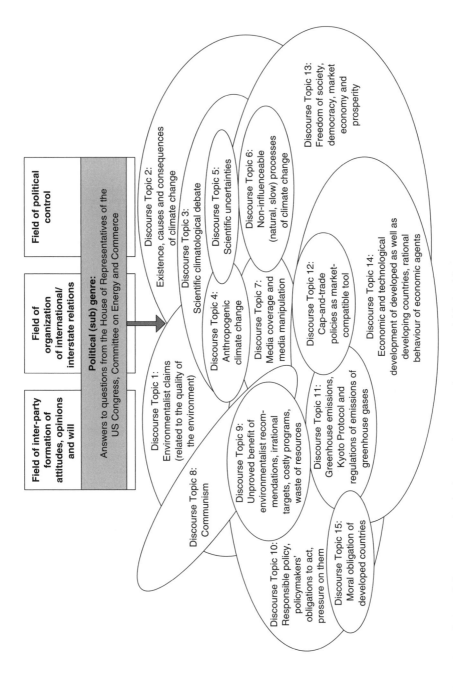

FIGURE 4.3 *Selected discourse topics in the questions to, and answers of, Václav Klaus*

TABLE 4.3   *Important categories to analyse discourses about climate change*

Questions	Discursive Strategies	Purpose
How are persons, objects, phenomena/ events, processes and actions related to climate change named and referred to linguistically?	**nomination strategies**	**discursive construction of social actors:** • *proper names*: Friedrich Hayek • *deictics and phoric expressions*: I, we, you; they • *professional anthroponyms*: policymakers • *ideological anthroponyms*: environmentalists, old Marxists, protectionists of all kinds • *collectives, including metonymic toponyms*: (the) people, future generations, (developed, developing) countries • *economic anthroponyms*: taxpayers **discursive construction of objects/ phenomena/events:** • *concrete*: world/planet, desert, ocean, country • *abstract*: ○ *natural/environmental:* nature, climate ○ *mental object/feelings*: ambition, fear, panic ○ *economic matters*: economy, money, waste, resource, poverty, market forces, wealth, prosperity, product ○ *political matters*: cap-and-trade policies, measure, precautionary principle, emission reduction scheme, welfare ○ *ideological matters*: freedom, communism, ideology, anti-greenhouse religion, media manipulation **discursive construction of processes and actions:** • *material*: ○ *natural/environmental*: climate change, global warming, effect, emissions ○ *economic*: economic growth, consumption • *mental*: ambition, reasoning, thinking • *verbal*: scientific climatology debate, environmentalist proposals/ recommendations, argumentation

TABLE 4.3   *(Continued)*

Questions	Discursive strategies	Purpose
What characteristics, qualities and features are attributed to social actors, objects, phenomena/events and processes?	**predication strategies**	**discursive characterization/qualification of social actors, objects, phenomena, events processes and actions** (more or less positively or negatively) • *social actors*, e.g. environmentalists: irrational, arbitrary, similar to old Marxists, illiberal, centralist, protectionist, wasteful, detrimental to economy • *natural/environmental processes*, e.g. climate change: uncertain, slow, natural, permanent, unstoppable
Which arguments are employed in discourses about climate change?	**argumentation strategies**	**persuading addressees of the truth and normative rightness of claims** (the text contains eight central claims) • *claims of truth* regarding the existence, causes, effects and avoidance of climate change • *claims of rightness* regarding human action related to climate change
From what perspective are these nominations, attributions and arguments expressed?	**perspectivization strategies**	**positioning speaker's or writer's point of view and expressing involvement or distance** • *ideological perspectives*: neo-liberal and communist versus environmentalist–protectionist

Are the respective utterances articulated overtly, are they intensified or mitigated?	**mitigation and intensification strategies**	**modifying the illocutionary force of utterances in respect of their epistemic or deontic status**
		• *epistemic*:
		  ○ *mitigation*: fallacy of scientific uncertainty, 'so-called climate change'
		  ○ *intensification*: fallacy of equating communism and environmentalism, tri-partite parallelism asserting the environmentalist distrust in economic and technological development, etc.
		• *deontic*:
		  ○ *mitigation*: topos or fallacy of backgrounding cap-and-trade policies
		  ○ *intensification*: topos or fallacy of moral duty not to introduce large emissions reduction schemes (in addition to the economic duty)

Only a few aspects of nomination and predication can be addressed in this pilot study: the six most important *social actors* who are discursively constructed in this text are 'I', 'we', 'policymakers', 'environmentalists', 'developing countries' and '(the) people'. The most salient *predications* relating to these actors are listed in Table 4.4.

As Table 4.4 illustrates, Klaus constructs environmentalists only by means of negative predications. Policymakers, on the one hand, appear as dependent agents wherever they adopt environmentalist claims and, on the other, as social actors who are requested to resist environmentalist recommendations in order to protect and foster (neo-)liberal principles under all circumstances. The 'I' propagates (neo-)liberal beliefs and convictions as well. The 'we-group', which does not play an important role in the text, oscillates between a 'we of politicians' ('our citizens'), a vague addressee-inclusive we, a 'we of perceivers', a 'we of civilization', and a 'we of all terrestrials'. The 'developing countries' appear as completely dependent on the 'developed countries' and as potential victims of environmentalist regulations. 'The people', finally, are represented as being both endowed with liberal rights and in danger of being deprived of these rights by environmentalist policies, and, furthermore, as potential beneficiaries of global warming.

In addition to the (neo-)liberal patterns,[8] it is worth looking at who is absent in the text, i.e. *not* represented by nomination. Klaus does not name scientists as social actors. They are only represented indirectly through the adjective 'scientific' that is attributed to 'debate'. Thus, scientists are backgrounded.

The most important phenomenon in the text is 'climate change'. It is primarily qualified with predications such as being 'uncertain', 'slow', 'natural', 'permanent', and 'probably unstoppable [...], caused not by human behaviour but by various exogenous and endogenous natural processes (such as fluctuating solar activity)'.[9] As we will see, this representation of climate change as a possibly permanent natural process is salient in Klaus's argumentation, since it forms the basis on which the fallacies of nature and uncertainty are grounded, with which Klaus attempts to justify his rejection of the Kyoto Protocol and other similar initiatives.

Various predications and nominations are relevant elements of the text's argumentation structure. Klaus's answers are highly persuasive. They contain many argumentative devices; on the meta-linguistic level, words such as 'argument', 'argumentation', 'debate', 'justify', 'conclusion' and 'disagree' explicitly indicate the persuasive character of the text. Hence, we recommend a focus on argumentation and particularly on content-related argumentation schemes (topoi and fallacies) for the analysis of this text, in addition to the analysis of nominations and predications (which are linked to and form the basis for the argumentation schemes).

The analysis of typical content-related topoi and fallacies depends on the macro-topics of a discourse. There is an impressive amount of literature dealing with field- and content-related argumentation schemes in various discourses (see, for example, Kienpointner, 1996; Kienpointner and Kindt, 1997; Kindt, 1992; Reeves, 1989; Wengeler, 2003). In the present context, we refer to several topoi which are mentioned in the literature, but we also coin new names for topoi and fallacies which occur in our specific data.

TABLE 4.4   *Main social actors and predications*

Social Actors	Predications
I	• someone who lived under communism for most of his life • not ambitious to bring additional arguments to the specific climatological debate • concerned about the misuse of environmental topics • convinced that the scientific debate has not been serious enough • feeling obliged to warn against the environmentalist threat of freedom • warning from adopting regulations based on the so-called precautionary principle and disagreeing with plans such as the Kyoto Protocol and similar initiatives • recommending higher attention to many small things that negatively influence the environment and recommending the protection of freedom • considering emission limits to be irrational and cap-and-trade policies to be of secondary importance
we	• in 'possess' of citizens ('our citizens') • witnesses of a clash of views about human freedom • in 'possess' of the planet • in 'possess' of a civilization with a potential • required to address global warming differently, to prepare ourselves for its consequences
environmentalists	• political pressure groups misusing environmental topics to attack free society • a centralist threat of human freedom similar to communism/old Marxists • stubborn truth-fiends, presumptuous wiseacres and static thinkers • sophisticated media manipulators • spreaders of fear and panic • historically narrow thinkers • neglecters of the complexity of climatic factors • accusers of contemporary mankind and the whole industrial civilization for being responsible for climate change and other environmental risks • askers for immediate political action and illiberal policies that harm developing countries • non-believers in the future economic expansion of the society • ignorers of technological progress and the positive relationship between wealth and the quality of the environment • justifiers of doubtful and wasteful protectionist recommendations by the so-called precautionary principle • neglecters of many other needs of millions of people all over the world • claimants of being able to manage even nature • proposers of arbitrary and irrational regulations on economic growth to the detriment of economy and all other possible risks, including the environmental ones

(Continued)

TABLE 4.4   *(Continued)*

Social Actors	Predications
policymakers	• pressured by environmentalists • pushed by environmentalists to adopt illiberal measures, impose arbitrary restrictions on everyday human activities and make people subject to omnipotent bureaucracy • pushed to follow a media-driven hysteria and to adopt costly, wasteful programs • asked to stick under all circumstances to the principles of free society • asked to protect taxpayers' money • asked to realistically evaluate the potential of our civilization • not able to stop the world and nature from changing • asked to act responsibly • asked to pay attention to the many small things that negatively influence the environment, and to protect and foster economy and society • asked to resist environmentalist appeals for new policies • asked to implement rational policies • morally obliged to create an environment for developing countries which guarantees free market, and not to introduce large emissions reduction schemes
developing countries	• not able to cope with the limits and standards imposed on the world by irrational environmental policies • not able to absorb new technological standards required by the anti-greenhouse religion • producers of products which will have difficult access to developed markets • victims of the widening gap between them and the developed world
the people	• subject to omnipotent bureaucratic decision-making • endowed with the right of choice that should not be taken from them and transferred to any advocacy group • millions of people that may get fertile areas • millions of people all over the world with many other important needs • allegedly managed by the newism • endangered of being deprived of their freedom

Topoi and fallacies in Klaus's text are listed in the right column of Table 4.2. They possess the function of justifying Klaus's main claims. These claims – most of which are normative proposals of how policymakers and people in developed countries should act – are formulated from a strictly (neo-)liberal perspective:

• Claim 1: Anthropogenic climate change is a dangerous argument (*claim of truth*).
• Claim 2: If policymakers address climate change, they must and should always stick to the principles of free society (*claim of normative rightness*, realized as topos or fallacy of freedom).

- Claim 3: The Kyoto Protocol or similar initiatives should be rejected (*claim of normative rightness*).
- Claim 4: Regulations based on the so-called precautionary principle should be rejected (*claim of normative rightness*).
- Claim 5: Instead of the Kyoto Protocol or similar initiatives, many small ecologically harmful things should be avoided; in all cases, freedom and the free market have to be protected (*claim of normative rightness*).
- Claim 6: If policymakers accept the (maximalist) ecological demands, this will have negative consequences for national economies (*claim of truth*; topos or fallacy of negative consequence).
- Claim 7: If we have to choose between free market and cap-and-trade policies, cap-and-trade policies are less important in the context of an irrational fight against global warming (*claim of truth*; fallacy of secondary importance as fallacy of the priority of free market over cap-and-trade policies).
- Claim 8: Since developed countries have moral obligations towards developing countries, they should not introduce large-emission reduction schemes (*claim of normative rightness*; topos or fallacy of moral obligation).

These claims are mostly justified by fallacies. The overall structure of Klaus's answers is dominated by two fallacies:

1. The *fallacy of uncertainty*[10] assumes that since science is uncertain in respect of the existence, causes, consequences and avoidance of climate change, environmentalist recommendations are not convincing and, thus, it does not make sense to follow these recommendations.
2. The second recurrent fallacy in Klaus's answers is the *fallacy of nature*: 'since climate change is natural, ecological regulations concerning greenhouse gases are not reasonable, but irrational and wasteful'.

Both fallacies can be discredited by a topos of numbers that refers to the vast majority of climatologists who agree that an anthropogenic climate change does exist with a very high degree of certainty.[11] In addition, the first fallacy can be countered by the topos of risk minimization (as a specific topos of priority): if different alternatives carry various risks, we have to minimize the risks by choosing the alternative with minimal risks. If we consider this argumentation scheme, Klaus's refusal of the precautionary principle appears unjustified. Furthermore, the topos of risk minimization can also be directed against the fallacy of secondary importance (claim 7).

We must interrupt our pilot analysis here. In sum, we are able to conclude that Klaus's argumentation is highly fallacious and that there are plausible reasons to reject Klaus's neo-liberal position and to accept a just limitation of human freedom for specific ecological reasons as concerning the well-being of the human species. A more detailed case study, which would analyse the whole Hearing, Klaus's entire book, and the political role of Klaus as supporter of the US government's negative position with respect to international greenhouse-gas emission regulations, would differentiate this first pilot analysis and would gain insight into the broader political and historical contexts of the specific discourse on climate change.

Such an analysis would also focus on strategies of perspectivization, mitigation and intensification.[12] This would help to recognize *the underlying ideological positioning* in this and other discourse fragments produced by Klaus. It would allow reconstructing how the strict neo-liberal perspective co-determines Klaus's choice of various rhetorical, pragmatic and argumentative devices and how frequent Klaus's dogmatic anti-communist stance leads to fallacious intensification strategies such as the one which dominates the argumentation in the above text: the quasi-equation of environmentalism with communism that aims to derogate many ecological positions (for more examples of perspectivization, mitigation and intensification strategies, see Table 4.3, point 5). Moreover, a broader study would focus on the various ways environmentalists are discursively constructed and represented as exceptionally powerful and dangerous (topos of threat). In the text, we analysed, for example, Klaus presupposes that ecological groups dominate and manipulate politicians and bureaucrats. Such negative other-presentations prepare the ground for 'shifting the blame' and 'scapegoating' strategies, which could eventually be used to legitimize and explain political mistakes. Our analysis illustrates that Klaus organizes most of his strategic discursive manoeuvres with a strict neo-liberal, anti-environmentalist and anti-communist ideological positioning in mind.

Step 6: Detailed case studies

This step consists of detailed case studies on the macro-, meso- and micro-levels of linguistic analysis, as well as on the level of context. This step, which cannot be illustrated in this chapter because of space restrictions, interprets the different results within the social, historical and political contexts of the discourse(s) under consideration.[13]

In the present case, this step would lead to general descriptions of the discourse on climate change in respect of:

- social actors and fields of political action
- communication obstacles and misunderstandings
- contradictory validity claims imbued by political or ideological orientation
- salient topics and discursive features
- aspects of historical change
- interdiscursive relationships, particularly overlaps with other discourses (such as discourses about globalization, migration or freedom/liberalism).

The overall interpretation would, for example, consider the question of whether the mass-mediated discourse(s) on climate change and global warming in European states resemble the discourses in the USA, where company lobbying frequently leads to a 'balance as bias' in the media coverage: the prevailing scientific consensus on the anthropogenic influence on global warming is not represented adequately in the media. In contrast, media coverage seems to suggest that scientists do not agree on this issue quite so strongly (see Boykoff and Boykoff, 2004; Oreskes, 2004 [both quoted in Rahmstorf and Schellnhuber, 2007: 83]).

The overall interpretation could further refer to Viehöver's stimulating research on various discourses on climate change (Viehöver, 2003). Viehöver investigated the media coverage from 1974 to 1995. On the basis of his comprehensive case study, he distinguished between six 'problem narratives' about global climate change and its definition, causes, (moral) consequences and possible reactions to it. According to Viehöver, these 'narratives' gained different salience at different times. He observes that currently the predominant 'narrative' seems to be the 'global warming story'. 'Stories' competing with this 'narrative' were and still are, according to the German sociologist, 'the global cooling story', 'the story of the climatic paradise', 'the story of the cyclical sunspots', 'the story of the climatic change as scientific and media fiction' and the 'story of the nuclear winter' (see Viehöver, 2003: 268 ff. for more details).

Step 7: Formulation of critique

Our 'critique' is based on ethical principles such as democratic norms, human rights and criteria of rational argumentation. It points to intended biases in representations (especially media coverage) and to contradictory and manipulative relationships between discourses and power structures.

In a theoretical sense, the critique – based on our empirical analysis and a theory of discursive/deliberative democracy – offers analytical parameters that evaluate the 'quality' of public political discourses in which 'collective' learning and decision-making are at stake.

In a practical sense, the critique might influence current discourses on global warming and raise the awareness of involved social actors about the problem, more responsibility and fallacious argumentations.

Step 8: Application of the detailed analytical results

The application of the analytical results stems from the critique. The application should not only consist of the scholarly publication of the results. In addition, our insights should also be made accessible to the 'general public' (e.g. by recommendations, newspaper commentaries, training seminars, further education courses, radio transmissions and political advising). Such a knowledge 'transfer' requires the recontextualization of theory, methodology, methods and empirical results into other genres and communicative practices. This is, of course, a challenging task.

Conclusions

The strengths of the discourse-historical approach include the following:

- its *interdisciplinary orientation*, which allows avoiding disciplinary restrictions
- the *principle of triangulation*, which implies a quasi-kaleidoscopic move towards the research object and enables the grasp of many different facets of the object under investigation

- the *historical analysis*, which allows transcending static spotlights and focusing on the diachronic reconstruction and explanation of discursive change
- *practical applications* of the results for emancipatory and democratic purposes.

The DHA relates to other CDA approaches in many aspects. However, the DHA – like any inter- or multidisciplinary enterprise – should avoid the combination of theoretically incompatible scientific (re)sources. This caveat remains one of the main theoretical challenges. Furthermore, many new discourse–related social phenomena (such as the one discussed in the present chapter) need to be investigated in systematic and detailed ways from the perspective of our approach.

FURTHER READING

Muntigl, P., Weiss, G., and Wodak, R. (2000) *European Union Discourses on Un/Employment: An Interdisciplinary Approach to Employment Policy-making and Organisational Change.* Amsterdam: Benjamins.
This book presents an interdisciplinary study of EU organizations which involved fieldwork, ethnography, interviews and the analysis of written and oral data. This study cuts across CDA, sociology, political science and European studies.

Reisigl, M. and Wodak, R. (2001) *Discourse and Discrimination: Rhetorics of Racism and Antisemitism.* London, New York: Routledge.
A comprehensive presentation of the DHA, with case studies on racist, xenophobic and antisemitic rhetoric in the post-war Austrian context.

Wodak, R. (1996) *Disorders of Discourses.* London: Longman.
A collection of case studies on organizational communication, framed in an integrated investigation of hospitals, media and bureaucracies.

Wodak, R. (2009) *'Politics as Usual' – The Construction and Representation of Politics in Action.* Basingstoke: Palgrave.
A monograph which illustrates the kind of inter- and post-disciplinary research proposed in the DHA. The 'backstage' of politics is juxtaposed with the analysis of media soaps about politics and politicians.

Wodak, R. and Krzyżanowski, M. (eds) (2008) *Qualitative Discourse Analysis in the Social Sciences.* Basingstoke: Palgrave.
An introductory text for social scientists which focuses primarily on the analysis of diverse genres (press articles, new media, documentaries, focus groups, interviews and broadcasts). The volume is particularly useful for non-linguists.

Notes

1 See Habermas, 1996; Horkheimer and Adorno, 1969/1991 [1944].
2 Other approaches to CDA do not explicitly link 'discourse' with a macro-topic and more than one perspective (see Reisigl, 2003: 91 ff.).
3 In three of the eight fields, we distinguish between attitudes, opinions and will. This distinction emphasizes the difference in the emotional, cognitive and volitional dimensions.
4 Many of these strategies are illustrated in Reisigl and Wodak (2001). In this chapter, we will focus primarily on nomination, predication and argumentation strategies.
5 The very first critical study which inspired the project on postwar antisemitism in Austria was Wodak et al. (1985).
6 See IPCC, 2007a, p. 1, downloaded from www.ipcc.ch/pdf/assessment-report/ar4/syr/ar4_syr_topic1.pdf on 9 February 2008; IPCC, 2007b, p. 6, downloaded from www.ipcc.ch/pdf/assessment-report/ar4/syr/ar4_syr_topic2.pdf on 9 February 2008. See also Müller et al., 2007; Rahmstorf and Schellnhuber, 2007.
7 The German translation deviates from the English version on several points. The English translation of the German title is: 'Blue planet in green bonds. What is endangered: climate or freedom?'. The book has also been translated into other languages.
8 The frequency of high-value words (*miranda*) such as 'freedom', 'wealth', 'prosperity' and 'economic growth' fits very well into Klaus's (neo-)liberal ideology.
9 Here, the assertion that climate change cannot be influenced is mitigated by 'probably'.
10 Klaus associates this fallacy with the fallacy of superficiality: if scientists don't work seriously, but superficially, their results are insignificant.
11 Klaus attempts to disparage this topos as a fallacy of numbers, i.e. a 'myth of scientific consent' (Klaus, 2007: 79).
12 See Reisigl (2003: 214–235); Reisigl and Wodak (2001: 81–85).
13 See, for example, Muntigl et al. (2000); Reisigl and Wodak (2001); Wodak et al. (1999) for such comprehensive studies.

5

Checks and Balances: How Corpus Linguistics can Contribute to CDA

Gerlinde Mautner

Introduction

This chapter focuses on the role that corpus linguistics can play in CDA projects. It will introduce readers to previous work in this area, explain basic concepts and techniques, present two worked examples and encourage critical engagement with the methodology.

Those with previous experience of corpus linguistics will be aware that it is a methodology that uses computer support – in particular, software called 'concordance programs' – to analyse authentic, and usually very large, volumes of textual data. Its potential usefulness for CDA, rather than for lexicography and grammar, may be less familiar, though. Reflections on the potential of combining corpus linguistics and CDA go back quite a long way now (e.g. Hardt-Mautner, 1995), and in the 1997 edited volume on discourse studies (Van Dijk, 1997), de Beaugrande argued that '[l]arge corpuses offer valuable support for the project of discourse analysis to return to authentic data' (de Beaugrande, 1997: 42). Still, none of the other contributors to that edition actually used the method. Awareness of its potential does seem to be growing, however, and there has been a spate of more recent CDA work using corpus linguistics (e.g. Baker and McEnery, 2005; Baker et al., 2007; Baker et al., 2008; Cotterill, 2001; Fairclough, 2000a; Mautner, 2007; Nelson, 2005; Orpin, 2005). Even so, it seems fair to say that the techniques of corpus linguistics are not yet generally regarded as being at the core of CDA's methodological canon. That the present (second) edition of the volume includes this chapter could thus be said to reflect a change in trend.

What, then, can one expect corpus linguistics to contribute to CDA? In a nutshell, the potential of this methodology rests on three factors:

- Corpus linguistics allows critical discourse analysts to work with much larger data volumes than they can when using purely manual techniques.
- In enabling critical discourse analysts to significantly broaden their empirical base, corpus linguistics can help reduce researcher bias, thus coping with a problem to which CDA is hardly more prone than other social sciences but for which it has come in for harsh and persistent criticism (e.g. Widdowson, 1995, 2004).[1]
- Corpus linguistics software offers both quantitative and qualitative perspectives on textual data, computing frequencies and measures of statistical significance, as well as presenting data extracts in such a way that the researcher can assess individual occurrences of search words, qualitatively examine their collocational environments, describe salient semantic patterns and identify discourse functions.

This chapter cannot offer detailed step-by-step guidance on project design and execution. For that, there are other, and arguably more suitable, sources that readers may want to turn to, notably Baker (2006) and McEnery et al. (2006). However, a few basics will be covered in the following section, using original sample analyses as well as cross-referencing existing work in this area. Throughout, the emphasis will be less on technical detail than on enabling readers to make their own informed judgements on whether the method is right for them. There are two worked examples: the first shows how a large reference corpus can be mined for socially relevant information, establishing a collocational profile of a key expression from the lexis of work, namely *unemployed*. The second takes a single newspaper article as its starting point, and uses large-corpus data as an aid in interpreting what appears to be a particularly 'loaded' expression from the article – the adjective *hard-working*.

Both case studies are based on the assumption that language and the social are inextricably, and dialectally, linked. In other words, the way in which labels, in this case *unemployed* and *hard-working*, are used reflects social attitudes, perspectives and categorizations. And the labels, in turn, shape the way in which social structures and relationships are perceived. By referring to a person or group as *unemployed*, one cannot help implying that being employed is the desired default, just as *hard-working* comes with a host of positive connotations directly related to an essentially capitalist work ethos.

Different approaches to discourse, and concomitant definitions of the term, exist in abundance, as do various notions of what it means to carry out 'critical analysis' (see Wodak, 2004: 198–199 and Wodak, 2006b for comprehensive overviews). The perspective adopted in this chapter is functional and constructivist (as well as unabashedly simple). *Discourse* is taken to refer to authentic texts used in multi-layered environments to perform social functions. *Analysing* discourse is understood as the systematic attempt to identify patterns in text, link them to patterns in the context, and vice versa. Doing so *critically* means unveiling and challenging taken-for-granted assumptions about language and the social, as well as recognizing discourse as a potentially powerful agent in social change.

It will not have escaped readers' attention that the title of this chapter contains two hedging devices, one modal (*can*) and another lexical (*contribute*). These correspond to two caveats which are worth spelling out right at the beginning. One is that the usefulness or otherwise of this method, as of any other, depends crucially on recognizing what kinds of research questions it is suitable for tackling. With corpus linguistics, the key limiting factors are the capabilities of the software, as well as the features – mainly in terms of composition and annotation – of the electronically held corpora that are used. At the current state of play, and considering the limitations of those tools that are sufficiently widely available, there is a very strong bias in favour of the individual lexical item and clusters thereof. Put simply, 'the word' is the peg that everything else is hung on. It follows that if the linguistic phenomenon you are interested in is in fact tied to, or at least crystallizes around, discrete lexical items, then you are likely to find this method a boon both as a practical and efficient time-saver, and as a powerful heuristic tool helping to clear pathways to discovery. If, on the other hand, the phenomenon to be focused on is one that is played out on a larger textual stage, and with varying and unpredictable lexical realizations, then corpus linguistic methods will be of little or no help. However, at some point or other, as soon as questions of micro-level linguistic realization are addressed, even projects located very much at the macro end of the CDA spectrum will have occasion to benefit from a corpus linguistic approach.

The second caveat, related to the 'contributing' role of corpus linguistics, is that we need to recall one of the principal tenets of what might be termed 'mainstream' CDA (broadly, the traditions shaped by Fairclough, Wodak and Van Dijk[2]), namely that the analyst must, precisely, look *beyond* the text proper in order to unearth socially meaningful interpretations that can then be enlisted to do socially transformative work. We need our much-famed 'context', history, and as firm a grasp as possible of the politics, in the widest sense, that have a bearing on the production and reception of the text. This social hinterland and the textual evidence before us are intricately linked, but rarely in a fully transparent, one-to-one type of relationship; hence the idea of making corpus linguistics 'contribute' to CDA rather than it 'doing CDA' of its own accord. All the same, at an Oscar night of methods, my vote would be on corpus linguistics as Best Supporting Actor, and the present chapter sets out to make the case for that award.

In addition, there is the added benefit that if you decide to include corpus linguistic methods in your CDA project design, you need not in fact discard, 'unlearn' or in any other way throw overboard whatever more traditional methods you have grown accustomed to using. As an ancillary method, corpus linguistics is flexible and unobtrusive, and if handled appropriately, will enrich but not prejudice the rest of the research design or the interpretation of the results.

Key concepts and a worked example

As with any method, researchers will want to know, first and foremost, what it can do, what kind of data and research questions it is suitable for, and what obstacles may be encountered when applying it. These are the concerns of the present section.

Concordancing software

Programs known as concordancers do not, by themselves, 'produce' analyses, but perform operations on text that make it easier for humans to analyse it. Some of the information that concordancers provide is quantitative, such as absolute and relative word frequencies. Programs also compute measures that indicate the relative statistical significance of the co-occurrence of items. Examples here are t-scores, which capture certainty of collocation, and MI ('mutual information') scores, which tell us about the strength of the bond between two items, that is, whether there is a higher-than-random probability of the two items occurring together (Church and Hanks, 1990; Clear, 1993: 281; Hunston, 2002: 73; McEnery and Wilson, 2001: 86).[3]

To see how this works in practice, let us have a look at the first worked example of this chapter: building a collocational profile of the adjective *unemployed*. Although this serves as a stand-alone case study here, with a focus on method rather than content, it could also form the nucleus of a substantive contribution to the existing body of discourse-analytic research on unemployment (see Muntigl et al., 2000 and the 2002 special issue of *Text*[4]). As we shall see, the corpus linguistic approach allows the researcher to work with enormous amounts of data and yet get a close-up on linguistic detail: a 'best-of-both-worlds' scenario hardly achievable through the use of purely qualitative CDA, pragmatics, ethnography or systemic functional analysis.

Given the key role that the mass media play in constructing social reality, a corpus of newspaper articles would appear to be a suitable starting point. Wordbanks Online,[5] a multi-genre corpus of more than 500 million words of mainly British and American text, includes a nearly 60-million-word corpus of articles from the British daily newspaper *The Times*. This is the subcorpus we will turn to first. The search reveals that *The Times* corpus contains 567 instances of *unemployed*. Table 5.1 gives the ten collocates with the highest t-scores and MI scores respectively.[6]

The t-score part of the table is headed, as is invariably the case, by high-frequency grammatical items. Here, these are *an* and *are*, with *who, and* and *for*

TABLE 5.1   *t-scores and MI scores for collocates of* unemployed *in* The Times *corpus of Wordbanks Online*

Collocate	t-score	Collocate	MI score
1. an	6.648362	1. steelmen	13.465279
2. are	6.227450	2. househusband	11.780613
3. people	5.779392	3. unemployable	11.228017
4. who	5.725799	4. housewives	8.733004
5. and	4.842066	5. 4m	8.066547
6. term	4.212151	6. youths	7.898282
7. long	3.749890	7. disadvantaged	7.547531
8. million	3.623313	8. homeless	7.213343
9. for	3.605234	9. pensioners	6.965925
10. workers	3.516933	10. claimants	6.889355

not far behind. Such 'function' words, devoid of separate meaning as they are, tend not to be as interesting to discourse analysts as to grammarians, and it is generally safe in a CDA setting to ignore them and indeed the whole t-score rank scale. Somewhat unusually though, the 'top ten' by t-score here includes five content words (*people, term, long, million* and *workers*), with the presence of both *long* and *term* probably being due to the phrase *long-term unemployed*. Comparing this with the collocation list of two other, randomly picked adjectives, *happy* and *sad*,[7] we can see how unusual it is for content words to appear so high up in the t-score rank scale: the group of top ten in the t-score list for *happy*, for example, contains no content word at all, and the one for *sad* includes only one (the intensifier *very*). For lexical items to be in the same t-score league as grammatical ones points to a high degree of what one might call patterned bonding; that is, of a lexical connection so formulaic that the degree of certainty with which it occurs equals that of patterns involving grammatical items. Translated into CDA terms, the 'phrase-ness' of a noun group referring to people could point to the solidified discursive construction of a social group (a necessary first step towards stereotyping).

Turning now to the right half of Table 5.1, which lists the top ten collocates according to 'Mutual Information' scores, we can see which social attributes being unemployed is associated with: *unemployable, disadvantaged* and *homeless*. Frequent nominal collocates include several labels for marginalized, dependent and economically inactive social groups: *househusband, housewives, youths, pensioners, claimants*.[8] In a full-blown study, rather than one done for demo purposes only, each of these high-frequency collocates would be interesting entry points to the corpus. For example, it would be worth looking at what kind of activities 'unemployed youths' are seen to engage in (by running a search of *unemployed youths* followed by a verb form), how the usage of *househusband* and *housewife* compares, how *unemployed* is linked syntactically to the negative adjectives it frequently collocates with, how quantification (cf. the collocate *4m*) contributes to establishing the unemployed as a problem group, and so on.

These sorts of questions lead us to another feature of concordance programs, one that a discourse analyst with a predominantly qualitative mindset might get more mileage out of than frequencies and statistics: their eponymous capacity to produce concordances. These are extracts from the corpus, displayed in such a way that the search word or phrase (also referred to as the 'node') appears in the middle of a line. The text that the extract comes from can be accessed at all times and with a simple operation such as a double mouse click or selecting an option from a menu bar. Accessible co-texts vary from just over 500 characters (e.g. with Wordbanks Online) to full texts (e.g. with Wordsmith Tools). Lines can be sorted alphabetically: for example, according to the word immediately pre- ceding or following the search word. When sorted like this, the collocational environment of the search word can be assessed rapidly, with frequent patterns standing out clearly. As shown in Table 5.2, for example, the concordance of *unemployed* followed by *and* and another adjective shows up a preponderance of items (six out of a total of nine) with a negative semantic load: *desperate, disad- vantaged, divorced, homeless* and *unemployable* (which occurs twice).

TABLE 5.2   *Occurrences of* unemployed, *followed by* and *and another adjective, in* The Times *corpus of Wordbanks Online*

mince. Tony Shalhoub is broke,	unemployed and	**desperate.** His fortune went
<p> Liam Parker, services to	unemployed and	**disadvantaged** people. Alison
near Consett, Co Durham, Sheila,	unemployed and	**divorced,** lives in a council
about 12,000 former teachers are	unemployed and	**free to work."** <p> He added
new law had effectively made him	unemployed and	**homeless.** He is married with
<p> Ronnie (Ben Miles), 35,	unemployed and	**Jewish,** is back from Israel,
full-time mothers, selfemployed,	unemployed and	**retired** people across the
needed to keep the largely	unemployed and	**unemployable** Saudi young from
the welfare state that bribes the	unemployed and	**unemployable** middle-class

To make sure that this semantic pattern is not just confined to newspaper discourse, it is worth checking the corresponding data from the British spoken corpus. The picture is in fact very similar (Table 5.3).

TABLE 5.3   *Occurrences of* unemployed, *followed by* and *and another adjective, in* the British spoken corpus of Wordbanks Online

to say hello to everybody who's	unemployed and	**bored** at the moment and hasn'
to town looking for work. He was	unemployed and	**homeless** when he turned up at
say he is thirty-two years old,	unemployed and	**single,** and will appear in
apprenticeship's over he becomes	unemployed and	**unemployable** himself. It's

These results are further confirmed if we extend the search to the complete 500+ million word corpus of Wordbanks Online. The adjectives joined to *unemployed* include more occurrences of the items already identified in the two subcorpora (see Tables 5.2 and 5.3) as well as new and similarly negative col- locates such as *angry, demoralized, destitute, disabled, dreary, drunk, excluded, poor, struggling* and *underprivileged*. By examining concordances, therefore, we can see more or less at a glance that the search word, *unemployed*, has a so-called negative 'semantic aura', or 'semantic prosody' (Hunston, 2004: 157; Louw, 1993; Partington, 2004). Alternatively, readers of this volume will be interested to note, this concept has been referred to as '*discourse* prosody', for example by Stubbs (2001: 65), in order to emphasize its role in expressing attitudes and in establishing coherence.

Detractors of corpus-based methods could argue, of course, that one hardly needs a huge database of text and sophisticated software to 'prove' that being unemployed is not a pleasant thing. On the other hand, we should not forget, first, that a fair proportion of any empirical work is devoted, precisely, to finding evidence for the intuitively obvious. Second, some insights may appear 'obvious' *after* having emerged from data but were nothing of the kind before. Supposedly neutral words such as *cause* or *provide*, to use one of Stubbs's examples, can in fact be heavily skewed in terms of their evaluative content when concordance evidence is examined. Patterns are revealed that are not easily accessible even to native speakers' intuition: *cause*, it turns out, collocates predominantly with unpleasant events, such as *damage, death, disease* or *trouble*, whereas *provide* occurs with desirable things, such as *care, help, money* or *service* (Stubbs, 2001: 65). Thus, if a speaker or writer uses *provide*, that choice in itself implies that what is provided is being presented as good rather than bad. Third, the concordancer does more than highlight the evaluative polarity, be it good or bad, of an item's collocational environment. Collocates may also turn out to belong to a class of words that share a semantic feature, that is, the search word may have a particular 'semantic preference' (Stubbs, 2001: 88). For example, Baker (2006: 79, 87) concludes from corpus evidence that *refugees* has a semantic preference for quantification, collocating frequently with numbers and phrases such as *more and more* (see also Baker and McEnery, 2005). In a study using a similar approach, Mautner (2007) shows that *elderly* often co-occurs with items from the domains of care, disability and vulnerability. By the same token, if we return to our concordance output related to *unemployed* and its co-ordinated adjectives, we can see that, broadly speaking, these denote either social states (e.g. *available for work, excluded, immigrant, nomadic, unemployable, unpaid*), negative emotions (e.g. *angry, bored, depressed*), or indeed a condition at the interface of both (*unloved*). The collocational profile thus points to the twin nature of unemployment as a social phenomenon with a manifestly psychological impact on individuals.

Taken together, then, semantic preference and discourse prosody show us what kinds of social issues a particular lexical item is bound up in, and what attitudes are commonly associated with it. Importantly, collocational patterns are not merely instantiated in text, but also cling to the lexical items themselves. 'Words which are co-selected', Tognini-Bonelli (2001: 111) reminds us, 'do not maintain their independence. If a word is regularly used in contexts of good news or bad news or judgement, for example, it carries this kind of meaning around with it'.

Finally, some software packages, such as Wordsmith Tools, allow the analyst to compare word lists compiled from different corpora, determining which words are statistically more frequent 'keywords' in a corpus (Baker, 2006: 125; Baker et al., 2008: 278; Mulderrig, 2006: 123). Fairclough's (2000a) study, for example, focuses on the keywords of New Labour – words, that is, that are more frequent in New Labour material than in earlier Labour texts, and more frequent, too, than in general corpora (Fairclough, 2000a: 17).

To sum up, concordancing software offers the above features which are useful for CDA applications (see Table 5.4).

TABLE 5.4 *Tools and types of linguistic evidence provided by concordance software*

Quantitative evidence	Frequency lists
	Comparisons of wordlists, giving information on relative frequency ('keyness')
	Measures of statistical significance:
	• t-score • 'Mutual Information' (MI) score
Qualitative evidence	Concordance lines sorted alphabetically, enabling the researcher to identify:
	• semantic preference • semantic prosody

Corpus design issues

These days, when linguists talk about *a corpus*, they generally refer to 'a collection of (1) *machine-readable* (2) *authentic* texts [...] which is (3) *sampled* to be (4) *representative* of a particular language or language variety' (McEnery et al., 2006: 5, original italics). Let us look at each of these four characteristics in turn, with an eye to whatever specific implications they may have for applications in CDA.

Machine readability is the obvious prerequisite for analysing language with the concordancing software described in the previous section. This sounds straightforward enough, but when it is coupled with the second feature – authenticity – issues of data quality arise that critical discourse analysts will want to address. Standard concordancers need 'plain text' files, stripped of formatting, layout and accompanying visuals. While traditional lexico-syntactic research does not see this as a loss, critical discourse analysts will (or should). After all, it is one of the foundational assumptions of discourse analysis, whether of the critical persuasion or not, that meaning-making works simultaneously on several levels, including the non-verbal. Elements of textual design, including typography, colour and text–image relationships, are not merely embellishments, but play an integral role in making text function as socially situated discourse (van Leeuwen, in this volume). The semiotic reduction that concordancing inevitably entails (Koller and Mautner, 2004) need not jeopardize the validity of one's analyses, but there ought to be adequate safeguards to ensure that whatever is lost along the way can be salvaged at a later stage. In mundanely practical terms, this means collecting and storing hard-copy or scanned originals for future reference, to be drawn upon should multimodality become an issue. Likewise, audio or video recordings of spoken data ought to be preserved, so that contextual clues lost through transcription and conversion into machine-readable format can be retrieved if and when necessary.

As far as criteria (3) and (4) are concerned – sampling and representativeness – the requirements for ensuring methodological rigour are basically no different here than they are for other approaches (see Mautner, 2008). The first step is to identify the 'universe of possible texts' (Titscher et al., 2000: 33), while the second involves sampling. This can be random (i.e. done by first numbering the texts in the 'universe' and then selecting those with the numbers that a random number generator has picked out). Alternatively, it may be guided by criteria that are applied systematically and, in a top-down selection process, narrow down the corpus to a manageable size (e.g. 'take one article about Topic A from newspapers B and C published each week between dates X and Y'). There is a third sampling method, common in qualitative research but unlikely to be suitable for corpus linguistic work, which uses a cyclical process, building a small and homogeneous corpus, then analysing it and adding to it on the basis of the first results (Bauer and Aarts, 2000: 31). The process is repeated until 'saturation' has been reached – a situation, that is, where adding new data does not yield any new representations (Bauer and Aarts, 2000: 34). The problem with this procedure from a corpus linguist's point of view is the flip side of what makes it appealing to the purely qualitative researcher: that you stop collecting data as soon as what you find is simply more of the same. In corpus linguistics, the frequency of an item or structure is taken to be a key indicator of its significance. If you stop adding text to your corpus as soon as repetition becomes apparent, you are effectively closing off any frequency-based line of inquiry. This may well be an acceptable decision to take in a particular project; after all, the qualitative analysis of concordance lines is as important and valuable as the quantitative inquiry that concordancing software allows. But it would have to be a decision taken with full awareness of the loss involved. Certainly, care must be taken not to indulge in hasty judgements about what can be excluded from the corpus on the grounds that it is 'similar' to what is already there. Such rashness can easily defeat the whole purpose of the corpus-building exercise, the point of which is, in a sense, to outwit the analyst who may be tempted to know the data *before* rather than *after* the analysis.

Summing up, corpus design involves the following issues (Figure 5.1):

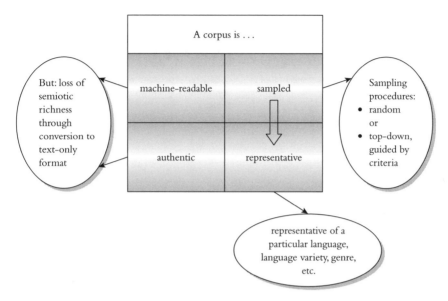

FIGURE 5.1   *Corpus characteristics and issues of corpus design*

Types of corpora and data capture

Corpora come in many shapes and sizes. There are huge, multi-million-word corpora such as The British National Corpus[9] (BNC) and Wordbanks Online, from which the *unemployed* example in the previous section was taken. These are ready-made, commercially available, and each comes with bespoke software unique to it (usually a source of frustration if you want to use both corpora simultaneously). Both were the result of large-scale projects spanning many years and involving teams of linguists and computer experts. In CDA, such corpora are ideal for painting on a very large canvas, investigating how broader social issues are reflected in the genres and discourses represented in the corpus (such as fiction, newspapers and spoken dialogue). This approach is used in studies such as those of Krishnamurthy (1996) on racism and Mautner (2007) on ageism.

At the other end of the spectrum, there are much smaller, 'do-it-yourself' (DIY) corpora (McEnery et al., 2006: 71), purpose-built by individual researchers or small teams to investigate specific research questions. Issues of size apart, corpora may also be classified according to whether they are synchronic, reflecting a language variety at any given point in time, or diachronic, reflecting historical development. They can be general, including a wide variety of genres and media, or specialized, focusing on a particular genre (e.g. corporate mission statements), a particular medium and topic (e.g. web-based texts on disability rights), a particular genre and topic (e.g. parliamentary speeches on global warming), or a particular topic in various genres and media (e.g. the 'Evolution vs. Creationism' debate in sermons, newspaper articles and web logs). Corpora may also differ in terms of

TABLE 5.5   *Main types of corpora*

Reference Corpora	'Do-it-yourself' (DIY) Corpora
Ready-made, 'off the peg', including a wide variety of genres (written, spoken, newspapers, fiction, etc.) and millions of words per genre.	Purpose-built by individual researchers, designed to tackle smaller-scale research questions, processed with the help of concordancing software such as Wordsmith Tools.
E.g. BNC (100 million words), Wordbanks Online (approx. 500 million words)	

Other criteria:

- synchronic vs. diachronic
- general vs. specialized
- types of mark-up and annotation

which meta-linguistic information is encoded with the text. Critical discourse analysts will be particularly keen to insert codes describing extratextual information (a procedure known as 'corpus mark-up'), such as text type, speakers' or writers' sociolinguistic characteristics, or indeed any feature that is relevant for a particular research question. Mark-up plays a key role in allowing the analyst to relate the examples shown up by corpus searches back to their original contextual environments (McEnery et al., 2006: 22–23). In addition, corpora may have undergone what is called 'annotation', a process of inserting, for example, parts-of-speech tags, prosodic or semantic information (Baker, 2006: 38–42). Table 5.5 summarizes the main types of corpora.

In building corpora of any size, the World Wide Web has emerged as a key resource. With the exception of spontaneous spoken language (which, admittedly, is a very significant exception), the web offers a huge variety of text and sheer unlimited amounts of it. Cut-and-paste procedures have greatly facilitated the process referred to as 'data capture' (Baker, 2006: 31–38; McEnery et al., 2006: 73). As a result, corpora running to hundreds of thousands of words can be assembled within the space of a few weeks. (On the copyright issues involved, see McEnery et al., 2006: 77–79.) More importantly still, this can be done by individual scholars without the help of battalions of research staff, access to whom is normally dependent on massive research grants and/or a position high up in the institutional pecking order. Seen from this angle, enlisting corpus methods also has a democratizing effect on critical research.

Thus, in terms of sheer corpus availability, most critical discourse analysts' interests will be catered for by the web (which makes it all the more surprising that until very recently, only comparatively few CDA projects were actually based on online material – see Mautner, 2005). Yet in spite of this new abundance, many of the old questions remain, which brings us back to the design issues raised in the previous section. Modern technology may have reduced the manual drudgery of corpus-building, but not the need for brainpower to make the *right* choices. To recap briefly, the key issues involved – all of them well known from traditional corpus-gathering – are: first, ensuring an adequate fit between the corpus and the research question(s) to be tackled, and, second, the triangle of issues concerning corpus size, homogeneity and representativeness.

Using a reference corpus to support interpretation: a second worked example

It is true, as the previous section explained, that corpus linguistic methods can be applied either to smaller, purpose-built corpora or to large reference corpora. Nonetheless, critical discourse analysts are likely to get most mileage out of a combination of the two approaches. Arguably, the smaller your own corpus, the more important it becomes to validate interpretations by checking them against evidence from larger corpora. We might feel, for example, that a certain word or phrase is used in a particular text because it carries a particular evaluative load, but is this borne out by data from a reference corpus reflecting general language use? What kind of collocational 'baggage' do words occurring in the text carry in wider universes of discourse? It is through comparative evidence from large corpora that suspicions can be confirmed or rejected, thus safeguarding against 'overinterpretation and underinterpretation' (O'Halloran and Coffin, 2004). It has to be conceded, of course, that making sense of this comparative evidence still involves acts of interpretation on the part of the analyst. Neither the quantitative nor the qualitative evidence that large corpora lay before us speaks for itself and to claim that it does so would be seriously misguided or, at the very least, naive. On the other hand, surely, any improvement in CDA's empirical credentials ought to be welcome, tempered though it may be by the sobering realization that completely mechanized discourse analysis is impossible. Or, were it possible, it would cease to be critical.

The idea of comparative evidence is illustrated by the second worked example. It relates to a column in the British popular daily the *Sun* (25 July 2007), published at a time when major floods were devastating large areas in central England. The headline reads 'It's time to turn off the spongers' money tap' (with *spongers*, or *scroungers*, referring to people who receive money but do nothing in return). The article is built around the contrast between the lives of 'hard-working people' whose homes have been destroyed by the flood in Gloucestershire, and a family with 12 children from Berkshire (*the scrounging Gillespies*) who have been given a new council house paid for by *the hard-working taxpayer*. The father of the family is quoted as saying, 'if it was economical for me to work then I would do'. A benefits system producing such attitudes, the article demands, ought to be changed; also, foreign aid should be put on hold 'until *our* national crisis is sorted out' (original italics). There are two large pictures, one of a flooded house in Gloucester, and a second of the Gillespies' £500,000 council home, which has a small inset showing the couple surrounded by their 12 children. Addressing politicians from both government and opposition, the columnist pleads: 'The hard-working people of Britain should come first'.

Like many opinion pieces in the popular press, this column develops a stark black-and-white dichotomy, pitting 'us' against 'them'. 'Us' refers to the *grafting taxpayer* (with *grafting* being a colloquial British expression meaning 'hard-working'), whose *hard-earned home* has been flooded, whereas 'they' are *the blatantly idle Gillespies of this world* and, less prominently, recipients of development aid in Africa. In establishing the 'we' group, the adjective *hard-working* clearly plays a central role. In an article of around 1300 words, it occurs five times. In four of these instances, *hard-working* is part of a noun group which includes at least one other in-group marker (*people of Britain, British taxpayers, our own people, the communities*). The occurrences, quoted below, are spread fairly evenly throughout the text, contributing to its cohesion:

1. … there's only one basic rule to remember: the **hard-working** people of Britain should come first.
2. Yet frankly, when the **hard-working** British taxpayers need them most, our politicians look as washed up as the million-plus doormats floating around the streets.
3. … not to mention the indirect £8 billion of our taxes the PM [Prime Minister] has recently pledged to Africa. But when our own **hard-working** people are in trouble, there should be an instant amnesty on all other benevolent activity until *our* national crisis is sorted out [original italics].
4. There's more rain on the way, so I suggest Brown [= the Prime Minister], Cameron [= the Leader of the Opposition] et al. get their galoshes on and *show* they care about the blighted, **hard-working** communities (…) [original italics].
5. … the skewed thinking that the **hard-working** taxpayer is a cash cow only to be milked and never fed.

On this evidence, it would be fair to claim that in this text, *hard-working* does ideological work, establishing a 'we' group and attributing a positive quality to it. But then, what is it about *hard-working*, exactly, that makes it such a powerfully positive label? And is this evaluative load true of general language use, or specific to certain discourses? In other words, is there a specifically 'tabloid' attitude towards 'hard-working' people?

Let us see what the Wordbanks reference corpus has to say. First of all, the collocation list for *hard-working* from the total 500+ million-word corpus, ordered by 'mutual information' score, reveals a long list of other positive adjectives. Picking out those that also have double-digit joint frequencies (that is, not only exhibit a strong collocational bond with *hard-working*, evident through an MI score of five or above, but also occur at least ten times), we arrive at the following list (see Table 5.6).

TABLE 5.6   *Collocates of* hard-working *in the total 500+ million-word Wordbanks corpus, with joint frequencies of at least 10 and MI scores of at least 5*

Word	Joint frequency	MI score
industrious	11	9.531038
conscientious	19	9.158034
abiding	19	8.612447
honest	75	7.322699
dedicated	46	7.307235
disciplined	11	7.087851
loyal	28	7.047991
sincere	12	7.001116
competent	12	6.847253
ambitious	28	6.793461
decent	38	6.724341
intelligent	27	6.611245
enthusiastic	14	6.242391
caring	17	6.127628
talented	15	6.044615
skilled	10	6.039344

Some of these are fairly closely related to the idea of working hard or in a particularly focused manner (*industrious, conscientious, dedicated, disciplined, ambitious, skilled*), but others refer to very general attributes that are quite independent of the domain of employment: *honest, loyal, sincere, decent* and *caring*. There is a semantic preference for character traits, and the semantic aura is unequivocally positive. To find that there is a statistically significant collocational bond between these adjectives and *hard-working* means that when someone is described as 'hard-working', there is a higher than random possibility that one of these other, non-work-related qualities will appear in close proximity. For each of these collocates, of course, we need to check what the syntactic relationship with *hard-working* is, because 'being close' could also mean 'close and linked through *but*', in which case the other adjective would be expressing a contrast, not a confirmation, of the virtues implied in hard work (cf. the hypothetical, not attested, phrase *hard-working but caring*). However, it can be established easily by examining the relevant concordances – such as the one for *decent*, which is given in Table 5.7 – that the 'virtuous' adjectives are linked to *hard-working* through *and* or a comma and do in fact refer to the same individuals or groups of people. In addition to showing how *hard-working* and *decent* (highlighted in bold capitals) are related syntactically and semantically when they appear together, the following concordance also reveals a number of other positive attributes in close proximity (highlighted in bold), some with distinctly moralizing overtones (e.g. *honest family man, genuine and Christian, self-sacrificing*).

Such instances of collocation – repeated, statistically significant and attested across a multi-million-word corpus – 'provide objective, empirical evidence for evaluative meanings', and these meanings 'are not merely personal and

TABLE 5.7   *Co-occurrence of* hard-working *and* decent *in the 500+ million-word Wordbanks Online corpus*

to denigrate Kilbane, who is a	hard-working	and **DECENT** professional. Yet on
a more **responsible**, **DECENT** and	hard-working	British citizen. **He is a credit to**
is that they are **DECENT** and	hard working	people," he said. Mr Xynias said
n the barrel, most fathers are	hard working	**DECENT family types** trying to do
thousands of **DECENT**, **brave**,	hard-working	coppers. It's hardly surprising
that Hart was a **DECENT**,	hard-working	and **honest family man**, but added
lost on Saturday night. **DECENT**,	hard-working	people, people who are prepared to
things are bad when a **DECENT**,	hard-working	father resorts to taking surgeons
s just as you see him. **DECENT**,	hard-working,	**genuine** and **Christian**. He's the
The bishops are **DECENT**,	hard-working	men in thankless roles, but the
Paul Duckworth was a **DECENT**,	hard-working	and **loving father**. <p> "The
The former teacher is **DECENT**,	hard-working	and **dutiful**. But as my colleague
of him is that he isa **DECENT**,	hard-working	bloke who was caught up in
TV.<p> Meanwhile most **DECENT**,	hard working	citizens will be lucky to see any
great to her family -a **DECENT**,	hard-working	girl." <hl> Open house contest
town I grew up in was a **DECENT**,	hard-working,	hard-drinking, cloth-cap- and-
Erfurt, Germany, as "a **DECENT**,	hard-working	man". <p> But Judge Gareth
he said: "They were all **DECENT**,	hard-working	men - **great lads and great mates**. I
make life a misery for **DECENT**,	hard-working	people. <p> The phone number to
badly on thousands of **DECENT**,	hard-working	taxi men and women who want these
employer as '**good**, **DECENT**,	hard-working	men" who were mown down in a hail
with admiration as **DECENT**,	hard-working	people, who despite having very
but my parents were **DECENT**,	hard-working	people. We used to go to church
of the game – the **DECENT**,	hard-working	people who work in and around
When I see a **DECENT**,	hard-working	man like you, with a responsible
admired his wife, a **DECENT**,	hard-working,	**self-sacrificing** woman; he couldn'
coal miners, each **DECENT**,	hard-working	union men with large families,
coal miners, each **DECENT**,	hard-working	union men with large families,
Slick Willy" into a **DECENT**,	hard-working	child of the middle class. He told
with New York: the **DECENT**,	hard-working	people who live here. And here's
he said, "a generally	hard-working	and **DECENT** people prepared to put
found them **DECENT**, **kindly**,	hard-working,	and **knowledgeable** within their
they will effectively stop many	hard working	**DECENT** Sikhs from earning a
of humanity; there's a lot of	hard-working,	**DECENT** people, a lot of children
level-headed, reliable,	hard-working,	**DECENT, orderly**" – are
and more time listening to the	hard-working,	**DECENT** majority that elected New
character who came from a "very	hard-working	and **DECENT** family". <p> The judge
<p> The puzzling aspect is why	hard-working,	**DECENT** people can see what is

idiosyncratic, but widely shared in a discourse community' (Stubbs, 2001: 215). Effectively, the frequent collocates of a word *become* part of its meaning. Thus, by drawing on corpus-based collocational information, a discourse analyst can replace his or her individual, intuitive judgement on evaluative meaning with shared assumptions and judgements.

In further attempting to put the use of *hard-working* in this *Sun* article into perspective, another angle worth looking at is to see how it is used in a newspaper catering for a different readership. The relevant subcorpus that Wordbanks Online offers is the nearly 60 million words from the British daily *The Times*. Whereas more than 60 per cent of the *Sun*'s readers are in the C2, D and E social grades, 89 per cent of *The Times*' readers belong to the A/B/C1 socio–economic group.[10] The results (Table 5.8) show that *hard-working* occurs more than twice as often in the *Sun* (in relative terms, that is, per million words) than it does in *The Times*.

TABLE 5.8   *Frequency of* hard-working *in the* Sun *and* Times *subcorpora of* Wordbanks Online

	absolute frequency	relative frequency, per one million words
Sun	393	8.69
Times	243	4.06

Furthermore, although the lists of high–frequency collocates appear to be rather similar in the two subcorpora, containing many of the items that showed up when we examined the whole 500–million–word corpus (see Table 5.6), two differences between the *Sun's* and *The Times'* collocation lists do stand out. One is that *honest* and *decent*, though present in both lists, are relatively more frequent in the *Sun* corpus.[11] The other is that the collocation list for *hard-working* in the *Sun* includes a collocate – the one with the highest MI score, in fact – that is not present in *The Times'* list at all: *abiding*. Switching from the collocation list to concordance mode, we can see that all six occurrences of *abiding* are due to *law-abiding* being one of the positive attributes closely associated with *hard-working* (Table 5.9).

TABLE 5.9   *Co-occurrence of* hard-working *and* law-abiding *in the* Sun *corpus of* Wordbanks Online

against the respectable,	hard-working,	**LAW-ABIDING** majority. No wonder
redit to their **LAW-ABIDING** and	hard-working	community. \<p\> A V DAVAR, East
>Then hopefully **LAW-ABIDING**,	hard-working	parents like the Gells need neve
t better meals than a lot of	hard-working	**LAW-ABIDING** people, better medic
time all decent, **LAW ABIDING**,	hard-working	people were given some
even exists. \<p\> How many	hard-working,	honest, **LAW-ABIDING** people can

The social construction involved in this collocational link, rather than any 'objective' semantic association, could hardly be more obvious. After all, it is perfectly possible to be 'lazy' and abide by the law, or work a very busy 70-hour week dedicated to breaking it. Incidentally, taken by itself, *law-abiding* is also considerably more frequent in the *Sun* (145 instances, or 3.2 occurrences per million words) than in *The Times* (111 instances, or 1.86 per million).

Summing up, and relating the evidence back to the article that made us turn to the reference corpus for support, we can draw the following conclusions:

- *Hard-working* is much more than a descriptive label. Its semantic preference and prosody, evident in the concordance lines, indicate that it is part and parcel of a moralizing discourse, linking hard work with positive attributes such as decency, honesty, loyalty, family values and the like.

- These patterns are relatively more prominent in the popular, working-class tabloid the *Sun* than they are in *The Times*, which caters for a predominantly middle-class readership.
- In a critical discourse analysis of a text using *hard-working*, a good case can therefore be made for arguing that the contribution of *hard-working* to the overall meaning of the text is based partly on the ideological baggage that the word carries, and that this, in turn, is derived from attested patterns of usage in larger universes of discourse.

Large-corpus evidence thus provides 'checks and balances' by opening a window on values and attitudes present throughout a discourse community rather than held only by individual researchers.

Summary and critique

Corpus linguistics has a lot to offer to CDA. It helps researchers cope with large amounts of textual data, thus bolstering CDA's empirical foundations, reducing researchers' bias and enhancing the credibility of analyses. On the other hand, critical discourse analysts ought to be self-confident enough to assert that, conversely, corpus linguistics is enriched by being applied to research questions inspired by social concerns, such as power, inequality and change. Ultimately, through their 'theoretical and methodological cross-pollination' (Baker et al., 2008: 297), both CDA and corpus linguistics ought to benefit.

Combining the two approaches typically involves the following steps:

- compiling an electronically held corpus that allows the investigation of research questions arising from social issues
- running the corpus through concordancing software that compiles frequency lists, identifies keywords and reveals statistically significant collocations
- analysing concordances qualitatively in order to establish the dominant semantic preferences and prosodies of lexical items relevant to the social issues under investigation
- putting the results from the purpose-built corpus into perspective by comparing them with evidence gleaned from large reference corpora.

Alternatively, a multi-million-word reference corpus may itself serve as the starting point, allowing researchers to build collocational profiles of socially contested lexical items across a wide range of genres, media and geographical areas.

In spite of the clear benefits involved, there are some areas of potential concern, which I will deal with in turn under five headings (Figure 5.2).

1. The skills gap and lack of standardization

This is a practical rather than a substantive issue, and may well disappear over time. At the time of writing, though, it still looms rather large. To anyone advocating

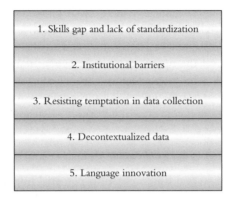

1. Skills gap and lack of standardization

2. Institutional barriers

3. Resisting temptation in data collection

4. Decontextualized data

5. Language innovation

FIGURE 5.2   *Using corpus linguistics in CDA: key areas of concern*

the integration of corpus linguistics into mainstream CDA, it is quite tempting to downplay the effort involved and make reassuring noises along the lines of 'it's not rocket science'. Indeed it isn't, but there is no denying the fact that becoming a confident user takes time and effort. Not much, perhaps, for the mundane task of learning to master the tools; but certainly a significant amount in order to develop the type of mindset that can appreciate the potential of the method, recognize its limitations, hone your analytical skills and refine your discovery procedures, so that ultimately you are able to fashion your research designs accordingly.

The continuing reluctance of many discourse analysts to become involved may well be due in part to the deplorable lack of standardization within corpus linguistics. The British National Corpus and Wordbanks Online, to use just two examples of multi-million-word corpora, do not use the same software. The same is true of the various concordancing packages available for analysing DIY corpora (such as Wordsmith Tools or Monoconc Pro). Search commands differ, screens differ, analytical tools differ: not a happy state of affairs if all you want to do is get on with the job.

2. Institutional barriers

The second point is related to the first, but located on the institutional rather than the individual level. Critical discourse analysts and computer linguists do not necessarily work in the same departments and, if they do, may not communicate well with each other. They often go to different conferences and publish in different journals. As a junior researcher, you are likely to be socialized into either the one methodology or the other, but rarely into both. As most linguists know, but not all care to admit, it is often early exposure to a particular methodology, rather than any inherent merits this may have, that tends to bias one's methodological choices for a long time.

At the risk of launching into after-dinner-speech mode, this is the moment to call for more communication between critical discourse analysts and computer linguists. This should not, I hasten to add, stop at CDA people begging for IT support, realistic though this image may be, but should also lead to corpus linguists picking their CDA colleagues' brains on how best to sharpen their computing tools so that they deliver the optimum value for applications in socially relevant, applied discourse studies. Existing reference corpora, too, could profit from some overhauling in that respect. In Wordbanks, for example, source referencing – such a key factor in determining context – is notoriously deficient.

3. Resisting temptation in data collection

Whereas the first and second issues related to potential hurdles encountered by those new to the method, the third centres on the need to curb the enthusiasm of the newly converted. We saw earlier that the World Wide Web and electronic processing have made for temptingly laden data tables. And indeed, being able to assemble and analyse large corpora is a key element in defusing the 'cherry-picking' charges frequently levelled at CDA. Generally speaking, corpus size undoubtedly boosts representativeness, and this, in turn, enhances the validity of analysts' claims. On the other hand, as is so often the case, a technological advance comes with strings attached. Somewhat paradoxically, the ease with which corpora can be assembled can prove to be at once overwhelming and tempting for the analyst, novice and seasoned researcher alike. They may well react like a glutton at an all-you-can-eat diner, guzzling data 'food' indiscriminately without due regard for the principles of discerning composition, be it of a menu or of a corpus. In our case, these will revolve, as ever, around questions such as: what kinds of texts are most likely to allow me to answer my research questions? Is the selection of texts which make up my corpus reasonably representative of the 'universe of discourse' that is 'out there'? None of these questions, and the principles underlying them, have ceased to be relevant. If anything, they have become more pressing, precisely because of the *embarras de richesses* surrounding the analyst engaged in corpus-building. Amid the bewildering surplus of easily storable text, it has become easier to lose sight of the need for constant reflexivity, even in the early stages of a project, and particularly with regard to what should go into the corpus. This is not a plea for allowing too much biased selectivity too soon; if it were, it would amount to reverting to the very 'cherry-picking' procedure that a corpus-based approach wishes to counteract (and which is why cyclical corpus-building up to saturation was rejected in our discussion of sampling). The point is, rather, that critical discourse analysts putting corpora together should, quite simply, not get carried away.

4. Decontextualized data

The fourth area of concern, mentioned earlier but worth restating here, relates to the fact that both the input to and output from concordancing software is decontextualized, semiotically reduced language. Although programs allow instant access to wider co-texts or even the full texts that the concordance lines come from, a considerable amount of non-verbal information is lost when text is transferred to machine-readable form. Corpus mark-up can help compensate up to a point but, with the current state of technological development and commercial availability, it is impossible to run concordancing software while preserving the full textual integrity of the original. This is an area, therefore, where the idea of 'checks and balances' needs to work the other way round, with the analyst having to make sure that whatever information concordancers cannot deal with, such as typography and pictures, remains accessible somewhere and is not entirely and irretrievably lost to the analysis.

In this context, we ought also to remind ourselves that concordancing software is biased towards the discrete lexical unit. Larger-scale discursive phenomena, such as argumentative patterns, may be captured through corpus linguistic techniques, but only if they crystallize systematically around certain words, phrases or lexico-semantic patterns.

Finally, and precisely because corpus linguistics has this fantastic potential for focusing on linguistic detail, there is a need to guard against becoming so engrossed in building collocational profiles of ideologically loaded individual words that the bigger picture is lost. There is a fine line between an eye for detail and myopia. Returning briefly to the *hard-working* example in the previous section: were this part of a full-blown study, it would of course be insufficient merely to look at *hard-working* (central though it is to this newspaper article). In addition, one would not only have to explore the full range of synonyms and related expressions that the article uses, but would also have to delve deeper into the history, politics and social psychology of wage labour and the work ethic.

5. Language innovation

The fifth issue to be borne in mind is that large and static reference corpora, such as the BNC and Wordbanks Online, are useless for investigating developments at the sharp end of language. Where social change is at its fastest – and arguably of keenest interest to CDA – these corpora fall silent. Youth culture, advertising and code-switching varieties emerging among new immigrant populations would be cases in point. For such applications, building ad-hoc DIY corpora is the only solution.

Essentially, the last four areas of concern all relate to the same issue: the need for a realistic assessment of a method's potential. Our metaphorical tools for setting to work on text are subject to very much the same limitations as tools in a literal sense. It makes as much, or as little, sense to criticize corpus linguistic methods for not permitting more contextually embedded analysis, or a static, ten-year-old corpus for being silent on the latest neologisms, as it does to criticize a screwdriver for being no good at hammering in nails.

What is more, it can be tempting to expect computer-based methods to work miracles and to obscure or even compensate for flaws elsewhere in the research design. Put more bluntly, if your sampling technique is faulty and your sample skewed, it will remain so even when computerized, concordanced and subjected to every statistical procedure under the sun. Similarly, if your choice of statistical techniques is such that the data are, as Baker (2006: 179) graphically puts it, 'subtly "massaged"' in order to produce the desired results; if the analyst reports results selectively, or ignores inconvenient concordance lines, then the fault lies not with their methodology but with their integrity.

Whatever the limitations of corpus linguistics, the complexity of discourse is such that any change in perspective and any insight not otherwise available ought surely to be welcome as additions to the methodological toolbox. On the other hand, we should not forget that, in choosing methods, there is a rather thin dividing line between, on the one hand, eclecticism that is imaginative and productive, and, on the other, aimless patchworking, which is neither. Whether your research design ends up on the right side of this divide depends crucially on (1) a clear statement of the aims of your project, (2) a rigorous assessment of what each method can and cannot do, and (3) robust theoretical foundations capturing core assumptions about language and the social. If deployed wisely, corpus linguistics provides an enriching complement to qualitative CDA, aiding discovery and adding analytical rigour. To return to the metaphor introduced earlier: even an Oscar-winning supporting actor cannot rescue a bad film, but they can make a good film great.

FURTHER READING

Baker, P. (2006) *Using Corpora in Discourse Analysis*. London and New York: Continuum.
This book is ideally suited for critical discourse analysts who are first-time users of corpus linguistic methods. It combines theoretical background with hands-on advice and several worked examples.

McEnery, T., Xiao, R. and Yukio Tono, Y. (2006) *Corpus-based Language Studies: An Advanced Resource Book*. London and New York: Routledge.
This book caters for both novice and more experienced researchers, proceeding from the basics to a section with key readings from corpus-based language studies. In a third section, six extended case studies are presented, covering areas as diverse as pedagogical lexicography, L2 acquisition, sociolinguistics, and contrastive and translation studies.

Stubbs, M. (1996) *Text and Corpus Analysis: Computer-assisted Studies of Language and Culture*. Oxford and Cambridge, MA: Blackwell.
Stubbs, M. (2001) *Words and Phrases: Corpus Studies of Lexical Semantics*. Oxford and Cambridge, MA: Blackwell.
Both volumes are seminal classics. Although the author positions them, as their respective subtitles reveal, as 'Computer-assisted Studies of Language and Culture' and 'Corpus Studies of Lexical Semantics', rather than CDA, they make essential reading for critical discourse analysts, and especially those who may be 'challenged' in terms of empirical rigour.

Acknowledgement

Material from the Bank of English® reproduced with the kind permission of HarperCollins Publishers Ltd.

Notes

1 This criticism, in turn, has been refuted strongly by, for example, Fairclough (1996) and Wodak (2006a: 606–609).
2 See Fairclough (1992a); Fairclough (1995a); Fairclough and Wodak (1997); Toolan (2002); van Dijk (2007a); Wodak (2006b); Wodak and Chilton (2005).
3 The MI score relates the *observed* frequency of a given co-occurring item within a certain collocational span to the left and right of the search word to the *expected* frequency of the co-occurring item in that span (McEnery et al., 2006: 56). For details of the statistical computation involved, see Matsumoto (2003: 398–399).
4 The issue in question is *Text* 22(3). See, in particular, Graham and Paulsen (2002); Muntigl (2002a); Wodak and van Leeuwen (2002).
5 See www.collins.co.uk/books.aspx?group=154
6 The cut-off point above which measures are considered to indicate statistical significance is 2 for t-scores and 3 for MI scores (Hunston, 2002: 71–72).
7 On the basis of the same number of occurrences, 567, as in the *unemployed* example.
8 In this particular corpus, *steelmen* is not as promising a collocate to follow up as it looks, because all nine occurrences refer to the film *The Full Monty*.
9 See www.natcorp.ox.ac.uk/
10 According to figures from the National Readership Survey, available at www.nrs.co.uk, accessed 9 August 2007.
11 In a million words, there are 0.3 occurrences of *honest* in the *Sun* (15 instances) and 0.1 in *The Times* (seven instances). The figures for *decent* are 0.26 per million for the *Sun* (12 instances) and 0.06 for the *Times* (four instances).

6

Discourse as the Recontextualization
of Social Practice: A Guide

Theo van Leeuwen

Introduction

The term 'discourse' is often used to mean an extended stretch of connected speech or writing – a 'text'. 'Discourse analysis' then means 'the analysis of a text, or type of text'. Here, I use it in a different sense, building on the work of Michel Foucault (e.g. 1977) and defining discourses (note the plural) as *socially constructed ways of knowing some aspect of reality* which can be drawn upon when that aspect of reality has to be represented, or, to put it another way, *context-specific frameworks for making sense of things*. In this chapter, I will use discourses of 'leadership' as an example. Clearly, there are different conceptions of what a 'leader' is and does. The discourse of the 'opinion leader', for instance, which was developed in the context of US public communication research (Katz and Lazarsfeld, 1955) is one in which leaders are 'first among equals', role models who provide examples for others to follow. Such leaders may never be formally recognized as leaders, but they will influence what their peers think, say and do. In other discourses, leaders are constructed as fundamentally different from ordinary mortals, and said to rule by 'divine right'. In his book on Nazi language, Klemperer (2000/2006 [1957]: 111 ff.) documents how the Nazi ideology 'again and again underlined [Hitler's] uniquely close relationship with the Godhead, his special status as the chosen one, his special sonship, his religious mission' (Klemperer, 2000/2006 [1957]: 111), but in recent times, too, we have seen leaders such as Bush and Blair claim divine approval for their actions. Clearly, discourses of leadership have a long history. The New Testament introduced the discourse of the leader as 'shep-herd', Plato's *Republic* the discourse of the 'philosopher king', with the leader as expert. And ever since then, political thinkers, philosophers and others have struggled to balance people's need for freedom and persuasion with society's need for guidance and some form of coercion.

In this chapter, I argue that discourses are ultimately modeled on social practices, so that, for instance, knowledge of what 'leadership' *is*, is ultimately based on what leaders *do*. However, discourses will *transform* these doings, for instance by leaving out some of the less palatable things leaders may do, or by representing, not just what leaders do, but also why they do it, and, therefore, why their actions are to be seen as legitimate (cf. Van Leeuwen, 2007). And different discourses, different ways of making sense of the same aspect of reality, will do all this in different ways, including and excluding different things, and doing so in the service of different interests.

As I have said, in this chapter, the term 'discourse' will not be synonymous with the term 'text'. Yet, evidence for the existence of discourses will inevitably have to come from texts, from what is said or written about 'leadership', for instance. More specifically, it will have to come from the similarity between what is said and written about a given aspect of reality in *different* texts that circulate in the same context. It is on the basis of such similar statements, repeated or paraphrased in different texts, and dispersed among these texts in different ways, that we can put the puzzle back together and reconstruct the discourses texts draw on. This chapter introduces methods for just this kind of reconstruction. After discussing the theoretical background of my approach to discourse, I will show (1) how to use text analysis to piece together a discourse, and to connect it to the practice from which it ultimately derives its meaning, and (2) how to analyse the processes of transformation, or *recontextualization* (Bernstein, 1981, 1986), that occur as practices are turned into discourses.

I will use a single example – an online leadership questionnaire for assessing the performance of managers and executives. Called 'Voices', it was designed by the US company Lominger-International, and is used by companies and other organizations the world over. The person to be assessed, referred to by Lominger as the 'learner', nominates five people to assess him or her in each of four categories: 'direct reports' (i.e. people he or she is supervising), 'peers', 'customers' and 'others'. In addition, the 'learner' is assessed by his or her boss and by the 'learner' him- or herself. The selected 'raters' complete the 'tool' online, rating the 'learner' in terms of 30 'competencies', such as 'hiring and staffing', 'interpersonal savvy', 'sizing up people', 'problem-solving', 'confronting direct reports', 'drive for results', 'customer focus', 'integrity and trust', etc., and also in terms of 30 'career stoppers and stallers' which are formulated in terms of 'overuse' of these same competencies. Each 'competency' and each 'stopper and staller' is glossed by a paragraph of description, for example:

> **Conflict Management** – Steps up to conflicts, seeing them as opportunities; reads situations quickly; good at focused listening; can hammer out tough agreements and settle disputes equitably; can find common ground and get cooperation with minimum noise.

This contrasts then to the following 'stopper and staller':

> **Overuse of Conflict Management** – May be seen as overly aggressive and assertive; may get in the middle of everyone else's problems; may drive for a solution before others are ready; may have a chilling effect on open debate; may spend too much time with obstinate people and unsolvable problems.

Both competencies and their 'overuse' are then rated on a five-point scale. Competencies are rated as (a) 'a towering strength', (b) 'talented', (c) 'skilled/OK', (d) 'weakness' or (e) 'serious issue'. 'Overuse' is rated as happening (a) 'constantly', (b) 'much of the time', (c) 'some of the time', (d) 'every so often' or (e) 'not at all'. Competencies are also rated in terms of their perceived importance for the job of the 'learner': (a) 'mission critical', (b) 'very important', (c) 'useful/nice to have', (d)' less important' and (e) 'not important'.

As I have said, a single text does not provide enough evidence for reconstructing a discourse, although it can of course be used for methodological demonstration, as I do in this chapter. I would nevertheless argue for the special importance of texts such as 'Voices'. 'Voices' is used very widely and is therefore not only a discourse *about* leadership, but also constitutive of actual leadership practices and actual ways of talking about these practices. When introduced in universities, as it was in the university where I work, 'Voices' plays a key part in the move from the old elected 'first among equals' style of leadership to new, corporate leadership discourses and practices (cf. Fairclough, 1993). And as 'learners' are obliged to discuss their 'weaknesses' with an 'executive coach', they will more or less be forced to introduce the discourse of 'Voices' into their thinking and talking about their own role and identity as 'leaders'. For all these reasons, it is important to critically analyse texts such as 'Voices', so as to reveal how they construct 'leadership'.

Theoretical background

Anthropologists and sociologists have always realized that representation is ultimately based on practice, on what people *do*. The primacy of practice runs like a thread through the classics of European as well as American sociology. It is true that sociologists sometimes derive concrete actions from abstract concepts and processes from systems – Durkheim's 'collective consciousness', Bourdieu's 'habitus', Talcott Parsons' systems theory (1977) and Levi-Strauss's structuralist anthropology (1964) are examples. Yet the primacy of practice also keeps asserting itself in the work of these writers, sometimes against the grain of their methodology, at other times as a fundamental cornerstone of their theory (e.g. Berger and Luckmann, 1966). Bourdieu elaborated the primacy of practice and the fundamental difference between participant knowledge and 'outsider' knowledge in his *Outline of a Theory of Practice* (1977) and elsewhere. Talcott Parsons, even in his systems theory, can still say that 'the subject of social interaction is in a fundamental sense logically prior to that of social system' (1977: 145), and even Levi-Strauss (1964) at times derives the meaning of myths from social practices rather than from abstract schemata. Durkheim leaves no doubt about it, especially in *The Elementary Forms of Religious Life* (1976) and *Primitive Classification* (Durkheim and Mauss, 1963): myths are modelled on rites, conceptual life on social life, representations of the world on social organization. And Malinowski (1923, 1935) shows how representation originates in action and in uses of language that are inextricably interwoven with action, and how action is then twice recontextualized, first as representation, in 'narrative speech', and then in the construction of new realities, in 'the language of ritual and magic', as Malinowski calls it. Later, Bernstein's theory of recontextualization applied a similar idea to educational practices, describing how knowledge is actively produced 'in the upper reaches of the education system' (1986: 5) and then embedded into a pedagogic content in the 'lower reaches', where it is objectified and made to serve the contextually defined purpose of a 'discourse of order', a form of 'moral education', in the Durkheimian sense. In the approach to critical discourse analysis I present in this chapter, I connect this idea to the term 'discourse', used in Foucault's sense (e.g. 1977). This definition of discourse has also been introduced into critical discourse analysis by Fairclough (e.g. 2000a) and the emphasis on discourse as 'social cognition' has been inspired by the work of Van Dijk (e.g. 1998).

Linguists have generally differed from sociologists in deriving processes (syntagms) from systems (grammars, paradigms), rather than processes (practices) from systems (institutions and objectified forms of knowledge). But when linguists began to study texts, in the 1970s, many found it hard to conceptualize the production and interpretation of texts without recourse to experience, to 'world knowledge' (e.g. Schank and Abelson, 1977) or 'background knowledge' (e.g. Brown and Yule, 1983; Levinson, 1983). Martin (1984, 1992) reintroduced the 'field' of discourse, using lexical cohesion analysis to construct 'activity sequences' – sequences of represented activities. Together with the work of Gleason (1973) and Grimes (1975) who paid attention, not just to represented activities, but also to represented 'roles', 'settings', etc., this work has had a profound influence on the ideas I present in this chapter, and the main difference is that I have extended it beyond procedural and narrative texts, in which there tends to be a close relation between the represented and representing activity sequences, and applied it also to other kinds of text, in which there is a greater difference between the structure of the text, which may be some rhetorical, argumentative structure, and the underlying discourse, i.e. the representation/transformation of a practice together with the purposes, legitimations and evaluations of that practice.

Finally, the study of the way discourses transform social practices, which in this chapter is represented especially by my theory of social action, derives to a large degree from the work of Halliday (1978, 1985), whose theory of transitivity made it possible to interpret differently worded representations of the same reality as different social constructions of that reality, and from the work of Kress, Hodge, Fowler, Trew and others (Fowler et al., 1979; Kress and Hodge, 1979) who demonstrated how Halliday's work can be used and extended for the purpose of critical discourse analysis, or, as they said, quoting Whorf (1956), how linguistics can become 'an instrument of discovery, clarification and insight' for the analysis of the social world (Kress and Hodge, 1979: 14).

Discourse and social practice

As I have said, the approach to discourse I introduce in this chapter is based on the idea that discourses are recontextualizations of social practices. To bring this out, I start with a simple schema of the crucial elements of social practices. Actual social practices will always contain all these elements. Specific discourses about social practices will select from them, transform them and add further elements.

Actions

The core of a social practice is formed by a set of actions, which may or may not have to be performed in a specific order. The 'conflict management' text above, for instance, contains the following actions (I ignore for the moment that they have been transformed in different ways, for instance by being generalized or represented in a relatively abstract way):

- stepping up to conflict
- reading situations
- listening
- hammering out agreements
- settling disputes
- finding common ground
- getting cooperation.

Performance modes

These actions may have to be performed in specific ways. In the 'conflict management' text, listening has to be *focused*, agreements have to be *tough*, and cooperation has to be achieved *with minimum noise*. Clearly, it is not just important what leaders do, but also how they do it – or how they should *not* do it, as can be seen in the '*Overuse* of Conflict Management' text, where 'overly aggressive and assertive' actions are disapproved of.

Actors

Social actors participate in practices in one of a number of roles – as 'agents' (doers of action), 'patients' (participants to whom actions are done) or 'beneficiaries' (participants who benefit from an action, whether in a positive or negative sense). In the 'conflict management' text, the key participant is the 'learner' whose performance is being assessed. Although the actions in the text would in reality require further participants (the people who are in conflict, the people who are being listened to, etc.), they have been deleted in this particular discourse. Only the actions of the 'learner' seem to matter – as 'behaviour', rather than as what they really are, *interactions*, actions undertaken for and with other people. In the 'Overuse of Conflict Management' text, on the other hand, other people are mentioned, though for the most part vaguely ('everyone else', 'others', 'obstinate people').

Presentation styles

The way in which actors present themselves (their dress, grooming, etc.) is an important aspect of all social practices, even if it may be taken for granted in some representations, as is the case in 'Voices'. In my experience, senior managers constantly evaluate each other's presentation style, but this is done informally, rather than as part of formal performance-assessment procedures.

Times

Social practices (or parts of them) will take place at more or less specific times. 'Focused listening', for instance, will happen in regular, scheduled face-to-face meetings with 'direct reports'. I have italicized some examples in the text below:

> *Timely* **Decision Making** – Makes decisions in a *timely* manner, sometimes with incomplete information and under *tight deadlines* and pressure; able to make a *quick* decision.
> **Confronting Direct Reports** – Deals with problem direct reports firmly and *in a timely manner*, doesn't allow problems to fester; *regularly* reviews performance and holds *timely* discussions; can make negative decisions when all efforts fail; deals effectively with troublemakers.

Spaces

Social practices (or parts of them) also take place in specific spaces, chosen or arranged as a suitable environment for the practice. The discourse of 'Voices', however, steers away from such concrete specifics, perhaps because it is designed to apply to many different institutional contexts.

Resources

Social practices also require specific resources, specific tools and materials. 'Providing information', for instance, may require computers, an intranet and so on. But these too have been left out of the 'Voices' text as somehow not relevant to leadership practices.

Eligibility

Specific qualities of the concrete elements of social practices (the actors, settings and resources) make them eligible to function as actors, settings or resources in those practices. In fact, the whole of the 'Voices' leadership questionnaire can be seen as a discourse focusing specifically on 'eligibility', on the characteristics an actor needs to have to be eligible to play the role of 'leader' in an organization. I will return to this point below.

As I have already said, discourses are transformations, or recontextualizations of social practices. Three types of transformation are particularly important.

Deletion

Some elements of a social practice may not be represented in a particular discourse. As we have seen, in the 'conflict management' text, all actors other than the 'learner' are deleted, and so are times, spaces and resources. Such deletions happen for context-specific reasons. First of all, 'Voices' centres on assessing 'learners', focusing on their behavioural patterns, often in abstraction from the specific situations in which these behaviours occur. 'Voices' also has to be applicable to many different contexts and therefore tends towards decontextualization, towards leaving out concrete specifics.

Substitution

The key transformation is of course the transformation from an actual element of an actual social practice into an element of discourse, and this can be done in many different ways. Actors, for instance, can be represented as specific individuals or as *types* of people, they can be referred to in abstract or specific terms, and so on. In the next section, I will deal in detail with the transformation of social action in discourse. Van Leeuwen (2008) provides an account of the ways in which actors, times and spaces can be transformed in discourse.

Addition

Discourses can also add *reactions* and *motives* to the representation of social practices. Reactions are the mental processes which, according to a given discourse, will accompany specific actions of specific actors, for instance the way the actors *feel* about specific actions, or the way they *interpret* specific actions. Needless to say, in different discourses, different reactions may accompany the same actions of the same actors. In the 'Voices' text, as in many other discourses, the focus is on the reactions of the 'patients', the people on the receiving end of the leader's actions. In the example below, for instance, I interpret 'being direct' as a 'performance mode', and 'being uncomfortable' and 'being off-guard' as reactions:

> *Overuse of* **Integrity and Trust** – May be too direct at times, which may catch people off guard and make them uncomfortable; may push openness and honesty to the point of being disruptive …

The most important motives are *purposes* and *legitimations*. Different discourses may ascribe different purposes to the same actions. In the following example, the purpose of 'getting first-hand customer information' is 'to improve products and services', because the relevant 'competency' is 'customer focus'. If the competency had been 'profit focus', the same action might be given another purpose, for instance 'meeting demand' or 'increasing sales':

> **Customer Focus** – Is dedicated to meeting the expectations and requirements of internal and external customers; gets first-hand customer information and uses it for improvements in products and services …

Legitimations provide *reasons* for why practices (or parts of practices) are performed, or for why they are performed the way they are. These reasons may be spelled out in explicit detail or be communicated through what, elsewhere (Van Leeuwen, 2007), I have called 'moral evaluation'. 'Moral evaluation' is an abstract way of referring to specific actions which serves to highlight qualities of that action that carry positive connotations (or, in the case of de-legitimation, negative connotations). In the 'conflict management' text, for instance, a particular action is referred to as 'getting cooperation'. This formulation does not reveal much about what the leader is actually, concretely, doing here. Persuading? Giving directives? Bribing? But it does legitimize the action, because it suggests that it is based on voluntary 'cooperation', rather than on 'compliance' with top-down orders, and it also reveals the purpose of the action ('getting cooperation').

To reconstruct a discourse (or rather, that part of it that is realized in a specific text), I enter a text's representations of the concrete elements of the social practice (actors, actions, times, places and so on), as well as the reactions and motives that have been added, in the different columns of a table, using the following principles:

1. Actions which are referred to several times in different wordings are combined, but where an alternative wording adds a purpose or legitimation, it is entered separately in the relevant column.
2. Where possible, actions are ordered chronologically, e.g.

Find common ground

↓

Hammer out agreement

Where actions are simultaneous rather than sequential, I use a '≈' sign. Where there is a choice of two (or more) possible actions, I use a flowchart notation. Where it is not possible to decide on any chronological connection, I use a '+' sign, e.g.

Monitors process

+

Monitors progress

3. Elements other than actions are horizontally aligned with the actions to which they pertain, e.g. timings with the actions they are timings of, spaces with the actions that take place in that space, legitimations with the actions they legitimize, and so on.

The example below analyses the 'conflict management' text. For the sake of convenience, I first show this text again.

> **Conflict Management** – Steps up to conflicts, seeing them as opportunities; reads situations quickly; good at focused listening; can hammer out tough agreements and settle disputes equitably; can find common ground and get cooperation with minimum noise.

The text contains two *overall labels* for this particular episode of leadership practice, a more neutral, technical one ('conflict management') and a more connotative one ('stepping up to conflict') which adds a hint of 'decisiveness' or 'boldness', hence a 'performance mode' that pertains to the whole of the practice. I have bolded and italicized such overall labels in the analysis.

Even this brief example reveals some aspects of the way the 'Voices' discourse defines leadership. Two motives intermingle: 'decisiveness' and 'toughness' on the one hand, and 'fairness' and 'attentiveness' on the other hand. It is also clear that the discourse focuses entirely on the leader and the way in which s/he performs the actions that define his/her leadership. The other participants are, so to speak, kept out of the frame.

Three further aspects of discourse need to be mentioned at this point.

1. Some discourses provide discursive resources for other discourses

In Van Leeuwen (2008), I look at how the practice of 'the first day at school' is recontextualized in different discourses and note that parent- and teacher-oriented 'first day' discourses rely a great deal on a lay version of child psychology for legitimation. Parents are advised to take their time 'because children don't like to be rushed', and to 'establish the same routine going to and from school' because that 'will make your child feel secure'. Psychologists are quoted to lend authority to such pronouncements. Clearly, certain discourses elaborate forms of knowledge (for instance about what children are like) or systems of moral values (e.g. religions), that can be used in a wide range of discourses to legitimize a wide range

TABLE 6.1   *Analysis of the 'conflict management' text*

Action	Actor	Performance Mode	Timing	Reaction	Motive
Conflict management	**(leader)**	**'stepping up' (decisive)**		**see as opportunity**	
read situation ↓	(leader)		quickly		
listen ↓	" "	focused			
find common ground ↓	" "				
hammer out agreement/settle disputes ↓	" "	tough; hammer			equitably
get cooperation	" "				cooperation

of different practices (cf. Berger and Luckmann, 1966). In my view, 'Voices' is such an expert discourse, supplying legitimate eligibility criteria for leaders and leadership that can be used in a wide range of settings, as borne out by this quote from the website of Lominger-International:

> Lominger's Leadership Architect Competencies drive our research-based, experience-tested and integrated talent management solutions. Flexible, useable and customizable, the suites can be deployed together as a fully integrated system or individually to meet your immediate business needs. No matter where you start, the Leadership Architect Competency Library allows you to maintain a common language for leadership ...

2. Discourses may be modalized

'Voices' uses a great deal of *ability modality*. The leader '*can* hammer out tough agreements', '*can* find common ground' and so on. In other words, the 'Voices' discourse is not so much about what leaders actually do as about what they are *able* to do, and this is probably true for all discourses that construct eligibility criteria for specific roles, and for all discursive practices that test and certify what 'learners' *can* do.

'Ability' modality is not the only way in which discourses can be modalized. Practices may be recontextualized as *past* or *future* practices, for instance as *actual* or *possible* practices, or as *right* or *wrong* practices. Such modalizations should be indicated in the analysis, for instance by using superscripts:

^{Ab}read situation
↓
^{Ab}listen
↓
^{Ab}find common ground

3. Discourses combine in specific ways

A given text may include several discourses. Nevertheless, one discourse is usually central and other, 'secondary' discourses relate to it in specific ways. Texts
may, for instance, contrast past and present discourses about a given practice,
usually to position the present discourse as an improvement on the past, or
'right' and 'wrong' discourses, as in the case of Voices' juxtaposition of competencies and 'overuses' of those competencies. Other discourses may play the
role of 'preparatory' discourses, dealing, for instance, with practices or arrang-
ing spaces for the central practice, or with acquiring the qualifications needed
to participate in the central practice. 'Secondary' discourses may also be legitimatory. In an interview with the CEO of a large company, conducted as part
of a research project on leadership in which I am currently involved, the CEO
interrupted his description of his company's corporate responsibility practices
with a lengthy account of how he built his own house and included a rainwa-
ter tank and low energy lightbulbs. He did this to show that he was personally
engaged in sustainability practices, and really believed in them, so positioning
himself as a charismatic leader who leads by example and inspires rather than
imposes.

Needless to say, what in one context is a 'central' discourse may in another
be 'secondary', and vice versa.

Social action

In this section, I deal with the ways social actions can be, and are, transformed
in discourse, again using 'Voices' as my main example. I will begin by explaining the main ways in which social actions can be transformed.

Actions and reactions

I have already touched on the way discourses may infuse a version of a social
practice with representations of the actors' reactions to the actions that constitute the practice. As Berger has said (Berger and Luckmann, 1966: 113),
social practices involve not only 'a regulatory pattern for externally visible
actions, but also the emotions and attitudes that belong to these actions',
and these may be differently construed in different discourses about these
practices.

Reactions can be formulated in a number of ways. They can be *unspecified* (through verbs like 'react', 'respond', etc.) or *specified* as *cognitive* (e.g. 'grasp'), *perceptive* (e.g. 'has a nose for') or *affective* (e.g. 'feel'):

- *responds* timely to problems with direct reports
- quickly *grasps* the essence and underlying structure of anything
- *has a nose for* talent
- makes people *feel* his or her work is important.

In many discourses, different types of reactions are attributed to different social actors. Some may be represented as engaging cognitively with social actions, for instance, with others as reacting at a more emotional level.

Material and semiotic action

Actions can be interpreted as *material,* as 'doings' (e.g. 'act'), or as *semiotic,* as 'meanings' (e.g 'articulate'). Most of a leader's actions are in fact speech acts, hence semiotic actions, but they may be represented as material actions, to make them seem more active and dynamic, as in the last two examples below:

- *acts* with customers in mind
- can *articulate* the strengths and limitations of people inside and outside the organization
- *provides the information* people need to know to do their job
- *creates mileposts and symbols* to rally support behind the vision.

Material actions can be *transactive,* involving two participants, so that the action is represented as actually having an effect on people or things (e.g. 'hire' and 'assemble') , or *non-transactive,* involving only one participant, which represents the action as 'display', as 'behaviour' that does not affect anyone or anything other than the actor him- or herself (e.g. 'perform'):

- *hires* the best people available
- *assembles* talented staff
- tends to trust people to *perform.*

Transactive material actions are *interactive* if they are realized by a verb that can only take a human object (e.g. 'be candid with … ') and *instrumental* if they can (also) take a non-human object (e.g. 'deal with', 'manage'). If the latter dominates in a given discourse, there is clearly more of a sense of the actor 'using' people 'instrumentally', to achieve goals, rather than thinking of them as people with their own goals and interests:

- *manages* all kinds and classes of people equitably
- *deals* effectively *with* trouble makers
- can *be candid with* peers.

The same distinction applies to semiotic actions. They can be behaviouralized, in which case the meanings conveyed by the speech acts are not included in the representation, for example:

- *communicates* effectively
- can *motivate* many kinds of direct reports.

Or they can include those meanings, whether through *quotation*, '*rendition*' (reported speech) or by specifying the nature of the signified (*topic specification*), or the signifier (*form specification*) as in:

- *talks about possibilities*
- can accurately *restate the opinions of others*
- can easily *pose future scenarios*.

Objectivation and descriptivization

Actions and reactions can be *activated,* that is represented dynamically, *as* actions (e.g. 'analyse') or *de-activated*, represented in a static way, as though they are entities or qualities rather than actions (e.g. 'analysis'):

- *analyses* both successes and failures for clues to improvement
- is excellent at honest *analysis*.

Deactivated representations of social actions may be *objectivated* or *descriptivized*. In the case of objectivation, actions or reactions are represented as though they were things, for instance by means of nominalization or process nouns, or by various metonyms, such as substituting the time of the action (*temporalization*) or the space of the action (*spatialization*) for the action itself:

- can diffuse even *high tension situations* comfortably
- fosters open *dialogue*
- may have a chilling effect on getting everyone's *input*.

In the case of descriptivization, actions and reactions are represented as more or less permanent qualities of social actors, that is, usually, either as 'epithets' or as 'attributes':

- can *be candid with* peers
- may *be* overly *optimistic about* how much people can grow.

De-agentialization

Actions and reactions can be *agentialized*, represented as brought about by human agency, or *de-agentialized*, represented as brought about in ways that are impermeable to human agency – through natural forces, unconscious processes and so on.

To mention three types of de-agentialization, in the case of *eventuation*, the action or reaction is represented as an event, as something that 'just happens', without anybody doing it. This may be done in a number of ways, for instance through verbs of involuntary action, through verbs like 'happen' or 'occur', etc. I have not found an example of this in the 'Voices' text.

In the case of *existentialization*, an action or reaction is represented as something that simply 'exists', usually through an 'existential process', as in *high tension situations*.

In the case of *naturalization*, an action or reaction is represented as a natural process through abstract verbs such as 'vary', 'expand', 'develop', etc., which link actions and reactions to specific interpretations of material processes – to discourses of rise and fall or ebb and flood; of birth and death; of growth and decay; of change and development and evolution; of fusion and disintegration; of expansion and contraction and so on. This will often have a legitimatory function. Examples in 'Voices' include terms like *growth, development, workflow, turnaround, breakthrough* and so on.

Generalization and abstraction

Actions and reactions may be *generalized* to different degrees. Generalizations abstract away from the specific actions that make up a practice or some episode that forms part of it, and label the practice or episode as a whole, as in our earlier example of 'conflict management', and as also in the following examples:

- *distributes the workload* appropriately
- regularly *reviews performance*
- *provides* challenging and stretching *tasks and assignment.*

Actions and reactions may also be represented abstractly, in which case a quality, often apparently peripheral, is used to name the whole. This I refer to as *distillation* – a quality is distilled from the whole that has particular relevance in the given context, usually for purposes of legitimation, as in our earlier example of 'getting cooperation', and also in:

- *builds* appropriate *rapport*
- *uses diplomacy and tact*
- *eliminates roadblocks.*

Overdetermination

I use the term *overdetermination* to refer to two specific types of representation where a given social practice stands for more than itself. I have not found an example of this in the 'Voices' text.

In the case of *symbolization*, an – often fictional – social practice stands for a number of social practices. This is the case in myths, and it is the reason why myths have such an important function in society: 'Myths are a model of social action based on a mythical interpretation of the past' (Wright, 1975: 188). The killing of the dragon in the myth can stand for passing the entrance examination, winning the election, in short for any trial in which the hero overcomes an obstacle towards achieving his or her goal. This accounts for its enduring quality as a 'model' for many different practices.

In the case of *inversion*, one or more elements of the social practice are changed into its opposite. In comic strips such as *The Flintstones* and *Hagar the Horrible*, the characters, settings and objects are set in the past, but the way they interact and live are more or less contemporary – the ways of contemporary suburban families. This gives a kind of universality to these practices that helps legitimate them as natural and unavoidable rather than culturally and historically specific.

The system network in Table 6.2 provides an overview of the categories I have discussed and also indicates that transformations can and cannot co-occur. Square brackets are 'either-or' choices and curly brackets simultaneous choices. It is therefore possible, for instance, for an action to be semiotic (behavioural) and objectivated and de-agentialized and generalized (but not overdetermined), e.g. 'workplace communication' in a sentence like 'good workplace communication improves productivity'. But it is not possible for an action to be both interactive and instrumental.

A text analysis using this network will allow two kinds of question to be asked:

1. What kinds of actions are attributed to what kinds of participants?
2. What kinds of actions tend to be objectivated, de-agentialized and so on?

Here are some observations resulting from my analysis of the 'Voices' text:

- Most actions and reactions in the text are attributed to the leader (199), rather than to employees (28) or customers (4).
- About one third (9 out of 25) of the reactions attributed to employees, and all reactions attributed to customers, are affective reactions such as *like, respect, trust, feel*, etc., for instance. Only two of the reactions attributed to employees are cognitive:

   o (employees) *like* working for (the leader)
   o (employees) *feel* their work is important
   o (employees) *need* further development
   o (the leader) gains (customers') *trust* and *respect*.

On the other hand, out of a total of 64 reactions of the leader, only seven are affective and 42 cognitive. The leader *is aware of, assesses, plans, judges, projects, learns, reads the situation* and so on.

TABLE 6.2   *Social action network*

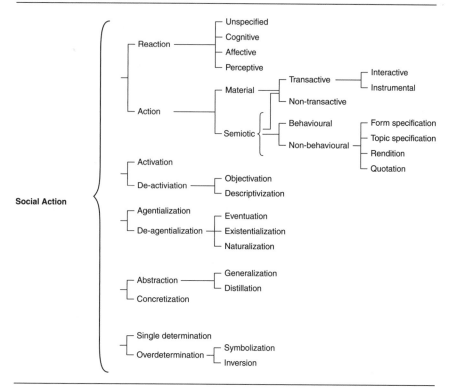

- Most of the leader's actions are material (101 out of 199) and semiotic actions (34) tend to be 'behaviouralized' or 'topic-specified', as, for example, in:

  o (leader) *represents his interests*
  o (leader) *diffuses high tension situations.*

  Of the leader's 199 actions, only 32 impact on other humans (and only half of these are interactive). The rest are non-transactive or instrumental. As mentioned before, the way in which most of the leaders' actions are represented leaves employees and customers out of the frame, for example:

  o (leader) *practises listening*
  o (leader) *holds development discussions.*

  We might ask: who is he listening to? And: who is he holding development discussions with?
- The leader's actions are overwhelmingly generalized and often represented in terms of distillations. The most common themes that emerge from these distillations are: motivation and inspiration (*inspire and motivate, create a climate in which people want*

to do their best, etc.), future vision (*look beyond today, project into the future*, etc.), relationship-building (*build rapport, relate to*), 'instrumental' methods (*use diplomacy and tact, use rigorous logic*, etc.), and finally honesty (*present unvarnished truths* etc.).

- All the leader's actions are agentialized.
- Twenty-nine of the leader's actions are descriptivized (*is fair to, has a nose for, is a teamplayer, is cooperative, is good at figuring out*, etc.), whereas this is the case for only two of the employees' actions. Only eight of the leader's actions are objectivated, while the employees' actions, on the other hand, are always objectivated (*career goal, trust, input, work*) – only their reactions are activated.

What can we conclude from this? First of all, that in this discourse, leaders are constructed as knowledgeable doers, who act at a broad, general level and whose actions are imbued with specific purposes and motives. They are at once tough, decisive, quick to act and patient, understanding and fair, at once practical and down to earth and visionary. That sounds good, but it is as if they act all this out in front of a mirror. Mirror, mirror on the wall, who is the toughest of them all? And the employees for and with whom they do their work are under-represented, while their work is conveyed by nouns and nominalizations which deprive it of its dynamic and productive character. The customers, finally, are almost entirely absent. Not to put too fine a point on it, this is not a form of leadership which is focused on *doing*, on service, facilitation, enablement, but a self-obsessed form of leadership which is focused on being a leader, and on glorifying the characteristic attributes of leaders, rather than their deeds.

FURTHER READING

Bernstein, B. (1990) *The Structuring of Pedagogic Discourse*. London: Routledge. Chapter 5 presents the theory of recontextualization which has especially inspired the earlier part of this chapter. It is difficult to read, but rewarding.

Fairclough, N. (1995a) *Critical Discourse Analysis*. London: Longman. Norman Fairclough was the first critical discourse analyst to turn his attention to corporate discourses, as exemplified by Chapters 5 and 6 in this volume.

Malinowski, B. (1923) 'The problem of meaning in primitive languages', in C.K. Ogden and I.A. Richards, *The Meaning of Meaning*. London: Routledge and Kegan Paul. Written in the 1920s, this is the classic account of how practice gets to be transformed, or 'recontextualized', into discourse.

Van Leeuwen, T. (2006) 'Critical Discourse Analysis', in K. Brown (ed.), *Encyclopedia of Language and Linguistics*. 2nd edn. Vol. 3. Oxford: Elsevier, pp. 290–294.

In this encyclopedia article, I have attempted a general overview of critical discourse analysis.

Van Leeuwen, T. (2008) *Discourse and Practice – New Tools for Critical Discourse Analysis*. New York: Oxford University Press.
Chapters 1 and 3 provide a fuller account of the theories and methods presented in this chapter.

Van Leeuwen, T. and Wodak, R. (1999) 'Legitimizing immigration control: A discourse-historical analysis', *Discourse Studies* 1(1): 83–119.
This was the first published version of the theory of discourse as recontextualized social practice.

7

A Dialectical–Relational Approach to Critical Discourse Analysis in Social Research[1]

Norman Fairclough

In this Chapter, I introduce and illustrate a methodology for using a *dialectical–relational* version of CDA in transdisciplinary social research (Chouliaraki and Fairclough, 1999; Fairclough, 2003, 2006). I begin with a theoretical section explaining the dialectical–relational approach, including my view of discourse, of critical analysis, and of transdisciplinary research. In the second section, I briefly discuss the fields of application of this approach, and in the third section, I explain the methodology, presenting it as a series of stages and steps, and identify a number of core analytical categories. In the fourth section, I present an example, showing the application of this methodology in researching a political topic, and illustrate the approach to political analysis in the fifth section with respect to particular texts. The sixth section summarizes what can be achieved with this methodology and discusses possible limitations.

Theory and concepts

First, a terminological point. *Discourse* is commonly used in various senses including (a) meaning-making as an element of the social process, (b) the language associated with a particular social field or practice (e.g. 'political discourse'), and

(c) a way of construing aspects of the world associated with a particular social perspective (e.g. a 'neo-liberal discourse of globalization'). It is easy to confuse them, so to at least partially reduce the scope for confusion, I prefer to use *semiosis* for the first, most abstract and general sense (Fairclough et al., 2004), which has the further advantage of suggesting that discourse analysis is concerned with various 'semiotic modalities' of which language is only one (others are visual images and 'body language').

Semiosis is viewed here as an element of the social process which is *dialectically* related to others – hence a 'dialectical–relational' approach. Relations between elements are dialectical in the sense of being different but not 'discrete', i.e. not fully separate. We might say that each 'internalizes' the others without being reducible to them (Harvey, 1996) – e.g. social relations, power, institutions, beliefs and cultural values are in part semiotic; they 'internalize' semiosis without being reducible to it. For example, although we should analyse political institutions or business organizations as partly semiotic objects, it would be a mistake to treat them as purely semiotic, because then we couldn't ask the key question: what is the relationship between semiotic and other elements? CDA focuses not just upon semiosis as such, but on *the relations between semiotic and other social elements*. The nature of this relationship varies between institutions and organizations, and according to time and place, and it needs to be established through analysis.

This requires CDA to be integrated within frameworks for *transdisciplinary* research, such as the framework I have used in recent publications – 'cultural political economy' – which combines elements from three disciplines: a form of economic analysis, a theory of the state and a form of CDA (Fairclough, 2006; Jessop, 2004). Transdisciplinary research is a particular form of interdisciplinary research (Fairclough, 2005b). What distinguishes it is that in bringing disciplines and theories together to address research issues, it sees 'dialogue' between them as a source for the theoretical and methodological development of each of them. For example, *recontextualization* was introduced as a concept and category within CDA through a dialogue with Basil Bernstein's sociology of pedagogy, where it originated (Chouliaraki and Fairclough, 1999).

In what sense is CDA *critical?* Critical social research aims to contribute to addressing the social 'wrongs' of the day (in a broad sense – injustice, inequality, lack of freedom, etc.) by analysing their sources and causes, resistance to them and possibilities of overcoming them. We can say that it has both a 'negative' and a 'positive' character. On the one hand, it analyses and seeks to explain dialectical relations between semiosis and other social elements to clarify how semiosis figures in the establishment, reproduction and change of unequal power relations (domination, marginalization, exclusion of some people by others) and in ideological processes, and how in more general terms it bears upon human 'well-being'. These relations require analysis because there are no societies whose logic and dynamic, including how semiosis figures within them, are fully transparent to all: the forms in which they appear to people are often partial and in part misleading. On the other hand, critique is oriented to analysing and explaining, with a focus on these dialectical relations, the many ways in which the dominant logic and dynamic are tested, challenged and disrupted by people, and to identifying possibilities which these suggest for overcoming obstacles to addressing 'wrongs' and improving well-being.

The social process can be seen as the interplay between three levels of social reality: social *structures*, *practices* and *events* (Chouliaraki and Fairclough, 1999). Social practices 'mediate' the relationship between general and abstract social structures and particular and concrete social events; social fields, institutions and organizations are constituted as networks of social practices (see Bourdieu on social practices and fields – Bourdieu and Wacquant, 1992). In this approach to CDA, analysis is focused on two dialectical relations: between structure (especially social practices as an intermediate level of structuring) and events (or structure and action, structure and strategy) and, within each, between semiotic and other elements. There are three major ways in which semiosis relates to other elements of social practices and of social events – as a facet of action; in the construal (representation) of aspects of the world; and in the constitution of identities. And there are three semiotic (or discourse-analytical) categories corresponding to these: genre, discourse and style.

Genres are semiotic ways of acting and interacting, such as news or job interviews, reports or editorials in newspapers, or advertisements on TV or the internet. Part of doing a job, or running a country, is interacting semiotically or communicatively in certain ways, and such activities have distinctive sets of genres associated with them.

Discourses are semiotic ways of construing aspects of the world (physical, social or mental) which can generally be identified with different positions or perspectives of different groups of social actors. For instance, the lives of poor people are not only construed through different discourses associated with different social practices (in politics, medicine, social welfare, academic sociology) but through different discourses in each which correspond to differences of position and perspective. I use 'construe' in preference to 'represent' to emphasize an active and often difficult process of 'grasping' the world from a particular perspective (Fairclough, forthcoming).

Styles are identities, or 'ways of being', in their semiotic aspect – for instance, being a 'manager' in the currently fashionable way in business or in universities is partly a matter of developing the right semiotic style.

The semiotic dimension of (networks of) social practices which constitute social fields, institutions, organizations, etc. is *orders of discourse* (Fairclough, 1992a); the semiotic dimension of events is *texts*. Orders of discourse are particular configurations of different genres, different discourses and different styles. An order of discourse is a social structuring of semiotic difference, a particular social ordering of relationships between different ways of meaning-making – different genres, discourses and styles. So, for example, the network of social practices which constitutes the field of education, or a particular educational organization such as a university, is constituted semiotically as an order of discourse. Texts are to be understood in an inclusive sense, not only written texts but also conversations and interviews, as well as the 'multi-modal' texts (mixing language and visual images) of television and the internet. Some events consist almost entirely of texts (e.g. a lecture or an interview), while in others, texts have a relatively small part (e.g. a game of chess).

Discourses which originate in some particular social field or institution (e.g. to anticipate the example, neo-liberal economic discourse, which originated within academic economics and business) may be *recontextualized* in others (e.g. in the political field or the wider educational field). Recontextualization has an ambivalent character (Chouliaraki and Fairclough, 1999): it can be seen as the 'colonization' of one field or institution by another, but also as the 'appropriation' of 'external' discourses, often the incorporation of discourses into strategies pursued by particular groups of social agents within the recontextualizing field. For example, the 'transition' to a market economy and Western-style democratic government in the formerly socialist countries of Europe (e.g. Poland, Romania) has involved a 'colonizing' recontextualization of discourses (e.g. discourses of 'privatization') which were however incorporated differently into the strategies of new entrepreneurs, government officials, managers of state industries, etc. (Fairclough, 2006).

Discourses may under certain conditions be *operationalized* or 'put into practice', which is a dialectical process with three aspects: they may be *enacted* as new ways of (inter)acting, they may be *inculcated* as new ways of being (identities), and they may be physically *materialized*, e.g. as new ways of organizing space, for example in architecture. Enactment and inculcation may themselves take semiotic forms: a new management discourse (e.g. the discourse of marketized 'new public management' which has invaded public sector fields like education and health) may be enacted as management procedures which include new genres of interaction between managers and workers, or it may be inculcated as identities which semiotically include the styles of the new type of managers.

CDA oscillates, as I have indicated, between a focus on *structures* (especially the intermediate level of the structuring of social practices) and a focus on the *strategies* of social agents, i.e. the ways in which they try to achieve outcomes or objectives within existing structures and practices, or to change them in particular ways. This includes a focus on shifts in the structuring of semiotic difference (i.e shifts in orders of discourse) which constitute a part of social change, and on how social agents pursue their strategies semiotically in texts. In both perspectives, a central concern is shifting relations between genres, between discourses and between styles: change in the social structuring of relations between them which achieves relative permanence and stability in orders of discourse, and the ongoing working and re-working of relations between them which is regarded in this approach to CDA as a normal feature of texts.

The term *interdiscursivity* is reserved for the latter: the interdiscursivity of a text is a part of its intertextuality (Fairclough, 1992a), a question of which genres, discourses and styles it draws upon, and how it works them into particular articulations. Textual analysis also includes linguistic analysis, and analysis where appropriate of visual images and 'body language', and these features of texts can be seen as realizing its interdiscursive features.

Fields of application

The dialectical–relational approach addresses the general question: what is the particular significance of semiosis, and of dialectical relations between semiosis and other social elements, in the social processes (issues, problems, changes, etc.) which are under investigation? This question is of interest right across the social sciences and humanities, and I would not want to foreclose the range of potentially fruitful fields of application of this approach, nor the range of genres or texts it might be applied to. It is true that certain types of texts would seem to pose particular problems – literary texts, for example – but that is a different matter. In general, I would oppose any view of method which seeks to neatly match methods (methodologies) to fields or text types, or cultivates the view that researchers need to seek the 'right' method for their data and research questions. In short, I would not want to limit in advance the fields of application of the dialectical–relational approach.

The relationship between 'approach' and 'applications' is not a simple one. The dialectical–relational approach in its current form has changed through the process of being 'applied' in various fields. The beginnings of this approach can be seen in my work on discourse and social change in the early 1990s (see especially Fairclough, 1992a, 1995a), which itself arose out of earlier work on relations between language, ideology and power (Fairclough, 1989,1991). Early applications of that version of CDA included the 'marketization' of higher education and the 'enterprise culture' project launched by the Thatcher government, as well as various aspects of political and media discourse (Fairclough, 1995b) and 'critical language awareness' in education (Fairclough, 1992b). Important theoretical developments arising out of this work were the conceptualization of orders of discourse (a concept used already in Fairclough, 1989, 1991, 1992a) as the semiotic dimension of networks of social practices, and the development of 'recontextualization' as a CDA category in Chouliaraki's research on classroom discourse (Chouliaraki, 1995; Chouliaraki and Fairclough, 1999), and the foregrounding of the dialectics of discourse. One application at this stage was to the political discourse of New Labour (Fairclough, 2000a). Further theoretical developments arose through exploring neglected semiotic issues in 'critical realism' (Fairclough et al., 2004), and the incorporation of the dialectical–relational approach within 'cultural political economy' (Jessop, 2004), which I addressed specifically from a CDA perspective in my research on globalization and 'transition' in Central and Eastern Europe[2] (Fairclough, 2006).

Methodology

I have referred to a 'methodology' for using a dialectical–relational version of CDA in transdisciplinary social research rather than a 'method', because I also see the process as a theoretical one in which methods are selected according to how the *object of research* (Bourdieu and Wacquant, 1992) is theoretically constructed. So it is not just a matter of 'applying methods' in the usual sense – we cannot so sharply separate theory and method. This version of CDA is associated with a *general* method, which I discuss below, but the specific methods used for a particular piece of research arise from the theoretical process of constructing its object.

We can identify 'steps' or 'stages' in the methodology only on condition that these are not interpreted in a mechanical way: these are essential parts of the methodology (a matter of its 'theoretical order'), and while it does make partial sense to proceed from one to the next (a matter of the 'procedural order'), the relationship between them in doing research is not simply that of sequential order. For instance, the 'step' I refer to below of constructing the 'object of research' does need to precede subsequent steps, but it also makes sense to 'loop' back to it in the light of subsequent steps, seeing the formulation of the object of research as a preoccupation throughout. It is also helpful to distinguish the 'theoretical' and 'procedural' from the 'presentational' order one chooses to follow in, for instance, writing a paper – other generally rhetorical factors will affect the order in which one presents one's analysis.

The methodology can be seen as a variant of Bhaskar's 'explanatory critique' (Bhaskar, 1986; Chouliaraki and Fairclough, 1999), which can be formulated in four 'stages' and which can be further elaborated as 'steps':

Stage 1: Focus upon a social wrong, in its semiotic aspect.
Stage 2: Identify obstacles to addressing the social wrong.
Stage 3: Consider whether the social order 'needs' the social wrong.
Stage 4: Identify possible ways past the obstacles.

Stage 1: Focus upon a social wrong, in its semiotic aspect

CDA is a form of critical social science geared to a better understanding of the nature and sources of social wrongs, the obstacles to addressing them and possible ways of overcoming those obstacles. 'Social wrongs' can be understood in broad terms as aspects of social systems, forms or orders which are detrimental to human well-being, and which could in principle be ameliorated if not eliminated, though perhaps only through major changes in these systems, forms or orders. Examples might be poverty, forms of inequality, lack of freedom or racism. Of course, what constitutes a 'social wrong' is a controversial matter, and CDA is inevitably involved in debates and arguments about this which go on all the time.[3]

We can elaborate Stage 1 in two steps:

Step 1:   Select a research topic which relates to or points up a social wrong and which can productively be approached in a transdisciplinary way with a particular focus on dialectical relations between semiotic and other 'moments'.

We might, for instance, conclude that such an approach is potentially 'productive' because there are significant semiotic features of the topic which have not been sufficiently attended to in existing social research. A topic might attract our interest because it has been prominent in the relevant academic literature, or is a focus of practical attention in the domain or field at issue (in political debate or debates over questions of management or 'leadership', in media commentary and so forth). Topics are often 'given', and they sometimes virtually select themselves – who could doubt for instance that 'immigration', 'terrorism', 'globalization' or 'security' are important contemporary topics, with significant implications for human well-being, which researchers should attend to? Selecting such topics has the advantage of ensuring that research is relevant to the issues, problems and wrongs of the day, but also the danger that their very obviousness can lead us to take them too much at face value. We cannot assume that such topics are coherent research objects; to 'translate' topics into objects, we need to theorize them.

Step 2:   Construct objects of research for initially identified research topics by theorizing them in a transdisciplinary way.

Anticipating the example I shall discuss below, let us assume that the selected research topic is the relationship between national strategies and policies and the 'global economy': strategies and policies which are developed for the global economy, or the adaptation of national strategies and policies for the global economy. We might pin this down by focusing, for instance, on strategies and policies to enhance 'competitiveness' in particular countries (the example I discuss relates to competitiveness policies in the UK). As a topic for critical research, this seems plausible enough: a preoccupation of contemporary governments is indeed adapting to the 'global economy', and this process does indeed have implications for human well-being (it is widely presented as a way towards greater prosperity and opportunity, but as entailing suffering and insecurity for some people). One – controversial – formulation of the social wrong in this case might be that the well-being (material prosperity, security, political freedom, etc.) of some people – arguably the majority – is being unfairly or unjustly sacrificed for the interests of others. I shall focus below on one particular, political aspect of the social wrong: the suppression of political differences in favour of a national consensus on strategies and policies.

Constructing an object of research for this topic involves drawing upon relevant bodies of theory in various disciplines to go beyond and beneath the obviousness of the topic, and since the focus is on a specifically semiotic 'point of entry' into researching it, these should include theories of semiosis and discourse. There are no 'right answers' to the question of which theoretical perspectives to draw upon: it is a matter of researchers' judgements about which perspectives can provide a rich theorization as a basis for defining coherent objects for critical research which can deepen understanding of the processes at issue, their implications for human well-being and the possibilities for improving well-being. One must work in a transdisciplinary way, either in research teams which bring together specialists in relevant disciplines, or by engaging with literature in such disciplines.

What theoretical perspectives might be drawn upon in this case? These might include (political) economic theories which theorize and analyse the 'global economy' and may take positions on whether and how it constitutes a 'realm of necessity', a fact of life; State and political theory which probe the character and functioning of the State and of national and international politics in the era of 'globalization'; theories of 'global ethnography' which address how local groups and individuals seek to adapt to but also sometimes test and challenge the 'global economy' as a realm of necessity. The importance of discourse theory is indicated by this implicit questioning of the 'global economy': a central issue in both the academic literature and practical responses to the 'global economy' in politics, workplaces and everyday life is the relationship between reality and discourse – the reality and the discourses of the 'global economy' and of its impact, implications and ramifications. We can initially identify an analysis of the complex relationship between reality and discourse as a general formulation of the object of research for a semiotic 'point of entry' into this topic, but I shall suggest a more specific formulation, linked to the example I shall discuss, in the section below on political discourse analysis.

Stage 2: Identify obstacles to addressing the social wrong

Stage 2 approaches the social wrong in a rather indirect way by asking what it is about the way in which social life is structured and organized that prevents it from being addressed. This requires bringing in analyses of the social order, and one 'point of entry' into this analysis can be semiotic, which entails selecting and analysing relevant 'texts' and addressing the dialectical relations between semiosis and other social elements.

Steps 1–3 can be formulated as follows:

1. Analyse dialectical relations between semiosis and other social elements: between orders of discourse and other elements of social practices, between texts and other elements of events.
2. Select texts, and focuses and categories for their analysis, in the light of and appropriate to the constitution of the object of research.

3. Carry out analyses of texts, both interdiscursive analysis, and linguistic/semiotic analysis.

Taken together, these three steps indicate an important feature of this version of CDA: textual analysis is only a part of semiotic analysis (discourse analysis), and the former must be adequately framed within the latter. The aim is to develop a specifically semiotic 'point of entry' into objects of research which are constituted in a transdisciplinary way, through dialogue between different theories and disciplines. The analysis of texts can effectively contribute to this only in so far as it is located within a wider analysis of the object of research in terms of dialectical relations between semiotic and other elements which comprehend relations between the level of social practices and the level of events (and between orders of discourse and texts).

I shall not elaborate much on the three steps at this stage, because I think they will be clearer when I work through them using the example below.

There is one point about Step 3 however. I said above that although the particular methods of textual analysis used in a specific case depend upon the object of research, this version of CDA does have a general method of analysis. I alluded to this in the first section: textual analysis includes both linguistic analysis (and if relevant analysis of other semiotic forms, such as visual images) and interdiscursive analysis (analysis of which genres, discourses and styles are drawn upon, and how they are articulated together). Moreover, interdiscursive analysis has the crucial effect of constituting a mediating 'interlevel' which connects both linguistic analysis with relevant forms of social analysis, and the analysis of the text as part of an event with the analysis of social practices – in more general terms, the analysis of event (action, strategy) with the analysis of structure. Why so? Because interdiscursive analysis compares how genres, discourses and styles are articulated together in a text as part of a specific event, and in more stable and durable orders of discourses as part of networks of practices, which (qua *social* practices) are objects of various forms of social analysis.

Stage 3: Consider whether the social order 'needs' the social wrong

It is not awfully obvious what this means, and I shall try to clarify it by again anticipating the example. I indicated above that the social wrong I shall focus on when I get to the example is the suppression of political differences over the global economy and national responses to it in favour of seeking to create a national consensus, which is substantively realized in discourse. In what sense might the social order 'need' this? Perhaps in the sense – again anticipating the discussion below – that the internationally dominant strategy for globalizing an economic order based upon neo-liberal principles requires that states be able to operate in support of this strategy without being encumbered by the 'old' adversarial politics. Stage 3 leads us to consider whether the social wrong in focus is inherent to the social order, whether it can be addressed within it, or only by changing it. It is a way of linking 'is' to 'ought': if a social order can be shown to inherently give rise to major social wrongs, then that is a reason for thinking that perhaps it should be changed. It also connects with questions of ideology: discourse is ideological in so far as it contributes to sustaining particular relations of power and domination.

Stage 4: Identify possible ways past the obstacles

Stage 4 moves the analysis from negative to positive critique: identifying, with a focus on dialectical relations between semiosis and other elements, possibilities within the existing social process for overcoming obstacles to addressing the social wrong in question. This includes developing a semiotic 'point of entry' into research on the ways in which these obstacles are actually tested, challenged and resisted, be it within organized political or social groups or movements, or more informally by people in the course of their ordinary working, social and domestic lives. A specifically semiotic focus would include ways in which dominant discourse is reacted to, contested, criticized and opposed (in its argumentation, its construal of the world, its construal of social identities and so forth).

To conclude this section, let me list the core analytical categories of this approach to CDA which I have introduced so far:

- *semiosis* (and other social elements)
- *discourse/genre/style, order of discourse* (and *social practices*)
- *text* (and *social event*)
- *interdiscursivity* (and *interdiscursive analysis*)
- *recontextualization*
- *operationalization* (enactment, inculcation, materialization).

An example: political discourse analysis

The texts I shall discuss below are political texts: the Foreword to a government document written by former British Prime Minister Tony Blair, and a critique of Blair's 'New Labour' government by two former members of the Labour Party. As I have said, how a research topic is constituted as an object of research determines both the selection of texts for analysis and the nature of the analysis. In this section, I shall suggest a more specific formulation of the object of research for the research topic anticipated above ('adapting national strategy and policy for the global economy'), which entails some discussion of political theories of the contemporary 'political condition', and the main issues and priorities it suggests for analysis of politics and political discourse. I shall discuss the theoretical perspectives on the character of contemporary politics and the State especially in advanced capitalist countries like Britain, but I should emphasize that this discussion is necessarily partial given the spatial limitations of the Chapter. The material in this section will also help with Step 1 of Stage 2 of the methodology when we get to the texts – analysing dialectical relations between semiosis and other elements, especially at the level of social practices and orders of discourse.

Let me begin with a highly condensed summary analysis of the contemporary 'political condition', in the form of four major claims:

- Globalization in its dominant neo-liberal form has been associated with changes in the State and national (as well as international) politics (Harvey, 2003; Pieterse, 2004).
- There is a tendency of the State to become a 'competition state' with the primary objective of securing competitive advantage for the capital based within its borders (Jessop, 2002).
- There is an associated tendency within mainstream politics for the political division and contestation (e.g. between political parties) characteristic of the previous period to weaken, and for consensus to emerge on the main strategy and policy issues (Rancière, 2006).
- This tendency constitutes a fundamental political danger; not only is it a threat to democracy, it also creates a vacuum which can be filled by nationalism and xenophobia (Mouffe, 2005; Rancière, 1995).

The fourth point is based upon particular views of the general character of (democratic) politics and of politics in modern democracies. I shall refer specifically to Rancière's version. He argues that democracies, both ancient and modern, are mixed forms, as anticipated by Aristotle when he characterized 'a good regime' as a 'mixture of constitutions … there should appear to be elements of both (oligarchy and democracy) yet at the same time of neither … the oligarch sees oligarchy and the democrat democracy' (see Aristotle, *Politics* IV: 1294b, cited in Everson [1996]). This follows from the fact that 'the question of politics begins in every city with the existence of the mass of the *aporoi*, those who have no means, and the small number of the *euporoi*, those who have them' (Rancière, 1995: 13). The task of politics is to calm and control the irreducible conflict between rich and poor, which means curbing the excesses of democracy. What we now call 'democracies' are actually oligarchies in which government is exercised by the minority over the majority. What makes them specifically democratic is that the power of oligarchies rests upon the power of the people, most obviously because governments are elected. In democracies, oligarchy and democracy are opposing principles in tension, and any regime is an unstable compromise between them. The public sphere is the sphere of encounters and conflicts between these principles: governments tend to reduce and appropriate the public sphere, relegating non-State actors to the private sphere; democracy is the struggle against this privatization, to enlarge the public sphere and oppose the public/private division imposed by government.

In contemporary democracies, the 'conflictual equilibrium' associated with popular sovereignty is being undermined. The oligarchic system is being combined with a 'consensual vision' on the claim that contemporary reality, the global economy and the prospect of endless 'growth' which it promises, do not leave us with a choice. Government is the business of 'managing the local effects of global necessity', which requires consensus and an end to the 'archaic' indulgence of political division. Oligarchies are tempted by the vision of governing without the people, i.e. without the division of the people, which means effectively without politics, rendering popular sovereignty problematic. But the suppressed division inevitably returns, both in the form of mobilization outside the political system (e.g. against the negative effects of neo-liberal globalization or the Iraq war) and in the dangerous form of extreme-right nationalism and xenophobia.

A priority for political analysis is consequently contemporary processes of *depoliticization*, which is by no means a new strategy (according to Rancière (1995), it is 'the oldest task of politics') but is now emerging in a particularly profound and threatening form. Depoliticization is the exclusion of issues and/or of people from processes of political deliberation and decision – placing them outside politics. But *politicization* is equally a priority if we are to analyse the tension between the principles of oligarchy and democracy, the democratic response to depoliticization, and how responses might develop a momentum capable of contesting the push towards depoliticization. Others have also identified depoliticization and politicization as priorities (Hay, 2007; Muntigl, 2002b; Palonen, 1993; Sondermann, 1997), but from different theoretical perspectives.

This prioritization provides a basis for questioning the centrality which has been attributed to other problems and issues. Let me briefly mention two. First, the centrality attributed to 'sub-politics' or 'life politics' by theorists of 'reflexive modernity', which is linked to the recent prominence of 'identity politics'. This accords with the perspective above in giving prominence to 'grassroots' political action, but clashes with it in construing such politics as an alternative to adversarial politics centred around the political system. The 'grassroots' politics of politicization is both defined and limited by the opposing logic of depoliticization, which means that state- and government-focused adversarial politics is by no means outdated. Second, the centrality attributed by, for instance, those influenced by Habermas to 'deliberative democracy' also tends to be associated with the assumption that adversarial politics can be superseded and to construe political dialogue as a rational process of consensus-formation, rather than a process which allows divisions, differences and conflicts to be contained within a shared political community without the assumption that these are just 'problems' waiting to be 'solved'. In different theoretical terms, we could say: these are contradictions, and although they can be managed, they cannot be solved within the parameters of the existing system (Jessop, 2002). This does not diminish or ignore cooperation in politics: conflict in political dialogue requires cooperation (only those who are cooperating at a certain level can stage a conflict), and adversarial politics necessarily includes cooperative moments (e.g. the formation of alliances).

We can fruitfully develop a specifically semiotic 'point of entry' into analysing the processes of depoliticization and politicization. I shall illustrate this below in my analysis of the texts. This does not exclude other issues and associated categories which have tended to receive more attention in political discourse analysis, and indeed I shall refer to some (legitimation, manipulation, ideology, cooperation and identity). But it does imply a different 'mapping' of the relations between categories which may lead to reconceptualizing or changing some of them.

Politicization and depoliticization are high-level strategies or 'macro-strategies'; so are legitimation and delegitimation. Strategies combine goals and means, and these macro-strategies are both means for achieving oligarchic or democratic goals (e.g. governing with minimal interference from political divisions, or pushing political differences into the public sphere), and goals in their own right associated with further strategies as means. We can identify strategies *for* (de)politicization and (de)legitimation – for instance, 'authorization' and 'rationalization' have been suggested as legitimation strategies (Van Leeuwen, 2007; Van Leeuwen and Wodak, 1999). All of these are *political* strategies, not semiotic (or 'discourse') strategies, though they are generally realized semiotically.

I suggested above that the object of research could be broadly formulated as the complex relationship between discourse and reality in adapting national strategy and policy for the global economy. We can now reformulate it more precisely: semiotic realizations of strategies of depoliticization and politicization in national responses to the 'global economy', focusing on the competitiveness policy in the UK.

An illustration: analysing political texts

I come now to the analysis of two sample texts. The one I shall begin with is the Foreword written by the former British Prime Minister Tony Blair to the Department of Trade and Industry's White Paper on Competitiveness (DTI, 1998 – see Appendix 1). I shall organize my comments according to the stages and steps listed in the Methodology section, but I have just been effectively discussing aspects of Stage 1 so I shall keep my comments on it brief.

Stage 1: Focus upon a social wrong, in its semiotic aspect

The social wrong I shall focus upon is the suppression or marginalization of political differences over important issues of strategy and policy – how to respond nationally to radical international economic changes (and the prior question of what the changes actually are) – in favour of creating a consensus, which is, as I indicated above, a social wrong in that it undermines democracy but also poses the danger that dissent, which cannot be politically articulated, may emerge in nationalist or xenophobic forms. A semiotic point of entry is possible and fruitful, focusing upon semiotic realizations of the macro-strategy of depoliticization, in accordance with the construction of the object of research which I have discussed above. The second text, an extract from a book (Brown and Coates, 1996) written by former members of the Labour Party criticizing Blair's 'New Labour' government, exemplifies semiotic realizations of the macro-strategy of politicization. (Note that both macro-strategies may however be at work in the same text.) Blair's text is representative of the dominant tendency of the times towards depoliticization; but this tendency coexists with politicizing responses such as that of the second text, even if the latter often have a relatively marginal effect on government strategy and policy. I have already discussed steps 1 and 2 above, on the construction of an object of research for the research topic, in anticipation of the illustration, so we can move on to Stage 2.

Stage 2: Identify obstacles to addressing the social wrong

I shall discuss Stage 2 by taking each of the three steps it includes in turn.

Step 1: Analyse dialectical relations between semiosis and other social elements (orders of discourse and elements of social practices, texts and elements of events).

Step 1 also implicitly includes the dialectic between structures (at the intermediate level of social practices) and events (and strategies). I have already (in the previous section) given an indication of the social practices and orders of discourse at issue here, but let me fill this out a little with respect to the 're-structuring' and 're-scaling' (Jessop, 2002) tendencies associated with contemporary capitalism, and a brief note on New Labour in Britain.

Re-structuring is changes in structural relations, notably between economic and non-economic fields, which include extensive 'colonization' of the latter (including politics and the State) by the former; re-scaling is changing relations between global, regional, national and local scales of social life, including changes in government and governance. Analysing these tendencies would help contextualize the UK strategies and policies which are in focus – i.e. help determine what they are a part of. National governments are increasingly incorporated within larger networks which include not only other governments but also international agencies (e.g. the European Union, the World Bank, the IMF), business networks and so forth. Governments, according to Castells (1996), are increasingly coming to function as 'nodes' within a transnational network based upon a business–government complex, whose central 'functions' are focused upon creating the conditions (financial, fiscal, legal, 'human capital', etc.) for successful competition in the 'global economy'. If the government strategies and policies in focus here are locked into this powerful network, this in itself constitutes a substantial obstacle to addressing the social wrong.

But these processes of re-structuring and re-scaling have an important semiotic dimension: the networks of social practices which they entail are also orders of discourse which themselves cut across structural and scalar boundaries. For example, the dominant neo-liberal discourse of globalization illustrated in the first text is dominant in education as well as politics, and in the European Union, the World Bank and many other countries apart from Britain. There are also genres and styles which are disseminated structurally and in scale in a similar way (Fairclough, 2006). Moreover, the semiotic dimension is fundamental to re-structuring and re-scaling, in the sense that these processes are 'semiotically driven'. They begin as discourses which constitute 'imaginaries' (Jessop, 2004, 2008) – imaginary projections – for new relations of structure and scale in economies, government, education and so forth; these may become hegemonic, or dominant, and may be widely recontextualized; in so far as they do become hegemonic, they are 'operationalized' in new structures, practices, relations and institutions; and the operationalization itself has a partly semiotic aspect in the emergence and dissemination of genres and 'genre networks' (see below), which enable the governance of these complex new networks, as well as styles. The semiotic dimension, deeply embedded within and constitutive of the new structural and scalar relations, is itself a part of the obstacles to addressing the social wrong.

With respect to the dialectic between texts and other elements of social events, the general point is that political texts are not some superficial embroidery upon political events but a fundamental, constitutive part of them. In this case, for example, the strategies and policies of the Blair government for building British 'competitiveness' in adapting to the 'global economy' have a clearly textual character. They are formed, disseminated and legitimized within complex chains and networks of events (committee meetings, reports, parliamentary debates, press statements and press conferences, etc.) which are largely chains and networks of texts – i.e. different types of texts which are regularly and systematically linked together. They are linked for instance in accordance with the 'genre networks' I referred to above – systematically linked genres (e.g. discussion, report, debate) which semiotically constitute procedures – in this case, procedures of governance (on 'chains' of events, texts and genres, see Fairclough, 2003). These strategy and policy processes thus have a largely textual character, and require textual analysis. The illustrative examples are just two small samples from the complex networks of texts involved.

The analysis would need to go into some detail about politics and social change in Britain. I have no space for such detail here, but let me make a couple of points (see further Fairclough, 2000a). First, 'New Labour' abandoned the traditional social democracy of the British Labour Party to embrace the neo-liberalism of preceding Conservative governments (those of Margaret Thatcher and John Major). The effect was to produce a neo-liberal consensus on major policy issues within mainstream politics and a common political discourse – the associated tendency to exclude opposition is precisely the 'social wrong' I am addressing. Second, the infamous preoccupation of New Labour with media 'spin' (close management and manipulation of the presentation of policies and events in the media) indicates the growing importance of semiotic processes (political 'communication') in government. Thus, the form of politics which has developed with New Labour poses specifically semiotic obstacles to addressing the social wrong at issue.

Step 2: Select texts and categories for analysis

With respect to Step 2, the constitution of the object of research indicates the selection of texts in which the macro-strategies of depoliticization and politicization are semiotically realized. My examples here are both written texts, but one would also want to include, for instance, not only discussions, debates and interviews on TV and radio, and websites, but also material from campaigns, protests and demonstrations centred upon 'the global economy' and government strategy and policy oriented towards it, and material representing how people experience and react to the drive for 'competitiveness' in a variety of situated contexts (e.g. conversations and discussions within workplaces). Appropriate focuses and categories for the analysis include semiotic strategies which realize de/politicization, including argumentation and rhetorical strategies, as well as semiotic aspects and realizations of legitimation, manipulation, ideology, cooperation and identity. I shall be more specific about some of these in discussing the texts.

Step 3: Carry out analyses of texts

The first text is structured as an argument whose structure we can schematically reconstruct as follows:

Premises: The modern world is changing.
                  There are opportunities to succeed and prosper in the modern
                  world.
                  If we want to succeed and prosper, we must compete effectively.
Implicit premise: (We do want to succeed and prosper.)
Conclusion: Therefore, we must compete (more) effectively.

The argumentation realizes semiotically the macro-strategy of legitimation, and specifically the strategy of rationalization: it is an example of the government's attempt to legitimize its political strategy and the policies associated with it as necessary responses to the situation.

The argument is formally valid, but whether it is sound or not (i.e. whether it is a reasonable argument) depends upon the truth of its premises. We can challenge the argument, argue that it is fallacious, by challenging the truth of its premises (Ieţcu, 2006). I want to specifically question the premises on the grounds that they (a) predicate the possible success of a problematic identity category as subject ('we'), and (b) falsely claim that the change attributed to the modern world is simply an inevitable fact of life which 'we' must accept. Both of these flaws in the premises can be associated with the macro-strategy of depoliticization.

With respect to the first flaw, the identity category 'we' is problematic in that it is based upon a false equation between 'we' = 'Britain' and 'we' = all the citizens of Britain: if Britain achieves 'success' or 'prosperity', it does not follow that all of its citizens do. This is the 'fallacy of division', when a general category has properties which are mistakenly attributed to each of its parts. One sentence clearly implies that this *does* follow: 'That is the route to commercial success and prosperity for all'. This fallacy is a banal feature of governmental discourse, but it is fundamental to the macro-strategy of depoliticization, whose basic strategic goal is to dedifferentiate potentially antagonistic identities – the internal division of the political community into 'us' and 'them'. In this sense, identity and the semiotic construal of identities are a major focus in analysis which prioritizes depoliticization.

The issue in semiotic terms is *personal deixis*. There are two personal 'deictic centres', or positionings of the author (Blair) with respect to identity: he positions himself within two group identities – 'we' = the government, and 'we' = the country. It is commonplace in the literature on identity that identity entails difference – 'we' entails 'they' (Connolly, 1991). We might say that 'we' = the government is implicitly construed in opposition to 'they' = previous governments which pursued strategies which are rejected because they 'did not and cannot work': 'old-fashioned state intervention' and 'naive reliance on markets'; whereas 'we' = the country is construed in opposition to 'competitors'. But notice that the construal of personal deixis excludes a 'we/they' division both within the political community ('Britain') and within the contemporary political field (political system), where no contemporaneous political 'opposition' is construed. The implication is that there is consensus within both the political community and the political field. This is depoliticization.

Texts semiotically construe identities and simultaneously seek to make these construals persuasive. The fact that we can show fallacies in Blair's argument does not mean that it will be widely perceived as fallacious, and we must consider what might make the argument and construal of identities persuasive. This brings us to the second flaw, in the construal of world change.

Dominant construals of 'the new global order' have certain predictable linguistic characteristics (on the linguistic categories I mention below, see Fairclough, 2003): processes of change are construed without responsible social agents; they are construed in a timeless, ahistorical present; statements about the new economy (which are often very familiar truisms) are construed categorically and authoritatively as unmodalized truths, and there is a movement from the 'is' of the economic to the 'ought' of the political – from what is categorically the case to what 'we' ought to do in response; the new economic reality is construed as indifferent to place; and series of evidences or appearances in the new economy are construed paratactically as lists. I have shown elsewhere (Fairclough, 2000b) that these features are sustained through recontextualization, appearing in economic texts (e.g. texts of the World Bank), political texts, educational texts and so forth, as well as on different scales.

They are also evident in Blair's text, and they can be seen as aspects of the semiotic realization of depoliticization. In the construal of economic change in the 'modern world', there is an absence of responsible social agents. Agents of material processes are abstract or inanimate. In the first paragraph, 'change' is the agent in the first (passive) sentence, and 'new technologies' and 'new markets' are agents in the second – agents, notice, of intransitive verbs ('emerge', 'open up') which construe change as happenings or processes without agents. The third sentence is existential – 'new competitors' and 'new opportunities' are merely claimed to exist, not located within processes of change. Notice also that in the third paragraph, the inanimate 'this new world' is the agent of 'challenges', construing change itself as articulating what responses to it are necessary. By contrast, when it comes to national responses to these implacable and impersonal processes of world change, social agents are fully present – business, the government, the DTI and especially 'we'.

Turning to time, tense and modality, world change is construed in the ahistorical 'timeless' present tense, as indeed are national responses, and, in terms of modality, through authoritative categorical assertions of truisms (e.g. 'The modern world is swept by change', and indeed all five statements in the first paragraph). The only historical reference is to the 'old-fashioned' strategies in paragraph 4. There is a movement from 'is' to 'ought'. 'Ought' is implicit in paragraphs 2 and 3: 'our success depends on how well we exploit our most valuable assets' implies that we should exploit them; 'this new world challenges business to be innovative' and 'government to create' imply that business and government should do these things. From paragraph 5 onwards, 'ought' is explicit and recurrent – the modal verb 'must' occurs six times. The domain of 'is' is world change; the domain of 'ought' is national responses: a divide is textually constructed between economics and politics (there is an 'industrial policy', but focused on enabling the economic process rather than radically shaping it), fact and value, which excludes the former from the latter. This differs from the social democratic tradition from which New Labour has come; earlier Labour governments used political power to change the economy, for example by nationalizing private industries, taking them into state control. In contrast with economic processes, political processes do have responsible social agents: the agent in processes modalized with 'must' is in five cases 'we' and in one case 'the government'. Summing up, world change is a process without a history which 'we' must respond to. Moreover, world change is implicitly construed as indifferent to place – there are no place expressions in the first or third paragraphs.

The syntax is paratactic,[4] in relations between both sentences and phrases within sentences. The first paragraph, for instance, consists of three paratactically related sentences (the second and third contain paratactically related clauses), listing evidences of world change. The same is true of the second paragraph. Notice that the sequencing of these sentences is not significant and is changeable (with minor rewording) without any substantive meaning change. Indeed, what is included in this list of evidences is somewhat arbitrary; for instance, the second sentence of the first paragraph might have been 'Huge amounts of money move across the globe in a fraction of a second, and even our family cat, Socks, has his own homepage on the World Wide Web'. The second clause is fanciful only in that Blair does not have a cat called Socks. It was actually included in a very similar list in a book by Bill Clinton. What is significant, rhetorically, is the relentless accumulation of evidences of change – what Clarke and Newman (1998) call 'the cascade of change' – which persuasively (and manipulatively) establishes the new economy as simple fact, what we must live with and respond to.

Summing up, change is authoritatively construed as lists of known appearances (and truisms) in the present which are indifferent to place and whose social agency is effaced, and which must be responded to in certain ways. These features together construe the new economy as a simple fact to which there is no alternative. They locate the 'global economy' within the 'realm of necessity', and therefore outside the 'realm of contingency and deliberation', i.e. outside the realm of politics, semiotically realizing the macro-strategy of depoliticization (Hay, 2007). We can say that in so far as this sort of discourse achieves significant public acceptance, which it has, it is part of the obstacles to addressing the social wrong.

Let me briefly comment on interdiscursive analysis. One can see Blair's text as recontextualizing analyses of the 'global economy' more fully elaborated in texts produced such as within the World Bank, and their particular discourse (construals of, narratives of and arguments about the 'global economy'). Blair's text is not primarily an analytical text but an advocative text, arguing for 'necessary' policies. But it is interdiscursively complex in grounding this advocative argument in the recontextualized analysis, combining analytical and advocative genres (as well as economic and political discourses). This type of recontextualization and interdiscursive hybridity is common as a semiotic realization of a favoured legitimation strategy: legitimizing by appeal to expert knowledge. Notice that the expert discourse is not the same here as it might be in specialist economic texts. For instance, in the first paragraph, the construal of change in the global economy is stripped down to three short sentences which furthermore incorporate characteristic features of political rhetoric (the dramatic metaphor 'swept by change', the antithesis of 'new competitors but also great new opportunities'), and which constitute dramatic and potentially persuasive formulations of premises in the argument. Recontextualization involves transformation to suit the new context, which affects forms of interdiscursive hybridity.

In discussing Stage 2, I have identified a number of obstacles to addressing the social wrong at issue, and shown that they are partly semiotic in nature. Let me summarize them: the national and international networks that government strategies and policies are embedded within; the consensual character of main-stream politics in Britain; and an influential political discourse, exemplified in the Blair text, which in various ways contributes to depoliticizing the global economy and national responses to it.

Stage 3: Consider whether the social order 'needs' the social wrong

I anticipated this example in discussing Stage 3 in the Methodology section, where I suggested how the suppression of political differences in favour of con-sensus might be interpreted as necessary for states to operate effectively within the hegemonic, neo-liberal strategy. We might add that achieving a broad con-sensus within the political system depends upon semiotic conditions – achiev-ing semiotic hegemony, or broad acceptance of the sort of discourse we have here. And as I noted above, this can be interpreted in terms of ideology as the naturalization of meanings which sustain relations of power and domination. So it seems plausible that the social order does 'need' the social wrong in this case – addressing it might require wider changes in the social order – and that, since the wrong has a partly semiotic character, it also 'needs' certain charac-teristics of contemporary political discourse.

Stage 4: Identify possible ways past the obstacles

At this point, I shall introduce the second text (see Appendix 2), an extract from a book (Brown and Coates, 1996) written by two longstanding members of the Labour Party about New Labour's view of what they call 'capitalist glob-alization'. This will allow some necessarily brief, partial and sketchy comments on the other main macro-strategy – politicization.

I mentioned one adversarial feature in the first text: a rejection of the 'old-fashioned state intervention' and the 'naive reliance on markets' of previous governments, while implying that there were no contemporaneous divisions on the nature of 'world change' or the national strategies needed to adjust to it. The second text, by contrast, enters into adversarial dialogue with contem-poraries, specifically Blairites. The macro-strategy of politicization is semioti-cally realized in the text's dialogicality. Specifically, there are claims which are denials of claims made 'elsewhere', by New Labour politicians among others: 'What has changed is not that capital is more mobile' and 'it is not true that national governments – and by extension the European Union – are totally lacking in powers to employ against the arbitrary actions of transnational cap-ital'. In this respect, the strategy is to politicize by construing the nature of 'world change' and government responses as controversial matters, subject to political difference and division.

Text 2 also politicizes by counterposing to the New Labour narrative of col-laboration between government and business a narrative of conflict between government and business, capital and labour. Notice that both texts construe the global(ized) economy as a reality which countries need to adjust to, but in radically different ways. In the second but not the first, the construal of the global(ized) economy does include responsible social agents: the companies, whose actions are construed in general and negative terms ('moving internationally from bases … ', 'the arbitrary actions of transnational capital', 'divide and conquer'). The text also construes relations between the companies and national governments, contrasting the 'clientelist' relations which tend to exist and which New Labour advocates ('nation-states … clients of transnational companies') with adversarial relations which could and by implication should exist ('employing' their 'powers … against the arbitrary actions of transnational capital', 'making or withholding tax concessions', 'bargaining'). The same contrast between what is and what could/should be is construed in relations between the EU and national governments ('reinforcing' the status of nation states as 'clients' of the companies, versus 'offering a lead and challenge to the nation states').

In sum, whereas text 1 depoliticizes by construing a consensus on the global economy as an inevitable fact of life and building national competitiveness as a necessary response, text 2 politicizes by construing the globalized economy as a stake in struggles between governments and transnationals, and capital and labour, and by opposing that construal to the government's consensualist construal. But the mere existence of texts which politicize in this way does not amount to 'ways past the obstacles'. This text offers an imaginary for a different, politicizing strategy in response to a differently conceived global(ized) economy; it shows that different imaginaries are possible and indeed exist, but we would also need to consider how feasible it would be to operationalize this or some other imaginary in a strategy which could actually succeed and be implemented in the face of the sort of obstacles I have begun to indicate. It's not impossible, but it's difficult to see how at present: there are abundant alternative imaginaries, but there is currently no clear counter-hegemonic strategy. A fuller treatment than I have space for would include an analysis of attempts to develop oppositional strategies and their semiotic dimensions.

Discussion

The theoretical claim that relations between semiosis and other social elements are dialectical in character, and the methodological focus on these relations rather than on semiosis as such, mean that this approach to CDA is particularly attuned to transdisciplinary research, to working with the grain of various bodies of social theory and research, but at the same time bringing to them an enhancement of their capacity to address often neglected semiotic dimensions of their research objects, as well as taking from them perspectives and research logics which can contribute to the further development of the dialectical–relational approach itself.

As with any approach, there are things about which the dialectical–relational approach has little to say. We should distinguish however between issues and problems it has not got around to because others seemed more pressing or more interesting or simply because life is short, and issues and problems which fall outside its remit and are thus not issues and problems *for it* (though they may be for other approaches). An example of the former is a relative emphasis on the workings of power rather than the workings of reception, reaction and resistance to power – I stress relative because the latter have not been entirely neglected (see, for instance, Fairclough, 2006). Critics might reasonably say that I have 'done it again' in this chapter, spending more time on depoliticization than politicization. This has been a bias in my work, perhaps partly because of the sort of left-wing politics I was involved with in the 1970s, but it is not in my opinion a limitation of the approach as such. An example of the latter is a lack of attention to psychological and cognitive matters. I would agree that cognitively oriented research on discourse can complement the dialectical–relational approach, but I would not accept that an absence of attention to cognitive issues is a 'blindspot' in the approach, still less that it in some sense invalidates the approach.

Chilton, for example, has suggested that a proper understanding of the cognitive capacities of humans may lead to the conclusion that CDA is trying to teach people what they already know. 'Put bluntly, if people have a natural ability to treat verbal input critically, in what sense can CDA either reveal in discourse what people can … already detect for themselves or educate them to detect it for themselves?' (Chilton, 2005a). Yet the closing sentences of Chilton (2004) note that 'if people are indeed political animals … then they are also in principle *capable* of doing their own political critique. The important question is whether they are free to do so'. I agree. Chilton (2005a) argues that although there are various conditions under which people are not free, 'it is doubtful that any of them can be elucidated by purely linguistic or discourse-analytical means. For they would seem to have to do with economic forces or socio-political institutions'. The main problem with this argument is indicated by the contrast between 'purely' linguistic or discourse-analytical factors and economic forces or socio-political institutions. From a dialectical–relational perspective, economic forces and socio-political institutions *are* in part semiotic, and analysis has to be in part semiotic analysis. The fact that people have cognitive capacities which make them in principle capable of seeing through manipulative intentions and even doing their own political critique (which CDA, far from discounting, presupposes) does not mean that they are generally capable in practice of seeing through the complex dialectical relations between semiotic and non-semiotic elements which constitute the social, political and economic conditions of their lives.

FURTHER READING

Chouliaraki, L. and Fairclough, N. (1999) *Discourse in Late Modernity.* Edinburgh: Edinburgh University Press.
This book shows the relationships of an earlier version of this approach to various sources and influences in social theory and research.

Fairclough, N. (2000a) *New Labour, New Language?* London: Routledge.
A popular introduction to analysis of political discourse, based upon a simplified version of this approach to CDA.

Fairclough, N. (2003) *Analysing Discourse: Textual Analysis for Social Research.* London: Routledge.
This book focuses on using textual analysis in social research within the dialectical–relational approach, with many examples of possible applications.

Fairclough, N. (2005a) 'Critical discourse analysis', *Marges Linguistiques* 9: 76–94.
A recent overview of the dialectical–relational approach in an electronic journal available free of charge on the internet.

Fairclough, N. (2006) *Language and Globalization.* London: Routledge.
This text exemplifies the application of the dialectical–relational approach in transdisciplinary research on globalization.

Appendix 1 – Building the knowledge-driven economy

Foreword by the Prime Minister

The modern world is swept by change. New technologies emerge constantly; new markets are opening up. There are new competitors but also great new opportunities.

Our success depends on how well we exploit our most valuable assets: our knowledge, skills and creativity. These are the key to designing high-value goods and services and advanced business practices. They are at the heart of a modern, knowledge-driven economy.

This new world challenges business to be innovative and creative, to improve performance continuously, to build new alliances and ventures. But it also challenges government: to create and execute a new approach to industrial policy.

This is the purpose of this White Paper. Old-fashioned state intervention did not and cannot work. But neither does naive reliance on markets.

The government must promote competition, stimulating enterprise, flexibility and innovation by opening markets. But we must also invest in British capabilities when companies alone cannot: in education, in science and in the creation of a culture of enterprise. And we must promote creative partnerships which help companies: to collaborate for competitive advantage; to promote a long-term vision in a world of short-term pressures; to benchmark their performance against the best in the world; and to forge alliances with other businesses and employees. All this is the DTI's role.

We will not meet our objectives overnight. The White Paper creates a policy framework for the next ten years. We must compete effectively in today's tough markets if we are to prosper in the markets of tomorrow.

In government, in business, in our universities and throughout society, we must do much more to foster an entrepreneurial spirit: equipping ourselves for the long term, prepared to seize opportunities, committed to constant innovation and enhanced performance. That is the route to commercial success and prosperity for all. We must put the future on Britain's side.

The Rt Hon. Tony Blair MP, Prime Minister

Appendix 2

Capital has always been global, moving internationally from bases in the industrialized countries. What has changed is not that capital is more mobile ... but that the national bases are less important as markets and production centres. In other words, the big transnational companies are not only bigger but more free-standing ... The European Union, far from offering a lead and a challenge to the nation-states of Europe, reinforces their status as clients of the transnational companies. Indeed, this clientism applies not only to companies based in Europe ... While it is true that a national capitalism is no longer possible in a globalized economy, it is not true that national governments – and by extension the European Union – are totally lacking in powers to employ against the arbitrary actions of transnational capital. There is much that governments can do in bargaining – in making or withholding tax concessions, for example ... But such bargaining has to have an international dimension or the transnational companies can simply continue to divide and conquer ... New Labour appears to have abandoned what remained of Labour's internationalist traditions ... Yet the ICTFU, the European TUC and the Geneva trade groups all offer potential allies for strengthening the response of British labour to international capital (Brown and Coates, 1996: 172–4).

Notes

1 I am grateful to Isabela Ieţcu, Michael Meyer and Ruth Wodak for commenting on a draft version of the chapter.
2 *Critical realism* is a realist philosophy of science and social science which has been developed especially in the work of Roy Bhaskar (Bhaskar, 1986). *Cultural political economy* is a version of political economy which claims that economic processes

and systems are culturally and semiotically conditioned and embedded, as well as politically.

3   In the first edition of this book and in other publications, I referred to social 'problems' rather than 'wrongs'. I have changed this because I think that construing all wrongs as 'problems' which need 'solutions' – which can in principle be provided even if they have not been so far in practice – is part of the self-justifying (and one might say ideological) discourse of contemporary social systems in countries like Britain. The objection to it is that some wrongs are produced by systems and are not resolvable within them.

4   *Paratactic*–syntactic relations are relations between sentences, clauses or phrases which are grammatically equal, and are *coordinated*; they contrast with *hypotactic* relations, where there is one *main* sentence, clause or phrase, and others are *subordinated*.

References

Agar, M. (2002) *The Professional Stranger*. 3rd unrevised edn. San Diego, CA: Academic Press.

Alexander, J. C., Marx, G. T. and Williams, C. L. (eds) (2004) *Self, Social Structure, and Beliefs: Explorations in sociology*. Berkeley: University of California Press.

Altheide, D. L. and Johnson, J. M. (1994) 'Criteria for Assessing Interpretive Validity in Qualitative Research', in N. K. Denzin (ed.), *Handbook of Qualitative Research*. Thousand Oaks: Sage, pp. 485–499.

Anthonissen, C. (2001) 'On the Effectivity of Media Censorship: An analysis of linguistic, paralinguistic and other communicative devices used to defy media restrictions.' Unpublished PhD thesis, University of Vienna.

Anthonissen, C. and Blommaert, J. (eds) (2007) *Discourse and Human Rights Violations*. Amsterdam: Benjamins.

Argyle, M., Furnham, A. and Graham, J. A. (1981) *Social Situations*. Cambridge: Cambridge University Press.

Auer, P. (ed.) (1992) *The Contextualization of Language*. Amsterdam: Benjamins.

Augoustinos, M. and Walker, I. (1995) *Social Cognition: An integrated introduction*. London: Sage.

Baker, P. (2006) *Using Corpora in Discourse Analysis*. London: Continuum.

Baker, P. and McEnery, T. (2005) 'A corpus-based approach to discourses of refugees and asylum seekers in UN and newspaper texts', *Journal of Language and Politics* 4(2): 197–226.

Baker, P., McEnery, T. and Gabrielatos, C. (2007) 'Using collocation analysis to reveal the construction of minority groups: the case of refugees, asylum seekers and immigrants in the UK press', paper given at Corpus Linguistics 2007, University of Birmingham, 28–30 July. Available at: eprints.lancs.ac.uk/602/.

Baker, P., Gabrielatos, C., Khozravinik, M., Krzyżanowski, M., McEnery, T., and Wodak, R. (2008) 'A useful methodological synergy? Combining critical discourse analysis and corpus linguistics to examine discourses of refugees and asylum seekers in the UK press', *Discourse and Society* 19(3): 273–305.

Balke, F. (1998) 'Was zu denken zwingt. Gilles Deleuze, Felxi Guattari und das Außen der Philosophie', in J. Jurt (ed.), *Zeitgenössische Französische Denker: Eine Bilanz*. Freiburg im Breisgau: Rombach Litterae, pp. 187–210.

Bauer, M. W. and Aarts, B. (2000) 'Corpus Construction: A Principle for Qualitative Data Collection', in M. W. Bauer and G. Gaskell (eds), *Qualitative Researching with Text, Image and Sound*. London: Sage, pp. 19–37.

Bell, A. (1994) 'Climate of opinion: public and media discourse on the global environment', *Discourse and Society* 5(1): 33–64.

Bellah, R. N. (1973) *Emile Durkheim: On morality and society – selected writings*. Chicago: University of Chicago Press.

Berger, P. and Luckmann, T. (1966) *The Social Construction of Reality*. Harmondsworth: Penguin.

Bernstein, B. (1981) 'Codes, modalities and the process of cultural reproduction: a model', *Language and Society* 19: 327–363.

Bernstein, B. (1986) 'On Pedagogic Discourse', in J. Richardson (ed.), *Handbook for Theory and Research in the Sociology of Education*. Connecticut: Greenwood Press.

Bernstein, B. (1990) *The Structuring of Pedagogic Discourse*. London: Routledge.

Bhaskar, R. (1986) *Scientific Realism and Human Emancipation*. London: Verso.

Billig, M. (2003) 'Critical Discourse Analysis and the Development of New Science', in G. Weiss and R. Wodak (eds), *Critical Discourse Analysis: Theory and Interdisciplinarity*. London: MacMillan, pp. 35–46.

Billig, M. (2008) 'Nominalizing and de-nominalizing: a reply', *Discourse and Society*, in press.

Blau, P. M. (1964) *Exchange and Power in Social Life*. New York: Wiley.

Blommaert, J. (2005) *Discourse*. Cambridge: Cambridge University Press.

Blommaert, J. and Bulcaen, C. (2000) 'Critical Discourse Analysis', *Annual Review of Anthropology*, 29: 447–466.

Boden, D. and Zimmerman, D. H. (eds) (1991) *Talk and Social Structure: Studies in ethnomethodology and conversation analysis*. Berkeley: University of California Press.

Bourdieu, P. (1977) *Outline of a Theory of Practice*. Cambridge: Cambridge University Press.

Bourdieu, P. (1984) *Homo Academics*. Paris: Les Éditions de Minuit.

Bourdieu, P. (1989) *La Noblesse d'État: Grandes écoles et esprit de corps*. Paris: Éditiones de Minuit.

Bourdieu, P. (1991) *Language and Symbolic Power*. Cambridge: Polity Press.

Bourdieu, P. and Wacquant, L. (1992) *An Invitation to Reflexive Sociology*. Cambridge: Polity Press.

Boykoff, M. T. and Boykoff, J. M. (2004) 'Balance as bias: global warming and the US prestige press', *Global Environmental Changes – Human and Policy Dimensions* 14: 125–136.

Brown, B. M. and Coates, K. (1996) *The Blair Revelation: Deliverance for whom?* Nottingham: Spokesman.

Brown, G. and Yule, G. (1983) *Discourse Analysis*. Cambridge: Cambridge University Press.

Brünner, G. and Graefen, G. (eds) (1994) *Texte und Diskurse*. Opladen: Westdeutscher Verlag.

Bublitz, H. (1999) *Foucaults Archäologie des kulturellen Unbewußten: Zum Wissensarchiv und Wissensbegehren moderner Gesellschaften*. Frankfurt am Main: Campus.

Burr, V. (2003) *Social Constructionism*, 2nd edn. Hove: Routledge.

Caborn, J. (1999) 'Die Presse und die "Hauptstadtdebatte": Konstrukte der deutschen Einheit', in U. Kreft, H. Uske and S. Jäger (eds), *Kassensturz: Politische Hypotheken der Berliner Republik*. Duisburg: DISS, pp. 61–84.

Caborn, J. (2006) *Schleichende Wende: Diskurse von Nation und Erinnerung bei der Konstituierung der Berliner Republik*. Münster: Unrast.

Castells, M. (1996) *The Rise of the Network Society*. Oxford: Blackwell.

Charteris-Black, J. (2006) *Politics and Rhetoric*. Basingstoke: Palgrave.

Chilton, P. (1994a) '"La plaie qu'il convient de fermer": Les métaphores du discours raciste', *Journal of Pragmatics* 21(6): 583–619.

Chilton, P. (ed.) (1994b) *Schémas cognitifs du discours raciste francais*. Vol. 4. Rotterdam: Institute for Social Policy Research.

Chilton, P. (ed.) (1996a) *The Meaning of Security*. East Lansing: Michigan State University Press.

Chilton, P. (1996b) *Security Metaphors: Cold War discourse from containment to common European home*. Bern: Peter Lang.

Chilton, P. (2004) *Analysing Political Discourse: Theory and practice*. London: Routledge.

Chilton, P. (2005a) 'Missing Links in Mainstream CDA: Modules, Blends and the Critical Instinct', in R. Wodak and P. Chilton (eds), *A New Research Agenda in (Critical) Discourse Analysis: Theory and Interdisciplinarity.* (Reprinted in 2nd edn, 2007.) Amsterdam: Benjamins, pp. 19–52.

Chilton, P. (2005b) 'Manipulations, Memes and Metaphors: The Case of *Mein Kampf*', in L. D. Saussure and P. Schulz (eds), *Manipulation.* Amsterdam: Benjamins.

Chilton, P. (2007) 'Is it Possible to Compare Political Rhetoric across Cultures?' *International Round Table on Discourse.* Hong Kong: City University.

Chilton, P. (2008) 'Critical Discourse Analysis', in *Cambridge Encyclopedia of the Language Sciences.* Cambridge: Cambridge University Press, in press.

Chilton, P. and Lakoff, G. (eds) (1995) *Metaphor in Foreign Policy Discourse.* Dartmouth: Aldershot.

Chilton, P. and Wodak, R. (2007) '*Preface*', in R. Wodak and P. Chilton (eds), *A New Research Agenda in (Critical) Discourse Analysis: Theory and Interdisciplinarity.* Amsterdam: Benjamins, pp. xi–xviii. (Revised 2nd edn.)

Chilton, P., Tian, H. and Wodak, R. (eds) (forthcoming) *New Discourses in Contemporary China.* Hong Kong: Hong Kong University Press.

Chouliaraki, L. (1995) 'Regulation and Heteroglossia in One Institutional Context: The Case of a "Progressivist" English Classroom.' Unpublished PhD thesis, University of Lancaster.

Chouliaraki, L. and Fairclough, N. (1999) *Discourse in Late Modernity.* Edinburgh: Edinburgh University Press.

Church, K. and Hanks, P. (1990) 'Word association norms, mutual information, and lexicography', *Computational Linguistics* 16(1): 22–29.

Clarke, J. and Newman, J. (1998) *A Modern British People? New Labour and the reconstruction of social welfare.* Copenhagen: Department of Intercultural Communication and Management, Copenhagen Business School.

Clear, J. (1993) 'From Firth Principles: Computational Tools for the Study of Collocation', in M. Baker, G. Francis and E. Tognini-Bonelli (eds), *Text and Technology: In Honour of John Sinclair.* Amsterdam: Benjamins, pp. 271–292.

Connerton, P. (1976) *How Societies Remember.* Cambridge: Cambridge University Press. (Reprinted 1996.)

Connolly, W. (1991) *Identity/Difference.* Ithaca: Cornell University Press.

Cotterill, J. (2001) 'Domestic discord, rocky relationships: semantic prosodies in representations of marital violence in the O. J. Simpson trial', *Discourse and Society* 12(3): 291–312.

de Beaugrande, R. (1997) 'The Story of Discourse Analysis', in T. A. van Dijk (ed.), *Discourse as Structure and Process* (Discourse Studies: A Multidisciplinary Introduction. Vol. 1). London: Sage, pp. 35–62.

de Cillia, R. and Wodak, R. (eds) (2008) *Gedenken im Gedankenjahr.* Innsbruck: Studienverlag.

Delanty, G., Wodak, R. and Jones, P. (eds) (2008) *Migration, Identity and Belonging.* Liverpool: Liverpool University Press.

Deleuze, G. (1988) *Foucault.* Minneapolis: University of Minnesota Press.

Denzin, N. K. (1970) *The Research Act in Sociology.* London: Butterworth.

Department of Trade and Industry (DTI) (1998) *White Paper on Competitiveness.* London: The Stationery Office.

Döring, H. and Hirschauer, S. (1997) 'Die Biographie der Dinge: Eine Ethnographie musealer Representation', in S. Hirschauer and K. Amann (eds), *Die Befremdung der eigenen Kultur.* Frankfurt am Main: Suhrkamp, pp. 267–297.

Drews, A., Gerhard, U. and Link, J. (1985) 'Moderne Kollektivsymbolik: Eine diskurstheoretisch orientierte Einführung mit Auswahlbiographie', *Internationales Archiv für Sozialgeschichte der deutschen Literatur (IASL)*. Tübingen: Sonderheft Forschungsreferate, pp. 256–375.

Dreyfus, H. L. and Rabinow, P. (1982) *Michel Foucault: Beyond Structuralism and Hermeneutics*. Sussex: The Harvester Press.

Duranti, A. and Goodwin, C. (eds) (1992) *Rethinking Context: Language as an Interactive Phenomenon*. Cambridge: Cambridge University Press.

Durkheim, E. (1933) *The Division of Labor in Society*. New York: The Free Press.

Durkheim, E. (1976) *The Elementary Forms of Religious Life*. London: Allen and Unwin.

Durkheim, E. and Mauss, M. (1963) *Primitive Classification*. London: Cohen and West.

Duveen, G. and Lloyd, B. (eds) (1990) *Social Representations and the Development of Knowledge*. Cambridge: Cambridge University Press.

Ehlich, K. (1983) 'Text und sprachliches Handeln: Die Entstehung von Texten aus dem Bedürfnis nach Überlieferung', in A. Assmann, J. Assmann and C. Hardmeier (eds), *Schrift und Gedächtnis: Beiträge zur Archäologie der literarischen Kommunikation*. Munich: Fink, pp. 24–43.

Emerson, R. M. (1962) 'Power-dependence relations', *American Sociological Review* 27: 31–41.

Emerson, R. M. (1975) 'Social exchange theory', *Annual Review of Sociology* 2: 335–362.

Emerson, R. M., Fretz, R. I. and Shaw, L. L. (1995) *Writing Ethnographic Fieldnotes*. Chicago: University of Chicago Press.

Ensink, T. and Sauer, C. (eds) (2003) *The Art of Commemoration*. Amsterdam: Benjamins.

Everson, S. (ed.) (1996) *The Politics and the Constitution of Athens*. Cambridge: Cambridge University Press.

Fairclough, N. (1989/1991) *Language and Power*. London: Longman. (Revised 2nd edn, 2001.)

Fairclough, N. (1992a) *Discourse and Social Change*. Cambridge: Polity Press.

Fairclough, N. (1992b) *Critical Language Awareness*. London: Longman.

Fairclough, N. (1993) 'Critical discourse analysis and the marketization of public discourse', *Discourse and Society* 4(2): 133–168.

Fairclough, N. (1995a) *Critical Discourse Analysis*. London: Longman.

Fairclough, N. (1995b) *Media Discourse*. London: Edward Arnold.

Fairclough, N. (1996) 'A reply to Henry Widdowson's "Discourse analysis: a critical view"', *Language and Literature* 5(1): 49–56. (Reprinted in M. Toolan [ed.] [2002] *Critical Discourse Analysis*. Vol. 3. London and New York: Routledge, pp. 148–155.)

Fairclough, N. (2000a) *New Labour, New Language?* London: Routledge.

Fairclough, N. (2000b) 'Represenciones del cambio en discurso neoliberal', *Cuadernos de Relaciones Laborales* 16: 13–36.

Fairclough, N. (2003) *Analysing Discourse: Text Analysis for Social Research*. London: Routledge.

Fairclough, N. (2005a) 'Critical discourse analysis', *Marges Linguistiques* 9: 76–94.

Fairclough, N. (2005b) 'Critical Discourse Analysis in Transdisciplinary Research', in R. Wodak and P. Chilton (eds), *A New Agenda in (Critical) Discourse Analysis*. Amsterdam: Benjamins, pp. 53–70.

Fairclough, N. (2006) *Language and Globalization*. London: Routledge.

Fairclough, N. (forthcoming) 'Language, Reality and Power', in J. Culpeper, F. Katamba, P. Kerswill and R. Wodak (eds), *English Language and Linguistics*. London: Palgrave.

Fairclough, N. and Wodak, R. (1997) 'Critical Discourse Analysis', in T. A. van Dijk (ed.), *Discourse as Social Interaction* (Discourse Studies: A Multidisciplinary Introduction. Vol. 2). London: Sage, pp. 258–284.

Fairclough, N., Jessop, B. and Sayer A. (2004) 'Critical Realism and Semiosis', in J. Joseph and J. Roberts (eds), *Realism, Discourse and Deconstruction*. London: Routledge, pp. 23–42.

Falkner, G., Treib, O., Hartlapp, M. and Leiber, S. (2005) *Complying with Europe*. Cambridge: Cambridge University Press.

Fay, B. (1987) *Critical Social Science*. London: Polity Press.

Fiske, S. T. and Taylor, S. E. (1991) *Social Cognition*. 2nd edn. New York: McGraw-Hill.

Foucault, M. (1975) *Surveiller et punir: Naissance de la prison*. Paris: Gallimard.

Foucault, M. (1977) *Language, Counter-Memory, Practice*. (D. F. Bouchard and S. Simon, eds.). Ithaca: Cornell University Press.

Foucault, M. (1979) *Discipline and Punish: The Birth of the Prison*. Harmondsworth: Penguin Books.

Foucault, M. (1980a) 'Truth and Power', in C. Gordon (ed.), *Power/Knowledge: Selected Interviews and Other Writings 1972–1977 by Michel Foucault*. New York: Pantheon Books, pp. 107–133.

Foucault, M. (1980b) 'The Confession of the Flesh', in C. Gordon (ed.), *Power/Knowledge: Selected Interviews and Other Writings 1972–1977 by Michel Foucault*. New York: Pantheon Books, pp. 194–228.

Foucault, M. (1983) *Der Wille zum Wissen: Sexualität und Wahrheit*. Frankfurt am Main: Suhrkamp.

Foucault, M. (1991) *Remarks on Marx: Conversations with Duccio Trombadori*. Transl. by R. J. Goldstein and J. Cascaito. New York: Semiotext(e).

Foucault, M. (1996) 'What is Critique?', in J. Schmidt (ed.), *What is Enlightenment? Eighteenth-century Answers and Twentieth-century Questions*. Berkeley: University of California Press, pp. 382–398.

Foucault, M. (2002) *The Archaeology of Knowledge*. London: Routledge. (1st English edn, 1972.)

Fowler, R., Hodge, R., Kress, G. and Trew, T. (eds) (1979) *Language and Control*. London: Routledge.

French, J. R. P. and Raven, B. (1959) 'The Bases of Social Power', in D. Cartwright (ed.), *Studies in Social Power*. Ann Arbor: University of Michigan, pp. 150–167.

Froschauer, U. (2002) 'Artefaktanalyse', in S. Kühl and P. Strodtholz (eds), *Methoden der Organisationsforschung*. Reinbek: Rororo, pp. 361–395.

Gee, J. (2004) *Discourse Analysis: Theory and method*. London: Routledge.

Giddens, A. (1984) *The Constitution of Society: Outline of the theory of structuration*. Cambridge: Polity Press.

Girnth, H. (1996) 'Texte im politischen Diskurs: Ein Vorschlag zur diskursorientierten Beschreibung von Textsorten', *Muttersprache* 106(1): 66–80.

Glaser, B. and Strauss, A. L. (1967) *The Discovery of Grounded Theory: Strategies for qualitative research*. Chicago: Weidenfeld and Nicolson.

Gleason, H. A. J. (1973) 'Contrastive Analysis in Discourse Structure', in A. Makkai and D. G. Lockwood (eds), *Readings in Stratificational Linguistics*. Tuscaloosa, AL: University of Alabama Press.

Goffman, E. (1970) *Strategic Interaction*. Oxford: Basil Blackwell.

Gore, A. (2007) *Angriff auf die Vernunft*. Munich: Riemann.

Graesser, A. C., Gernsbacher, M. A. and Goldman, S. R. (eds) (2003) *Handbook of Discourse Processes*. Mahwah, NJ: L. Erlbaum.

Graham, P. (2002) 'Space and Cyberspace: On the enclosure of consciousness', in J. Armitage and J. Roberts (eds), *Living with Cyberspace: Technology and Society in the 21st Century*. London: The Athlone Press.

Graham, P. and Paulsen, N. (2002) 'Third-sector discourses and the future of (un)employment: skilled labor, new technologies, and the meaning of work', *Text* 22(3): 443–467.

Grant, D., Hardy, C., Oswick, C. and Putnam, L. (eds) (2004) *The Sage Handbook of Organizational Discourse*. London: Sage.

Grimes, J. (1975) *The Thread of Discourse*. The Hague: Mouton.

Gruber, H. (1991) *Antisemitismus und Mediendiskurs. Die Affäre "Waldheim" in der Tagespresse*. Wiesbaden: Deutscher Universitätsverlag.

Gumperz, J. J. (1982) *Discourse Strategies*. Cambridge: Cambridge University Press.

Habermas, J. (1967) *Erkenntnis und Interesse*. Frankfurt am Main: Suhrkamp.

Habermas, J. (1996) *Die Einbeziehung des Anderen. Studien zur politischen Theorie*. Frankfurt am Main: Suhrkamp.

Halliday, M. A. K. (1978) *Language as Social Semiotic*. London: Arnold.

Halliday, M. A. K. (1985) *An Introduction to Functional Grammar*. London: Arnold. (2nd edn, 1994.)

Hammersley, M. and Atkinson, P. (2007) *Ethnography: Principles in Practice*. 3rd edn. London: Routledge.

Hardt-Mautner, G. (1995) 'Only Connect: Critical Discourse Analysis and Corpus Linguistics.' UCREL Technical Paper 6, University of Lancaster, Lancaster. Available at www.comp.lancs.ac.uk/ucrel/tech_papers.html.

Harvey, D. (1996) *Justice, Nature and the Geography of Difference*. Oxford: Blackwell.

Harvey, D. (2003) *The New Imperialism*. Oxford: Oxford University Press.

Hay, C. (2007) *Why We Hate Politics*. Cambridge: Polity Press.

Heer, H., Manoschek, W., Pollak, A. and Wodak, R. (eds) (2008) *The Discursive Construction of History: Remembering the Wehrmacht's War of Annihilation*. Basingstoke: Palgrave.

Horkheimer, M. and Adorno, T. W. (1969/1991 [1944]) *Dialektik der Aufklärung: Philosophische Fragmente*. Frankfurt am Main: Fischer.

Hunston, S. (2002) *Corpora in Applied Linguistics*. Cambridge: Cambridge University Press.

Hunston, S. (2004) 'Counting the Uncountable: Problems of identifying evaluation in a text and in a corpus', in A. Partington, J. Morley and L. Haarman (eds), *Corpora and Discourse*. Bern: Peter Lang, pp. 157–188.

Iedema, R. (1997) 'Interactional Dynamics and Social Change: Planning as morpho-genesis.' Unpublished PhD thesis, University of Sydney.

Iedema, R. and Wodak, R. (1999) 'Introduction: organizational discourse and practices', *Discourse and Society* 10(1): 5–19.

Ieţcu, I. (2006) *Discourse Analysis and Argumentation Theory*. Bucharest: Editura Universităţii din Bucureşti.

IPCC (Intergovernmental Panel on Climate Change) (2007a) Climate Change 2007: Synthesis report, Intergovernmental Panel on Climate Change Fourth Assessment Report. Topic 1 (Downloaded from www.ipcc.ch/pdf/assessment-report/ar4/syr/ar4_syr_topic1.pdf on 9 February 2008).

IPCC (Intergovernmental Panel on Climate Change) (2007b) Climate Change 2007: Synthesis report, Intergovernmental Panel on Climate Change Fourth Assessment Report. Topic 2 (Downloaded from www.ipcc.ch/pdf/assessment-report/ar4/syr/ar4_syr_topic2.pdf on 9 February 2008).

Jäger, M. (1996) *Fatale Effekte: Die Kritik am Patriarchat im Einwanderungsdiskurs*. Duisburg: DISS.

Jäger, S. (2001a) 'Dispositiv', in M. S. Kleiner (ed.), *Michel Foucault: Eine Einführung in sein Denken*. Frankfurt am Main: Campus, pp. 72–89.

Jäger, S. (2001b) 'Discourse and Knowledge: Theoretical and methodological aspects of a critical discourse and dispositive analysis', in R. Wodak and M. Meyer (eds), *Methods of Critical Discourse Analysis*. London: Sage, pp. 32–62.

Jäger, S. (2004) *Kritische Diskursanalyse*. 4th unrevised edn. Münster: Unrast.

Jäger, S. (ed.) (2008) *Wie kritisch ist die Kritische Diskursanalyse?* Münster: Unrast.

Jäger, M. and Jäger, S. (2007) *Deutungskämpfe: Theorie und Praxis Kritischer Diskursanalyse*. Wiesbaden: VS Verlag.

Jessop, B. (2002) *The Future of the Capitalist State*. Cambridge: Polity Press.

Jessop, B. (2004) 'Critical semiotic analysis and cultural political economy', *Critical Discourse Studies* 1(2): 159–174.

Jessop, B. (2008) 'The cultural political economy of competitiveness and its implications for higher education', in B. Jessop, N. Fairclough and R. Wodak (eds), *Education and the Knowledge-based Economy in Europe*. Amsterdam: Sense Publishers, pp. 13–41.

Jessop, R., Fairclough, N. and Wodak, R. (eds) (2008) *Higher Education and the Knowledge Based Economy in Europe*. Rotterdam: Sense Publishers.

Johnson-Laird, P. N. (1983) *Mental Models*. Cambridge: Cambridge University Press.

Katz, E. and Lazarsfeld, P. F. (1955) *Personal Influence*. Glencoe: Free Press.

Kienpointner, M. (1992) *Alltagslogik: Struktur und Funktion von Argumentationsmustern*. Stuttgart-Bad Cannstatt: Frommann-Holzboog.

Kienpointner, M. (1996) *Vernünftig Argumentieren: Regeln und Techniken der Diskussion*. Hamburg: Rowohlt.

Kienpointner, M. and Kindt, W. (1997) 'On the problem of bias in political argumentation: an investigation into discussions about political asylum in Germany and Austria', *Journal of Pragmatics* 27: 555–585.

Kindt, W. (1992) 'Argumentation und Konfliktaustragung in Äußerungen über den Golfkrieg', *Zeitschrift für Sprachwissenschaft* 11: 189–215.

Kintsch, W. (1998) *Comprehension: A paradigm for cognition*. New York: Cambridge University Press.

Klaus, V. (2007) *Blauer Planet in grünen Fesseln! Was ist bedroht: Klima oder Freiheit?* Vienna: Carl Gerold's Sohn Verlagsbuchhandlung.

Klemperer, V. (1975/1947) *LTI Lingua Tertii Imperii: Die Sprache des Dritten Reiches*. Leipzig: Reclam.

Klemperer, V. (2000/2006 [1947]) *The Language of the Third Reich: LTI – Lingua Tertii Imperii: A Philologist's Notebook*. London: Continuum.

Klemperer, V. (2001) *I Will Bear Witness: A diary of the Nazi years*. New York: Modern Library.

Knight, K. (2006) 'Transformations of the concept of ideology in the twentieth century', *American Political Science Review* 100(4): 619–626.

Koller, V. (2008) 'Identity, Image, Impression: Corporate self-presentation and public reactions', in R. Wodak and V. Koller (eds), *Handbook of Communication in the Public Sphere (Handbook of Linguistics*, Vol. 4). Berlin: de Gruyter, pp. 155–180.

Koller, V. and Mautner, G. (2004) 'Computer Applications in Critical Discourse Analysis', in A. Hewings, C. Coffin and K. O'Halloran (eds), *Applying English Grammar*. London: Arnold, pp. 216–228.

Koller, V. and Davidson, P. (2008) 'Social exclusion as conceptual and grammatical metaphor: a cross-genre study of British policy-making', *Discourse and Society* 19(3): 307–331.

Kovács, A. and Wodak, R. (eds) (2003) *Nato, Neutrality and National Identity: The case of Austria and Hungary*. Vienna: Böhlau.

Kress, G. and Hodge, R. (1979) *Language as Ideology*. London: Routledge.

Kress, G. and Van Leeuwen, T. (1996) *Reading Images*. London: Routledge.

Krings, H., Baumgartner, H. and Wild, C. (1973) *Handbuch philosophischer Grundbegriffe*. Munich: Kösel.

Krishnamurthy, R. (1996) 'Ethnic, Racial and Tribal: The language of racism?' in C. R. Caldas-Coulthard and M. Coulthard (eds), *Texts and Practices: Readings in Critical Discourse Analysis*. London: Routledge, pp. 129–149.

Krzyżanowski, M. and Oberhuber, F. (2007) *(Un)Doing Europe*. Bern: Peter Lang.

Krzyżanowski, M. and Wodak, R. (2008) *The Politics of Exclusion: Debating migration in Austria*. New Brunswick, NJ: Transaction Press.

Laclau, E. (1980) 'Populist rupture and discourse', *Screen Education* 34: 87–93.

Lakoff, G. (1987) *Women, Fire and Dangerous Things*. Chicago: University of Chicago Press.

Lakoff, G. and Johnson, M. (1980) *Metaphors We Live By*. Chicago: University of Chicago Press.

Lakoff, G. and Johnson, M. (1999) *Philosophy in the Flesh*. New York: Basic Books.

Lalouschek, J., Menz, F. and Wodak, R. (1990) *Alltag in der Ambulanz: Gespräche zwischen Ärzten, Schwestern und Patienten*. Tübingen: Narr.

Lazar, M. (ed.) (2005) *Feminist Critical Discourse Analysis*. Basingstoke: Palgrave.

Le, E. (2006) *The Spiral of 'Anti-Other' Rhetoric*. Amsterdam: Benjamins.

Lemke, J. (1995) *Textual Politics: Discourse and social dynamics*. London: Taylor and Francis.

Lemke, J. (2001) 'Discursive technologies and the social organization of meaning', *Special Issue of Folia Linguistica* 35(1–2): 79–96.

Lemke, J. (2002) 'Multimedia Genres for Science Education and Scientific Literacy', in M. Schleppegrell and C. Colombi (eds), *Developing Advanced Literacy in First and Second Languages*. Mahwah, NJ: Lawrence Erlbaum, pp. 21–44.

Leont'ev, A. N. (1978) *Activity, Consciousness, and Personality*. Englewood Cliffs: Prentice Hall.

Leont'ev, A. N. (1982) *Tätigkeit, Bewußtsein, Persönlichkeit*. Cologne: Pahl-Rugenstein.

Levinson, S. C. (1983) *Pragmatics*. Cambridge: Cambridge University Press.

Lévi-Strauss, C. (1964) *Totemism*. Harmondsworth: Penguin.

Link, J. (1982) 'Kollektivsymbolik und Mediendiskurse', *kulturRRevolution* 1: 6–21.

Link, J. (1983) 'Was ist und was bringt Diskurstaktik', *kulturRRevolution* 2: 60–66.

Link, J. (1992) 'Die Analyse der symbolischen Komponente realer Ereignisse: Ein Beitrag der Diskurstheorie zur Analyse neorassistischer Äußerungen', in S. Jäger and F. Januschek (eds), *Der Diskurs des Rassismus*. Oldenburg: Osnabrücker Beiträge zur Sprachtheorie 46, pp. 37–52.

Link, J. (1996) 'Wie "ideologisch" war der Ideologiebegriff von Marx? Zur verkannten Materialität der Diskurse und Subjektivitäten im Marxschen Materialismus', in R. Scholz and K.-M. Bogdal (eds), *Literaturtheorie und Geschichte: Zur Diskussion materialistischer Literaturwissenschaft*. Opladen: Westdeutscher Verlag, pp. 132–148.

Link, J. and Link-Heer, U. (1990) 'Diskurs/Interdiskurs und Literaturanalyse', *Zeitschrift für Linguistik und Literaturwissenschaft (LiLi)* 77: 88–99.

Louw, B. (1993) 'Irony in the Text or Insincerity in the Writer? The diagnostic potential of semantic prosodies', in M. Baker, G. Francis and E. Tognini-Bonelli (eds), *Text and Technology: In honour of John Sinclair*. Amsterdam: Benjamins, pp. 157–176.

Lueger, M. (2004) *Grundlagen qualitativer Feldforschung*. 2nd edn. Vienna: WUV.

Lutz, B. and Wodak, R. (1987) *Information für Informierte*. Vienna: Verlag der österr. Akademie der Wissenschaften.

Maas, U. (1984) *Als der Geist der Gemeinschaft eine Sprache fand: Sprache im Nationalsozialismus*. Opladen: Westdeutscher Verlag.

Maas, U. (1989a) *Sprachpolitik und politische Sprachwissenschaft*. Frankfurt am Main: Suhrkamp.

Maas, U. (1989b) 'Sprache im Nationalsozialismus: Analyse einer Rede eines Studentenfunktionärs', in K. Ehlich (ed.), *Sprache im Faschismus*. Frankfurt am Main: Suhrkamp, pp. 162–197.

Maier, F. (forthcoming) 'Doing Hair – Doing Age: Perspectives of emancipated ageing', in M. Beisheim, B. Gusenbauer, L. Kreil and F. Maier (eds), *Perspectives of Women's Age at the Work Place*. Bern: Peter Lang.

Malinowski, B. (1923) 'The Problem of Meaning in Primitive Languages', in C. K. Ogden and I. A. Richards (eds), *The Meaning of Meaning*. London: Routledge and Kegan Paul.

Malinowski, B. (1935) *Coral Gardens and their Magic*. Vol. 2. London: Allen and Unwin.

Martin, J. R. (1984) 'Lexical Cohesion, Field and Genre: Parceling experience and discourse goals', in J. E. Copeland (ed.), *Linguistics and Semiotics: Text semantics and discourse semantics*. Proceedings of the Second Rice Symposium. Houston: Rice University Press.

Martin, J. R. (1992) *English Text: System and structure*. Amsterdam: Benjamins.

Martin, J. and Wodak, R. (eds) (2003) *Re/reading the Past*. Amsterdam: Benjamins.

Marx, K. (1992) *Capital: A critique of political economy*. London: Penguin. (1st German edn, 1867.)

Matouschek, B., Wodak, R. and Januschek, F. (1995) *Notwendige Maßnahmen gegen Fremde? Genese und Formen von rassistischen Diskursen der Differenz*. Vienna: Passagen Verlag.

Matsumoto, Y. (2003) 'Lexical Knowledge Acquisition', in R. Mitkov (ed.), *The Oxford Handbook of Computational Linguistics*. Oxford: Oxford University Press, pp. 395–413.

Mautner, G. (2005) 'Time to get wired: using web-based corpora in critical discourse analysis', *Discourse and Society* 16(6): 809–828.

Mautner, G. (2007) 'Mining large corpora for social information: the case of *elderly*', *Language in Society* 36(1): 51–72.

Mautner, G. (2008) 'Analysing newspapers, magazines and other print media', in R. Wodak and M. Krzyżanowski, (eds), *Qualitative Discourse Analysis in the Social Sciences*. Basingstoke: Palgrave, pp. 30–53.

McEnery, T. and Wilson, A. (2001) *Corpus Linguistics*. 2nd edn. Edinburgh: Edinburgh University Press.

McEnery, T., Xiao, R. and Tono, Y. (2006) *Corpus-based Language Studies: An advanced resource book*. London and New York: Routledge.

Merton, R. K. (1967) *On Theoretical Sociology*. New York: The Free Press.

Mitten, R. (1992) *The Politics of Antisemitic Prejudice: The Waldheim phenomenon in Austria*. Boulder, CO: Westview Press.

Morse, J. M., Barrett, M., Mayan, M., Olson, K. and Spiers, J. (2002) 'Verification strategies for establishing reliability and validity in qualitative research', *International Journal of Qualitative Methods* 1(2): 1–19.

Moscovici, S. (1982) 'On Social Representations', in J. P. Forgas (ed.), *Social Cognition: Perspectives on everyday understanding*. London: Academic Press, pp. 181–209.

Moscovici, S. (2000) *Social Representations*. Cambridge: Polity Press.

Mouffe, C. (2005) *On the Political.* London: Routledge.

Mouzelis, N. P. (1995) *Sociological Theory: What went wrong? Diagnoses and remedies.* London: Routledge.

Mulderrig, J. (2006) 'The Governance of Education: A Corpus-Based Critical Discourse Analysis of UK Education Policy Texts 1972 to 2005.' Unpublished PhD thesis, Department of Linguistics, Lancaster University.

Müller, M., Fuentes, U. and Kohl, H. (2007) *Der UN-Weltklimareport: Bericht über eine aufhaltsame Katastrophe.* Cologne: Kiepenheuer und Witsch.

Mullins, W. E. (1972) 'On the concept of ideology in political science', *American Political Science Review* 66: 498–510.

Muntigl, P. (2002a) 'Policy, politics, and social control: a systemic functional linguistic analysis of EU employment policy', *Text* 22(3): 393–441.

Muntigl, P. (2002b) 'Politicization and Depoliticization: Employment policy in the European Union', in P. Chilton and Ch. Schäffner (eds), *Politics as Text and Talk.* Amsterdam: Benjamins, pp. 45–79.

Muntigl, P., Weiss, G. and Wodak, R. (2000) *European Union Discourses of Un/employment: An interdisciplinary approach to employment policy-making and organizational change.* Amsterdam: Benjamins.

Musolff, A. (2004) *Metaphors and Political Discourse.* Basingstoke: Palgrave.

Nelson, M. (2005) 'Semantic associations in Business English: a corpus-based analysis', *English for Specific Purposes* 25: 217–234.

Ng, S. H. and Bradac, J. J. (1993) *Power in Language.* Newbury Park: Sage.

O'Halloran, K. and Coffin, C. (2004) 'Checking Overinterpretation and Underinterpretation: Help from corpora in critical linguistics', in A. Hewings, C. Coffin and K. O'Halloran (eds), *Applying English Grammar.* London: Arnold, pp. 275–297.

Oevermann, U., Allert, T., Konau, E. and Krambeck, J. (1979) 'Die Methodologie einer "objektiven Hermeneutik" und ihre allgemeine forschungslogische Bedeutung in den Sozialwissenschaften', in H.-G. Soeffner (ed.), *Interpretative Verfahren in den Sozial- und Textwissenschaften.* Stuttgart: Metzler, pp. 352–434.

Oreskes, N. (2004) 'Beyond the ivory tower: the scientific consensus on climate change', *Science* 306: 1686–1690.

Orpin, D. (2005) 'Corpus linguistics and critical discourse analysis: examining the ideology of sleaze', *International Journal of Corpus Linguistics* 10(1): 37–61.

Palonen, K. (1993) 'Introduction: From policy and polity to politicking and politicization', in K. Paolonen and T. Parvikko (eds), *Reading the Political: Exploring the margins of politics.* Helsinki: FPSA, pp. 6–16.

Panagl, O. and Wodak, R. (eds) (2004) *Text und Kontext.* Munich: Königshausen & Neumann.

Parsons, T. (1977) *The Structure of Social Action.* Chicago: The Free Press.

Parsons, T. and Shils, E. (eds) (1951) *Towards a General Theory of Action.* Cambridge, MA: University Press.

Partington, A. (2004) 'Utterly content in each other's company: semantic prosody and semantic preference', *International Journal of Corpus Linguistics* 9(1): 131–156.

Pelinka, A. and Wodak, R. (eds) (2002) '*Dreck am Stecken': Politik der Ausgrenzung.* Vienna: Czernin.

Pieterse, J. (2004) *Globalization or Empire?* London: Routledge.

Popitz, H. (1992) *Phänomene der Macht.* Tübingen: Mohr.

Rahmstorf, S. and Schellnhuber, H. J. (2007) *Der Klimawandel,* 4th edition. Munich: Beck.

Rancière, J. (1995) *On the Shores of Politics*. London: Verso.

Rancière, J. (2006) *Hatred of Democracy*. London: Verso.

Rapley, J. (2004) *Globalization and Inequality: Neoliberalism's downward spiral*. Boulder, CO: Lynne Rienner.

Reeves, F. (1989) *British Racial Discourse: A study of British political discourse about race and related matters*. Cambridge: Cambridge University Press.

Reisigl, M. (2003) 'Wie man eine Nation herbeiredet. Eine diskursanalytische Untersuchung zur sprachlichen Konstruktion der östereichischen Identität in politischen Gedenkreden.' Unpublished PhD thesis, University of Vienna.

Reisigl, M. (2007) *Nationale Rhetorik in Fest- und Gedenkreden: Eine diskursanalytische Studie zum 'österreichischen Millennium' in den Jahren 1946 und 1996*. Tübingen: Stauffenburg.

Reisigl, M. and Wodak, R. (2001) *Discourse and Discrimination: Rhetorics of racism and anti-semitism*. London: Routledge.

Renkema, J. (2004) *Introduction to Discourse Studies*. Amsterdam: Benjamins.

Richardson, J. (2004) *(Mis)representing Islam*. Amsterdam: Benjamins.

Richardson, J. and Wodak, R. (2008) 'Visual argumentation in racist discourse', *Controversies* (in press).

Rose, N. (1999) *Powers of Freedom: Reframing political thought*. Cambridge: Cambridge University Press.

Rydgren, J. (2005) *Movements of Exclusion*. New York: Nova.

Sacks, H. (1992) *Lectures on Conversation*. 2 volumes. Oxford: Blackwell.

Sarasin, P. (2003) *Geschichtswissenschaft und Diskursanalyse*. Frankfurt am Main: Suhrkamp.

Schank, R. and Abelson, R. (1977) *Scripts, Plans, Goals and Understanding*. Hillsdale, NJ: Lawrence Erlbaum.

Scherer, K. R. and Giles, H. (1979) *Social Markers in Speech*. Cambridge: Cambridge University Press.

Schiffrin, D. (1994) *Approaches to Discourse*. Oxford: Blackwell.

Schiffrin, D., Tannen, D. and Hamilton, H. E. (eds) (2001) *The Handbook of Discourse Analysis*. Malden, MA: Blackwell Publishers.

Silverman, D. (1993) *Interpreting Qualitative Data*. London: Sage.

Sondermann, K. (1997) 'Reading Politically: National anthems as textual Icons', in T. Carver and M. Hyvärinen (eds), *Interpreting the Political: New methodologies*. London: Routledge, pp. 128–142.

Spradley, J. P. (1979) *The Ethnographic Interview*. New York: Holt, Rinehart and Winston.

Spradley, J. P. (1980) *Participant Observation*. Fort Worth: Harcourt Brace Jovanovich College Publishers.

Strauss, A. (1987) *Qualitative Analysis for Social Scientists*. Cambridge: Cambridge University Press.

Strauss, A. and Corbin, J. (1990) *Basics of Qualitative Research*. Newbury Park: Sage.

Stubbs, M. (1996) *Text and Corpus Analysis: Computer-assisted studies of language and culture*. Oxford: Blackwell.

Stubbs, M. (2001) *Words and Phrases: Corpus studies of lexical semantics*. Oxford: Blackwell.

Talbot, M. R. (2003) *Language and Power in the Modern World*. Edinburgh: Edinburgh University Press.

Ten Have, P. (1999) *Doing Conversation Analysis: A practical guide*. London: Sage.

Teubert, W. (1999) 'Zum Verlust von Pluralität im politisch-gesellschaftlichen Diskurs: Das Beispiel Besitzstände', in U. Kreft, H. Uske and S. Jäger (eds), *Kassensturz: Politische Hypotheken der Berliner Republik*. Duisburg: DISS, pp. 29–48.

Thompson, J. B. (1988) *Critical Hermeneutics* (4th edn.) Cambridge: Cambridge University Press.

Thompson, J. B. (1990) *Ideology and Modern Culture.* Cambridge: Cambridge University Press.

Titscher, S., Meyer, M., Wodak, R. and Vetter, E. (2000) *Methods of Text and Discourse Analysis.* London: Sage.

Tognini-Bonelli, E. (2001) *Corpus Linguistics at Work.* Amsterdam: Benjamins.

Toolan, M. (ed.) (2002) *Critical Discourse Analysis: Critical concepts in linguistics.* 4 vols. London: Routledge.

Triandafyllidou, A., Wodak, R. and Krzyżanowski, M. (eds) (2009) *European Media in Crisis and the European Public Sphere.* Basingstoke: Palgrave.

Tricento, T. (ed.) (2005) *Introduction to the Study of Language Policies.* Oxford: Blackwell.

Tulving, E. (1983) *Elements of Episodic Memory.* Oxford: Oxford University Press.

US Congress (2007) 'Hearing on Perspectives on Climate Change' (downloaded from frwebgate.access.gpo.gov/cgi-bin/getdoc.cgi?dbname=110_house_hearings&docid=f: 37579.pdf on 10 April 2008).

Van Dijk, T. A. (1984) *Prejudice in Discourse: An analysis of ethnic prejudice in cognition and conversation.* Amsterdam: Benjamins.

Van Dijk, T. A. (1987) *Communicating Racism: Ethnic prejudice in thought and talk.* Newbury Park, CA: Sage.

Van Dijk, T. A. (1991) *Racism and the Press.* London: Routledge.

Van Dijk, T. A. (1993a) *Elite Discourse and Racism.* Newbury Park, CA: Sage.

Van Dijk, T. A. (1993b) 'Principles of critical discourse analysis', *Discourse and Society* 4(2): 249–283.

Van Dijk, T. A. (ed.) (1997) *Discourse as Structure and Process* (Discourse Studies: A Multidisciplinary Introduction. 2 vols.) London: Sage.

Van Dijk, T. A. (1998) *Ideology: A multidisciplinary approach.* London: Sage.

Van Dijk, T. A. (2005) *Racism and discourse in Spain and Latin America.* Amsterdam: Benjamins.

Van Dijk, T. A. (ed.) (2007a) *Discourse Studies.* 5 vols. London: Sage.

Van Dijk, T. A. (ed.) (2007b) *Racismo y Discurso en América Latina.* Barcelona: Gedisa. (English version to appear with Lexington Books.)

Van Dijk, T. A. (2008a) *Discourse and Context. A sociocognitive approach.* Cambridge: Cambridge University Press.

Van Dijk, T. A. (2008b) *Discourse and Power.* Basingstoke: Palgrave.

Van Dijk, T. A. (2009) *Society and Discourse: How context controls text and talk.* Cambridge: Cambridge University Press.

Van Dijk, T. A. and Kintsch, W. (1983) *Strategies of Discourse Comprehension.* New York: Academic Press.

Van Eeemeren, F. H. and Grootendorst, R. (1992) *Argumentation, Communication and Fallacies: A pragma-dialectical perspective.* Hillsdale, NJ: Lawrence Erlbaum.

Van Leeuwen, T. (2005) *Introducing Social Semiotics.* London: Routledge.

Van Leeuwen, T. (2006) 'Critical Discourse Analysis', in K. Brown (ed.), *Encyclopedia of Language and Linguistics.* 2nd edn. Vol. 3. Oxford: Elsevier, pp. 290–294.

Van Leeuwen, T. (2007) 'Legitimation in discourse and communication', *Discourse and Communication* 1(1): 91–112.

Van Leeuwen, T. (2008) *Discourse and Practice: New tools for critical discourse analysis.* New York: Oxford University Press.

Van Leeuwen, T. and Wodak, R. (1999) 'Legitimizing immigration control: a discourse-historical analysis', *Discourse Studies* 1(1): 83–118.

Van Oostendorp, H. and Goldman, S. R. (eds) (1999) *The Construction of Mental Representations During Reading*. Mahwah, NJ: Lawrence Erlbaum.

Vass, E. (1992) 'Diskursanalyse als interdisziplinäres Forschungsgebiet.' Unpublished MA thesis, University of Vienna.

Verdoolaege, A. (2008) *Reconciliation Discourse*. Amsterdam: Benjamins.

Viehöver, W. (2003) 'Die Wissenschaft und die Wiederverzauberung des sublunaren Raumes. Der Klimadiskurs im Licht der narrativen Diskursanalyse', in R. Keller, A. Hirseland, W. Schneider and W. Viehöver (eds), *Handbuch Sozialwissensch-aftliche Diskursanalyse*. Vol. 2: Forschungspraxis. Opladen: Leske and Budrich, pp. 233–270.

Vygotsky, L. S. (1986) *Thought and Language*. Revised edn. Cambridge, MA: The MIT Press. (Originally published in 1934.)

Wacquant, L. (2004) *Body and Soul: Notebooks of an apprentice boxer*. Oxford: Oxford University Press.

Wagner, W. (1994) *Alltagsdiskurs: Die Theorie sozialer Repräsentationen*. Göttingen: Hogrefe.

Waldenfels, B. (1991) 'Ordnung in Diskursen', in F. Ewald and B. Waldenfels (eds), *Spiele der Wahrheit: Michel Foucaults Denken*. Frankfurt am Main: Suhrkamp, pp. 277–297.

Webb, E. J., Campbell, D. T., Schwartz, R. D. and Seclrest, L. (1966) *Unobtrusive Measures: Nonreactive research in the social sciences*. Chicago: Rand-McNally.

Weber, M. (1980) *Wirtschaft und Gesellschaft*. 5th edn. Tübingen: Mohr.

Weiss, G. and Wodak, R. (eds) (2003) *Critical Discourse Analysis: Theory and interdisciplinarity*. Basingstoke: Palgrave.

Wengeler, M. (2003) *Topos und Diskurs*. Tübingen: Niemeyer.

Wetherell, M., Taylor, S. and Simeon, Y. (eds) (2001) *Discourse as Data*. London: Sage

Whorf, B. L. (1956) *Language, Thought and Reality*. Cambridge, MA: MIT Press.

Widdowson, H. G. (1995) 'Discourse analysis: a critical view', *Language and Literature* 4(3): 157–172. (Republished in M. Toolan [ed.] [2002] *Critical Discourse Analysis*. Vol. 3. London and New York: Routledge, pp. 131–147.)

Widdowson, H. G. (2004) *Text, Context, Pretext*. Oxford: Blackwell.

Wittgenstein, L. (1989 [1952]) 'Philosophische Untersuchungen', in L. Wittgenstein (1989) *Werkausgabe Band 1: Tractatus logico-philosophicus – Tagebücher 1914–1916 – Philosophische Untersuchungen*. Frankfurt am Main: Suhrkamp, pp. 224–580.

Wodak, R. (1986) *Language Behavior in Therapy Groups*. Los Angeles: California University Press.

Wodak, R. (ed.) (1989) *Language, Power and Ideology*. Amsterdam: Benjamins.

Wodak, R. (1996) *Disorders of Discourse*. London: Longman.

Wodak, R. (2004) 'Critical Discourse Analysis', in C. Seale, G. Gobo, J. Gubrium and D. Silverman (eds), *Qualitative Research Practice*. London: Sage, pp. 197–213.

Wodak, R. (2006a) 'Dilemmas of discourse (analysis)', *Language in Society* 35: 595–611.

Wodak, R. (2006b) 'Critical linguistics and critical discourse analysis', in J.-O. Östman and J. Verschueren (eds), *Handbook of Pragmatics*. Amsterdam: Benjamins, pp. 1–24.

Wodak, R. (2007) 'Pragmatics and critical discourse analysis', *Pragmatics and Cognition* 15(1): 203–225.

Wodak, R. (2008a) 'Introduction: Terms and concepts', in R. Wodak and M. Krzyżanowski (eds), *Qualitative Discourse Analysis in the Social Sciences*. Basingstoke: Palgrave, pp. 1–42.

Wodak, R. (2008b) 'The Contribution of Critical Linguistics to the Analysis of Discriminatory Prejudices and Stereotypes in the Language of Politics', in R. Wodak and V. Koller (eds), *Handbook of Communication in the Public Sphere* (Handbook of Linguistics, Vol. 4). Berlin: de Gruyter, pp. 291–316.

Wodak, R. (2008c) '"Us" and "Them": Inclusion/Exclusion – discrimination via discourse', in G. Delanty, R. Wodak and P. Jones (eds), *Migration, Identity and Belonging*. Liverpool: Liverpool University Press, pp. 54–78.

Wodak, R. (2009) *'Politics as Usual': The discursive construction and representation of politics in action*. Basingstoke: Palgrave.

Wodak, R. and Chilton, P. (eds) (2005) *A New Agenda in (Critical) Discourse Analysis*. Amsterdam: Benjamins. (2nd edn 2007.)

Wodak, R. and de Cillia, R. (2006) 'Politics and Language: Overview', in K. Brown (ed.), *Encyclopedia of Language and Linguistics*. 2nd edn. Vol. 9. Oxford: Elsevier, pp. 706–719.

Wodak, R. and de Cillia, R. (2007) 'Commemorating the past: the discursive construction of official narratives about the rebirth of the second Austrian Republic', *Discourse and Communication* 1(3): 337–363.

Wodak, R. and Koller, V. (eds) (2008) *Handbook of Communication in the Public Sphere*. Berlin: de Gruyter.

Wodak, R. and Krzyżanowski, M. (eds) (2008) *Qualitative Discourse Analysis in the Social Sciences*. Basingstoke: Palgrave.

Wodak, R. and Meyer, M. (eds) (2001) *Methods of Critical Discourse Analysis*. London: Sage.

Wodak, R. and Pelinka, A. (2002) 'From Waldheim to Haider: An introduction', in R. Wodak and A. Pelinka (eds), *The Haider Phenomenon in Austria*. New Brunswick: Transaction Press, pp. vii–xxvii.

Wodak, R. and Schulz, M. (1986) *The Language of Love and Guilt*. Amsterdam: Benjamins.

Wodak, R. and van Dijk, T. A. (eds) (2000) *Racism at the Top*. Klagenfurt: Drava.

Wodak, R. and van Leeuwen, T. (2002) 'Discourses of un/employment in Europe: the Austrian case', *Text* 22(3): 345–367.

Wodak, R., de Cillia, R., Reisigl, M. and Liebhart, K. (1999) *The Discursive Construction of National Identity*. Edinburgh: Edinburgh University Press. (2nd edn 2009.)

Wodak, R., Menz, F., Lutz, B. and Gruber, H. (1985) *Die Sprache der 'Mächtigen' und 'Ohnmächtigen': Der Fall Hainburg*. Vienna: Arbeitsgemeinschaft für staatsbürgerliche Erziehung und politische Bildung.

Wodak, R., Nowak, P., Pelikan, J., Gruber, H., de Cillia, R. and Mitten, R. (1990) *'Wir sind alle unschuldige Täter!': Diskurshistorische Studien zum Nachkriegsantisemitismus*. Frankfurt am Main: Suhrkamp.

Wright, W. (1975) *Sixguns and Society: A Structural Study of the Western*. Berkeley: University of California Press.

Wuthnow, R. (1989) *Communities of Discourse: Ideology and social structure in the Reformation, the Enlightenment, and European socialism*. Cambridge, MA: Harvard University Press.

Young, L. and Fitzgerald, B. (2006) *The Power of Language: How discourse influences society*. London: Equinox.

Index